LONDON

A Companion to its History and Archaeology

LONDON

A Companion to its History and Archaeology

Malcolm Billings

KYLE CATHIE LIMITED

For Brigid, Henrietta and Sebastian

First published 1994
in Great Britain by
Kyle Cathie Limited
7/8 Hatherley Street
London SW1P 2QT

ISBN 1 85626 153 0

Copyright © Malcolm Billings 1994

Designed by Tamasin Cole

Chronology, Guide to Churches and Access to Sites
compiled by Nicholas Tanner

See also picture acknowledgements on page 208

Malcolm Billings is hereby identified as the
author of this work in accordance with Section 77
of the Copyright, Designs and Patents Act 1988

A Cataloguing in Publication record for this title
is available from the British Library

Origination by Master Image S'pore Pte Ltd
and Printed & Bound by Kyodo Printing S'pore.

*Frontispiece: The Painted Hall,
Greenwich Naval College.
Commissioned by William and Mary as
the Royal Naval Hospital, the building
is Christopher Wren's greatest secular
work. Sir James Thornhill spent twenty
years painting the allegorical ceiling
tableau, extolling the achievements of
his royal patrons.*

Contents

Acknowledgements

I am pleased to pay tribute to the painstaking and thorough research that Nick Tanner contributed throughout the production of this book. Dr John Schofield of the Museum of London generously gave advice on the manuscript and his pioneering work in medieval archaeology, as detailed in his book *The Building of London*, was not only an important source but also an inspiration for my endeavours.

I received much help and co-operation from many archaeologists at the Museum of London; among them Nick Bateman, who kindly and patiently took me through the Roman and Norman levels of his remarkable excavation beneath Guildhall Yard, and Dr William McCann who allowed me to use material from his Fleet Valley excavation report before final publication.

Great encouragement and good advice came from those who kindly read the manuscript: Mark Hassall of the Institute of Archaeology, John Schofield of the Museum of London, Pamela Willis of the Museum of the Order of St John of Jerusalem, Anthony Rendell of the BBC, and architectural historian Celina Fox.

Peter Casson, my son-in-law, practised computer wizardry on my behalf, and I am also indebted to my literary agent Dinah Weiner, editor Caroline Taggart and publisher Kyle Cathie.

Introduction

CHANGE, OFTEN VIOLENT AND DESTRUCTIVE, mostly short-sighted: London's story is one of constant upheaval. So profound are some of the most recent changes that many parts of London have become unrecognizable in the course of just one generation.

Those who seek tangible evidence of London's 2,000 years, searching out buildings that represent the city's different phases, can find it a frustrating experience. In many areas great canyons of concrete and glass have sanitized and sealed off any sense of the sixty or so generations of Londoners who have come and gone since the first merchants and traders followed the Roman legionaries into the Thames Valley.

The one aspect of London's past that is enduring is its commercial ethos: set up as a market place all those centuries ago, it still fulfils the same function. Today's City bristles with traders going about their business of insurance, shipping, banking, stockbroking and moving money, in any denomination or currency you fancy, around the world. It is, of course, this immutable aspect of London's character that has swept away much of the past in its successful attempt to keep up with the changing demands of the market. But an observer interested in those fine buildings and townscapes that have survived phase after phase of redevelopment must come to the regrettable conclusion that they have done so more by good luck and default than through wise planning or regard for our architectural heritage.

No great Roman buildings, medieval squares or merchants' houses remain in the old City of London – the last stretches of wall and the City gates were pulled down in the interests of commerce in the eighteenth century – and the "old City" now bears a closer resemblance to Manhattan's Wall Street than to a venerable European capital.

But despite the avarice of successive generations of City Fathers, the devastation inflicted by the Luftwaffe and acts of God, it is still possible to trace London's history through tangible remains – and not just such great set pieces of modern tourism as Westminster Abbey, the Houses of Parliament, St Paul's Cathedral and the Tower of London. Tucked away in corners and courtyards, dwarfed by modern tower blocks or barely visible at the end of narrow lanes, are many buildings and places that spectacularly evoke the spirit of London's past. The hidden story of this city lies behind the solid wrought-iron gates of the livery companies and medieval

John Stow's monument in St Andrew Undershaft, Leadenhall. Stow, London's first antiquarian, spent eight years writing his epic Survey of London, *published in 1598 and using records no longer available to us. His work has never been bettered: it is the result of insatiable curiosity, painstaking research and a great love for his city.*

Inns of Court; it lives on in the names of streets around Cheapside that have not changed since the Middle Ages; in the crypts of ancient churches, in the collections of London's many museums and libraries, and in the dozens of City churches rebuilt by Sir Christopher Wren after the Great Fire of 1666.

The other important and exciting source of information has, paradoxically, come from the destruction of nineteenth- and early twentieth-century London by wartime bombing and the redevelopment that followed it. Great swathes of London's history, of which very little was known, have been revealed as foundations for new buildings trenched deeper and deeper into the archaeological layers. The Roman city plan, for example, was very sketchy until the post-war redevelopment of bombed and derelict sites. Whole new stretches of the Roman and medieval wall have now been revealed

A precious survival of Norman London: the rounded chancel or choir of St Bartholomew the Great, looking very much as it did in the twelfth century.

and archaeologists working on the banks of the Thames have discovered previously unsuspected defences along the waterfront. The "missing" Roman amphitheatre was the last major find; it lies under the courtyard of the medieval Guildhall.

As for the Saxons, who until recently were simply not present in London's recorded or archaeological history, the mystery of their whereabouts was finally solved in the early 1980s when archaeologists came across evidence to show that they had virtually abandoned the walled Roman town and built their own version of London along the Strand.

Administratively London is, of course, two separate cities: Westminster, with its elegant squares, shopping streets, thirteenth-century abbey, royal palaces and Houses of Parliament; and the City of London, the "square mile" that roughly conforms to the boundaries of the Roman settlement, dominated today by wide-ranging commercial interests. This central area is encompassed within Greater London, which covers about 1,840 square kilometres (720 square miles) and has a population of some eight million.

I have had to define my focus or risk the wrath of both publisher and reader by producing a massive, unmanageable tome. Greater London is, therefore, largely beyond the scope of this book. It is the historic centre – the City and "royal" Westminster, with the occasional foray into such ancient and medieval suburbs as Southwark and Clerkenwell, Shoreditch and Hackney – that this book sets out to explore, with, I freely admit, an archaeological bias. Of course, the edges of my loose definition of Central London become blurred at times: it would be perverse to rule out a visit to Greenwich or Hampton Court when discussing the work of Inigo Jones or Christopher Wren. My arbitrary approach is most evident in the coverage of those seventeenth- and eighteenth-century buildings which sprang up as London broke free of its City boundaries into new suburbs in the west.

As for when to stop? I have deliberately concentrated on the periods in which archaeological discovery has been able to increase our knowledge of London's past: the truly remarkable finds from within the Roman walled city that have given historians a new dimension to its story; Saxon London along the Strand; the recently acquired knowledge of London's medieval past that has been brought to light by excavations or discovered hidden in the fabric of later buildings; and the remarkable story of the rebuilding after the Great Fire. Georgian London is therefore my postscript – a glimpse into what might be described as the beginning of modern London.

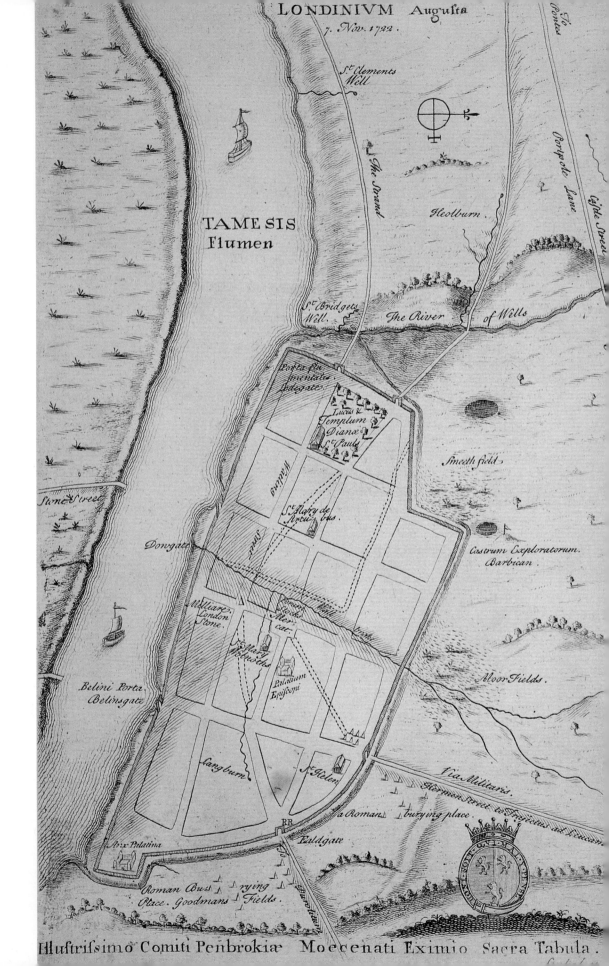

LONDINIVM Augusta
7. Nov. 1722.

Chapter 1
Londinium AD 50-410

"**B**OOM AND BUST**"** – according to London's archaeologists that is the expression that best describes the first thousand years of London. It is a harsh verdict for those who like to think that the City represents almost 2,000 years of continuous history. But at times the economic bust must have seemed terminal, for it now appears that London was virtually abandoned and given over to pasture for several centuries. Fire usually stalked the boom periods, the Great Fire of 1666 being only one of several in London's long history.

The date of London's foundation, usually attributed to AD 43, may also have to be reconsidered. There is no positive evidence of occupation in the archaeological record until the early AD 50s, and although there are traces of a ditch and a bank that could have been part of an early Roman fort, most archaeologists remain unconvinced that the earthworks represent Roman military presence on the site of what we now know as the City of London. The notion that London has enjoyed 2,000 years, or even longer, of continuous occupation was nurtured by the historians of the Middle Ages. William Fitz Stephen, a Londoner who wrote a biography of Thomas Becket and a detailed description of London in about 1180, confidently asserted that "London, as the chroniclers have shown is far older than Rome."

Fitz Stephen's view of London's history was greatly influenced by Geoffrey of Monmouth (c. 1100-54), whose *History of the Kings of England* was known throughout medieval Europe. Geoffrey, who also popularized the stories of King Arthur and his Knights of the Round Table, inspired his readers with the story of a mythical Trojan warrior, Brutus. After the fall of Troy the gods revealed to him a new world in a dream: "Brutus, beyond the setting sun, past the realms of Gaul, there lies an island in the sea, once occupied by giants...and for your descendants it will be a second Troy."

Geoffrey of Monmouth's fantasy lost credence as the centuries passed, but the lingering possibility of some sort of prehistory for London, on which the Romans had built, survived into modern

The Roman settlement of Londinium about AD 60 occupied the two hill tops on either side of the Walbrook. Perhaps as much as four times wider than it is today, the Thames could have been bridged using a series of sandy islands that reached out into the river from the Southwark bank.

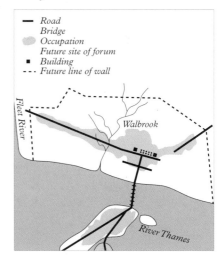

— Road
   Bridge
   Occupation
   Future site of forum
■ Building
--- Future line of wall

The earliest known map of Roman London, made by the antiquary William Stukeley in 1722. Working from stray finds, he pinpointed many features of the Roman city. Sceptical archaeologists proved Stukeley's line of the river wall to be correct only in the 1970s.

times. Only in the second half of the twentieth century did scientific investigation finally scotch that idea.

There is no doubt now that London began on a green-field site which the Romans clearly chose for very practical reasons. It was probably the first place up river which could be easily bridged. Although the Thames was much wider then – one study of the landscape in Roman times suggests it might have been up to four times its present width – it may have been possible to wade well into the river at low tide, using a series of sandy islands that reached out from the Southwark bank. London was located at about the limit of the tidal flow, enabling boats to be swept up river on the flood tide; and there was high ground on the north bank where two flat-topped hills overlooked the Thames. The first crossing may have been at Westminster, where more islands made it possible to ford the river. But some time around AD 50 London became the preferred crossing, and although no trace of that first bridge has been found, archaeologists digging under the streets of modern Southwark have discovered an early Roman road built on a foundation of logs, across the marshy ground. It leads straight to the same alignment as the succession of London Bridges for which there are records in the Middle Ages.

The absence of any clear sign of a fort on the site, and a dearth of military items such as armour or horse trappings, has led some archaeologists to conclude that London was not a civilian shadow of a military settlement, but a product of pure private enterprise, a crossroads community of traders drawn from all over the Roman Empire in search of a quick profit. Firm evidence one way or the other has probably been lost forever, but archaeologists, digging down through the basements of nineteenth-century buildings, have glimpsed the town as it was in AD 60. It covered about 12 hectares (30 acres), with a grid of roads across the twin hills of Cornhill and Ludgate Hill, and the stream called Walbrook dividing them. You can still see the dip of the Walbrook Valley in the roads around Cannon Street Station, and the modern street named Walbrook marks the course of that ancient tributary of the Thames.

The Roman streets were lined with shops and houses built mainly of wattle and daub (a frame of sticks with mud or clay infill) and thatched roofs. A large open space at the main crossroads may have been the market place – 6 metres (20 feet) below today's Leadenhall Market – and on the main east-west road archaeologists found the remains of a row of buildings with a colonnaded street frontage. Some windows may have had glass; most were shuttered, but on one street, almost directly beneath Fenchurch Street, were the remains of a piped water system – wooden pipes joined together with iron collars.

The houses had concrete floors; some plastered walls had a painted decoration. The bane of today's town planner, continuous ribbon development outside the town, was even then a feature of this earliest phase of London. All the main roads leading out of the town were affected – across the river in Southwark buildings straggled along the Kent Road for more than a kilometre (about three-quarters of a mile). The few inscriptions that survive, giving us names of Londoners, suggest that the town was almost as cosmopolitan then as it is today, and familiar with a range of imported goods that spanned the Roman world: glass from Italy and Syria; tableware from Gaul; olive oil from Spain; and wine in amphoras from the island of Rhodes in the Mediterranean. The merchants and artisans who followed the army to the edge of the world must have done well in the boom economy of Londinium.

Such a snapshot of London in AD 60 is only possible because of a catastrophe. London was consumed in a holocaust – the first Great Fire of London – when the Celtic British queen Boudicca swept through the town bent on revenge for Roman injustice. The Roman writer Tacitus, in one of his few references to London, tells us that the Roman commander decided to evacuate the town in order to save the rest of the province: "Neither the tears nor the lamentations of those who begged his help could deflect him from giving the signal to pull out, and allowing into his column [only] those who could keep up with him." Women, children and old people who stayed behind "were overwhelmed by the enemy."

Boudicca's army, having sacked the provincial capital Camulodunum (Colchester), then demolished Verulamium (St Albans) and Londinium: no prisoners were taken: "They rushed to slaughter, hang, burn and crucify." A mass grave of skulls found by workmen in the Walbrook Valley in the nineteenth century may well have dated from that early disaster. The ferocity of the fire is clearly documented in the scorched floors of houses and the layer of orange-red burnt clay from wattle-and-daub walls that archaeologists have found on more than a dozen sites scattered across the City. The tell-tale scorched areas have given us a rough idea of the boundaries of this first settlement. But the question of London's population at the time is difficult to resolve. The only information we have on this subject also comes from Tacitus, who tells us that 70,000 people were massacred in the three towns. But the classical writers are notorious for their broad-brush approach to figures. Boudicca's rebellion was quickly put down by the Romans, who were equally ruthless; the queen, we are told, ended her life by taking poison.

In a matter of hours London was bust, and in a state of shock. It took a long time for confidence to return, and although the military had soon regained control there is no evidence of any significant economic activity for about ten years. After that the city rushed into what seems like a frenzied period of development. Massive public buildings, an expanded road network, a new port and substantial town houses replaced the charred remains of Boudicca's rebellion. One exceptional find from that period is the funeral monument of Gaius Julius Classicianus, which is now in the Roman gallery of the Museum of London. Gaius Classicianus had been sent by the Emperor Nero to sort out the financial aspects of Rome's relationship with the rebellious local Celtic British rulers. The Roman writers mention his successful stint as Procurator of the Province and his monument, found in two parts over a period of eighty-three years in the nineteenth and twentieth centuries, confirms the written record and clearly indicates that by the late first century London had become the administrative capital of Roman Britain.

A length of battered-looking timber in the tiny churchyard of St Magnus the Martyr on Lower Thames Street is said to be Roman. According to tradition that baulk of wood, lying on the flagstones alongside the porch, was dredged up from the Thames during work on the 'new' London Bridge in the 1820s. The river-bed yielded a store of Roman and medieval objects including coins, pottery, swords and daggers – the bric-à-brac of almost two millennia lost or thrown into the Thames. Those finds clearly indicated the line of an ancient crossing, which was confirmed by a recent discovery of more Roman timber: a box-like structure made of large squared beams jointed at the corners. Tree-ring analysis dated the felling of the timber to the late AD 70s or early 80s, leading City archaeologists to believe that the structure was one of the pylons of the first-century AD Roman bridge.

Excavations on either side of the "pylon" during the 1980s uncovered a series of quays made of large oak beams that stretched at least 550 metres (1,800 feet) along London's waterfront. Archaeologists had found the "lost" port of Roman London beneath a network of lanes and small streets on the landward side of Lower Thames Street – at least 100 metres (330 feet) inland from the modern river frontage! The timbers, still solid after 1,900 years, dwarfed the excavators as they revealed the best part of entire tree trunks that had been rafted down the Thames and squared up for the jetties and quays that Roman engineers had terraced into the steep bank.

Shipwrecks found in the Thames give some idea of how the trade for the port was handled. One of the vessels discovered during dredging was a flat-bottomed lighter some 16 metres (52 feet) long with a beam of about 4 metres (13 feet). Another wreck found at Blackfriars was slightly bigger, with a draft of about 2 metres (6 feet 6 inches), but the third one, found in the river alongside County Hall near Westminster Bridge in 1910, was a small sea-going merchantman about 20 metres (65 feet) long. A study of the port and its three unfortunate visitors has led the excavator Gustav Milne of the Museum of London to believe that the largest sea-going Roman vessels did not find their way to London, and that all the goods were transhipped into shallow-draft vessels, such as the "County Hall" ship, in ports on the Kent coast. Whatever the case it seems likely that because of the tides vessels may have had to discharge into

Massive oak timbers dwarf the archaeologist at work during excavations of the Roman quayside. In its final, third-century phase the quayside measured at least 550 metres (1,804 feet) and was about 50 metres (164 feet) wide.

Samian pottery, made in large quantities in central France, was imported for the army. This shipment was found in excavations along the Roman waterfront. Glass came from Italy, marble from Turkey, wine from Spain, Italy and Gaul (France), jewellery from Egypt, amber from the Baltic and amphoras of dried fruit from Palestine.

lighters in midstream, or simply beach themselves on the shingle at low tide – practices that continued on the London river well into the twentieth century.

Southwark, at the other end of London Bridge, also had its share of the port, with quays and warehouses. A startling find was a Roman timber warehouse on the Courage Brewery site in Park Street, about 200 metres (650 feet) back from the river. About 11 metres (36 feet) long by 4.75 metres (15 feet 6 inches) wide, the oak floors were perfectly preserved, along with the remains of wooden walls and a couple of wooden roof shingles with their iron nails still in place. The whole remarkable floor clearly showed the skills of late first- or second-century carpenters.

Southwark's more modern warehouses along the nineteenth-century waterfront concealed many archaeological treasures: just up stream from Southwark Cathedral, archaeologists found parts of the Bishop of Winchester's medieval palace preserved within warehouses built in the nineteenth century – we shall hear more about this in Chapter 4. But underneath there was an even greater surprise: the floors of what could have been a Roman palace of the first and second century AD, complete with hypocausts (the Roman underfloor heating system), mosaics and painted plaster. Having fallen face down the precious plaster decoration had survived in full colour: thousands of fragments fitted together to reveal a fresco depicting the columns of a portico hung with garlands of flowers; Cupid featured in the middle of the design, standing on one leg and holding what looks like a plate. It has turned out to be one of Roman Britain's most important fresco discoveries.

Across the river, on the terraces of the northern bank, another even more palatial building was found – perhaps the palace of the Roman governor. It must have had a commanding view, overlooking both the Thames and the estuary of the Walbrook. The building first came to light when very thick Roman walls were encountered by the builders of Cannon Street Railway Station in 1868. A plan of what was found was drawn by an antiquary who watched the work in progress, but it was not until almost a century later that Peter Marsden, who was then working for the Guildhall Museum and excavating another site nearby, found more walls 3 metres (10 feet) wide, and mosaic pavements that were certainly a continuation of the same building. He found the remains of a 10 metre (33 foot) wide ornamental pool and what must have been part of a spectacular garden terrace about 130 metres (425 feet) long, looking out across the river.

The "palace" included a hall of monumental proportions measuring some 13 metres (43 feet) by 24 metres (80 feet). Sadly no inscription has been found to confirm the building's identity. Some of the walls still survive under the station – they were seen again by archaeologists in the 1980s – but only one fragment of the governor's palace can be seen above ground. A single stone, it may have been part of the entrance which took on some special significance for medieval Londoners, but to see it today you have to bend down and peer through a dusty window set into the new building of the

Oversea Chinese Banking Corporation at 111 Cannon Street, opposite the station. Behind the small glass window is the roughly rounded top of a piece of limestone that used to obstruct the traffic in Cannon Street until it was swept away in a spate of Corporation tidiness in 1742. The surviving stone was removed to the medieval church of St Swithin, but that was bombed during the Blitz and demolished. After the war the best that could be done for the venerable "Stone of London" was to make a glass-covered niche in the wall of the OCBC as near as possible to the position it occupied in the Middle Ages.

A few minutes away, at the top of Huggin Hill, a stone's throw from the mighty dome of St Paul's Cathedral, an open space somewhat clumsily preserved as a terraced garden is a welcome "lung" for modern City workers. It also marks the site of another great building of the late first century AD: a large bath house that was fed from a natural spring. Much of this bathing complex still remains, among the foundations of modern office blocks on either side, safe until commercial pressure forces another spate of redevelopment for this part of London. Perhaps a more enlightened attitude next time around might enable the remains of the baths to be conserved for public exhibition in the basements of the buildings. In the meantime there is just a glimpse of a Roman wall available at the very bottom of the terraced garden.

Leadenhall Market – an area of streets and lanes covered by a splendid web of cast-iron girders – sits on top of the centre of the Roman town, covering part of the first forum, built about AD 70. The remains of a large rectangular stone building were noted and sketched by Henry Hodge when the foundations were being dug for the market in the nineteenth century. The sketches took on a new significance when, in 1977, the Post Office tunnelled under Gracechurch Street to lay new cables. It was just possible for someone to crouch their way through the tunnel and examine the full width of the Roman concrete floor of the nave, 3 metres (10 feet) below the modern street. Much of the plan of the forum, and its successor, has been traced, making possible a three-dimensional drawing which shows a large aisled hall (the basilica) with a semicircular east end within a large, colonnaded courtyard. For a Roman town the size of London it seemed adequate, but in about AD 120 it was superseded by a massive new forum, whose basilica, the seat of government for the town, had an aisled hall as large as the nave of Christopher Wren's St Paul's Cathedral, built nearly 1,600 years later. Second-century Londoners were probably proud to claim that their forum was the biggest in any Roman city north of the Alps!

Such a development may have been the result of the Emperor Hadrian's visit to the Province of Britain in the AD 120s. He turned up with a large retinue on a tour of the empire's defences. He had a penchant for triumphal arches and left many in his trail, and it is likely that a spate of public buildings in London – such as a massive masonry arch found near the Huggin Hill baths, the extension of the baths themselves, and the governor's palace now covered by

An imaginative reconstruction of the ornamental garden and state rooms of the governor's palace, based on excavations during the 1960s. Remains of massive walls and of mosaics were also found and recorded during the building of Cannon Street Station in 1868.

Cannon Street Station – stemmed from his visit. As for Hadrian's influence on London's defences, he probably built the Roman fort at Cripplegate. Only located by Professor W.F. Grimes in 1949, the 5 hectare (12 acre) fort had four gates, the usual collection of stores and accommodation for perhaps a thousand troops. Hadrian's Wall in the north of England was certainly inspired by the restless emperor who, in AD 120, ordered his engineers to build the most lavish frontier defence in the entire empire.

Perhaps London had the ubiquitous Hadrian to thank for the amphitheatre as well. To the chagrin of archaeologists, this had always been missing from maps of Roman London. They knew, of course, that there must have been one – every self-respecting Roman town had an amphitheatre – but it was not until 1985 that the missing arena emerged from a trench outside the medieval Guildhall.

It turned up because the Corporation of London decided to build an art gallery on the site of the old library, which had been badly damaged during the Blitz. The site was cleared and test trenches to probe the archaeology were sunk into Guildhall Yard. Six metres (20 feet) beneath the surface, archaeologists struck a gravel floor and some Roman timber. Subsequent excavations in 1993-4 have revealed stretches of a curved wall, the foundations of two rectangular chambers that flanked the main east entrance, the gravelled floor of the amphitheatre some 62 metres (203 feet) by 44 metres (144 feet), and wooden drains, including the main drain that spanned the length of the arena. Nicholas Bateman, the excavation director, when he showed me the remains, explained that the box-shaped drain was made of long stretches of thick planks cut from squared oak logs. Tons of timber have been recovered: one of the largest deposits of ancient timber to have been found anywhere in the Roman world.

At first no one could imagine how the timber drain had survived so well. The site is actually on a hill top, an unlikely place for conditions that are damp enough to preserve wood. But as excavations continued it became clear that the amphitheatre had been constructed in a shallow valley containing a small stream that flowed into the Walbrook nearby, and that the drains kept the amphitheatre dry. Later the area became water-logged, creating perfect conditions for the preservation of the oak. To my touch it felt as firm as if it had been delivered to the site by the timber merchant last week, but in fact the planks were brittle and needed to be strengthened with soluble wax before they could be put on display.

In the drains archaeologists found a Roman gold earring, many coins that dated the construction to about AD 120 (traces of an earlier arena from about AD 70 were also noted) and a large collection of bones. A bear and a bull were definitely represented – they very likely met their end in a display of fighting in the arena – and there were some scattered human bones. The same fate may have befallen their owners! Another remarkable find was a piece of a Samian pottery bowl with a decoration that depicted a gladiator with sword and shield, confronting a bull. Archaeologists estimate that the timber tiers of seats above the masonry walls of the amphitheatre would have held about 8,000 spectators, and that the arena was in use until about AD 370.

Continuity is one of the first things that strikes you about the site: there has been an open space at this point in the City since medieval times, and perhaps future work will show that the Guildhall itself was deliberately sited over the amphitheatre. The remains are so well preserved that, instead of archaeologists merely recording the existence and position of the structure, the walls and the gravel floor are to be preserved *in situ*. A £40 million art gallery is to rise on the site and will embrace the remains, which will be on permanent display. The architects have planned to spread the weight of the new building on a massive steel frame so that concrete piles, the usual type of foundations for such a building, need not be used. The amphitheatre will therefore not be punctured by concrete pillars. The plan is to "suspend" it inside the new two-storey basement by supporting the amphitheatre's gravel floor with a raft of concrete. The clay underneath will then be dug out so that a much needed deeper basement to house the Guildhall's collection of medieval and later documents can be created. With the conserved amphitheatre walls, drain and floor still in place, visitors using overhead walkways will be able to see the remains, apparently untouched by the twentieth century, one floor beneath the main art gallery.

London's second Great Fire must have engulfed the city soon after Hadrian's visit in AD 122, although it is not mentioned by any of the classical writers. Since an excavation in 1930 near the northern end of London Bridge revealed a layer of burnt debris, archaeologists have been aware that something serious must have happened. This scorched red layer contained fragments of imported bowls, lamps and jars that represented at least 600 pieces of new pottery, suggesting that the building which had been consumed by fire was a warehouse.

But as excavations have extended across the City during the building boom of the past thirty years, so evidence has been amassed to show that fire wiped out a large section of London in the AD 120s. It clearly raced through the tightly packed two-storey tenements – wooden-framed buildings that must have burned like their equally vulnerable medieval counterparts – for about a mile across the city. Burnt red clay, plaster and tiles have been seen in recent excavations as far east as All Hallows Barking Church near the Tower of London, in King William Street, and as far west as Newgate Street. The new forum, however, and the fort at

A mosaic discovered on a redevelopment site in Milk Street. It was covered with a layer of "dark earth", indicating that for long periods London had been deserted and perhaps turned over to pasture.

Cripplegate seem to have escaped, as did most of the big public buildings – including the amphitheatre – perhaps because they were built in stone.

Dominic Perring, who has excavated in the City of London, first for the Museum of London and latterly for English Heritage, believes that "in most areas the post-fire recovery was prompt... and prime commercial sites, such as those in Newgate Street, were redeveloped almost immediately." Other archaeologists disagree, maintaining that the fire had a profound effect on the city and that commercial recovery was very weak. Although London appears to have bounced back, and mostly intact, as the province's leading commercial centre and capital, some burnt buildings were simply left as they were and not redeveloped for decades. More stone buildings appeared after the fire and many large houses, lavishly decorated with marble veneer and mosaic floors, had their own private bath houses. Workshops and shops were also well decorated with painted walls and cement floors. But this revival was short-lived. It was not long before London began to show an entirely different face: that of sagging confidence, spiralling decline and abandonment.

There are no documents that give us a clue as to why London appeared to decline dramatically after about AD 150, and no one was more surprised that the archaeologists who, having dug through the basements of nineteenth-century office buildings, found only layers of dark earth. On site after site of Roman London, buildings and evidence of occupation, representing more than half a century, were missing from the archaeological record. Many parts of the city appeared to lie dormant until the fall of the empire in AD 410. What the archaeologists found instead was something that looked like garden loam. I well remember in the early 1980s climbing down into a square shaft, let into the floor of a nineteenth-century basement, to find puzzled archaeologists confronted by the "dark earth". And these were not isolated garden plots that they had hit upon: the dark earth layer, anything up to 1.5 metres (5 feet) thick, was like a charcoal grey blanket covering much of the city.

The area least affected by the phenomenon was along the Walbrook Valley, but archaeologists have estimated that as much as two-thirds of the City must have been smothered by the soil. I doubt if any London archaeologist would claim to know what lies behind this mystery; scientific analysis has confirmed that the earth was enriched with "compost", i.e. night soil and street sweepings, but was mainly made up of wattle-and-daub debris – the sort of materials of which most houses, except the wealthier stone ones and the public buildings, were built. Some scientists think that the dark earth could represent the result of a natural process; one in which earthworms had so thoroughly churned up the building debris that it became indistinguishable from garden loam, and that the buildings of second-century London are there, but are unrecognizable today.

Whatever the truth of this may be, the fact remains that there is a distinct lack of wells and rubbish pits for this period, indicating a much reduced population; for those who subscribe to the abandonment theory, London, in the latter part of the second century, had become a huge market garden. It still functioned as a city, in that the main streets were kept up, the thriving trades in the Walbrook Valley stayed in business and some public buildings were still in use. The great public baths on Huggin Hill, however, were demolished by about AD 200. Excavations in Southwark gave similar results; communities outside London, the shanty towns along the roads leading to the capital, had also shrunk significantly.

In the absence of any documents of the period that refer to London we can only speculate on what might have happened. Plague is high on the list of suspects – between AD 165 and 190 the disease had severely affected Western Europe, and may have played a role in reducing the size of London's population. Just as effective might have been the economic changes of the time. After Hadrian's decision not to extend the boundaries of the empire any further, London's merchants might have lost valuable military contracts as army campaigns were scaled down. Other towns with ports, such as York, may have syphoned off trade that once flowed through London, and it looks as though the level of imports of pottery, wine and oil fell substantially during the latter half of the second century. As Dominic Perring put it, "London was no longer a hub of commerce but had perhaps begun to become a place more fit for gentlemen."

All the more puzzling, therefore, was the decision to build a wall around London. In their post-fire town houses Londoners must have been shocked out of their semi-rural idyll when wagons loaded

Plan of Cripplegate Fort, excavated by W.F. Grimes in 1949. He discovered the position of the fort by observing that near Cripplegate the city wall suddenly became a double wall. He then discovered that at one point one wall curved away from the other and pursued a different course. He had found the south-west corner of the fort, whose adjoining walls ran parallel across the width of the fort. Part of the double wall and a turret are preserved in a sunken garden in Noble Street, opposite the Museum of London.

with stone destined for the city walls began arriving. Curiously, Roman London had no city wall for about half of its history, and it was not until AD 190 at the earliest that a start was made. For a distance of about 3 kilometres (2 miles) the massive wall, 6 metres (20 feet) high and 2.5 metres (8 feet) wide, wrapped itself around London in a huge semi-circle enclosing about 133 hectares (330 acres). It had a walkway along the top and through its crenellations a soldier on patrol would have looked out over a deep U- or V-shaped defensive ditch to the suburbs and countryside beyond.

Wall enthusiasts estimate that it would have taken about 5,700 lorries to carry the stone and flint – not to mention the half-million tiles – that were needed for the project. The squared blocks of Kentish rag stone had to be brought from 110 kilometres (70 miles) away by boat, first along the Medway, then into the Thames estuary for the journey up stream to London. We know this because of the shipwreck in the Port of London known as the Blackfriars Boat. She foundered, probably because of a collision, and sank with a load of stone that never reached the wall. In the socket that held the mast was found a coin minted in Rome in either AD 88 or 89, obviously placed there by the builders. Archaeologists found it reverse side up, so that the image of the goddess Fortuna would have pressed against the end of the mast to bring the boat luck.

This discovery was a useful guide to the dating of the wall, as no inscription or classical references had previously offered any clues. A more reliable date came from coins found at another site during excavations in 1966. Ironically, a hoard belonging to a coin forger was found in Warwick Square, just behind London's main criminal court, the Old Bailey. The forger had hidden his moulds, originals and fakes in a turret of the wall and an examination of the coin dates revealed that he was minting coins in bronze – perhaps with the connivance of the military authorities. He was copying original silver coins dated from between AD 201 and 217, disguising the bronze with a silver wash. Pottery and another coin suggest that the wall was built some time between AD 190 and 225.

Another important piece of Roman civil engineering was the bridge over the Fleet River – one of London's so-called lost rivers – at the western end of the city. Contrary to what many Londoners believe, the Fleet River, which rises from springs on Hampstead Heath, does not follow the line of modern Fleet Street but flows roughly north-south under the wider Farringdon and New Bridge Streets. When the Romans arrived they found the Fleet emptying into the Thames through a wide estuary and, where Ludgate Circus is today, there were two small islands that proved very useful.

The islands were discovered in 1988-92 as archaeologists explored the valley of the Fleet during the redevelopment of a very large area along the line of the old river. On the remains of the upstream island they could see how the Romans had built a mill and, on the smaller island, a warehouse and a timber jetty, all of which date from the first or second centuries AD.

Later, at about the time of the construction of the city walls, the smaller island was used to build masonry piers that must have

Cooper's Row, Trinity Square. The lower section – up to 4.4 metres (14 feet 6 inches) is Roman and the red sandstone plinth, marking the Roman ground level, is clearly visible. During the medieval period the height was increased to 6.2 metres (20 feet) and loopholes for archers, reached by a sentry walk, were incorporated. A timber platform was probably supported by joists let into the sockets on either side of the loopholes.

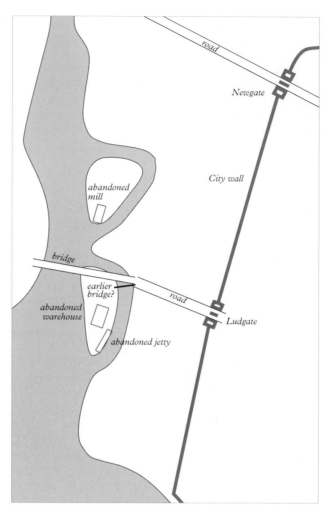

Plan of the small islands in the Fleet River. Archaeologists digging below Ludgate Circus in 1988-92 made this surprising discovery. They also found evidence that the Romans had used one of the islands to carry a bridge across to what is now Fleet Street. The upstream island, site of an early mill, had been abandoned by the third century.

carried a substantial bridge spanning the Fleet estuary, probably one of several bridges to have occupied the site and on an alignment roughly the same as the existing Ludgate Hill. The idea of islands under Ludgate Circus seems hardly credible today as traffic thunders across the modest dip in the road where modern Fleet Street and Ludgate Hill meet at what was once the western extremity of the ancient city.

The remains of the Roman bridge pier were made of Kentish rag stone and tiles, the very material being used to build the city walls in the late second century. During the first and second centuries there were glassworks higher up the bank – glass fragments and kilns have been found – and later in the third century a large octagonal building overlooking the river was built on top of the kilns. Because of its unusual shape and size – painted plaster fragments had also survived – archaeologists believe that it may have been a Romano-Celtic temple, and a human skull buried with charcoal in a pit near the outside walls may have been a sacrifice to mark the foundation of the temple.

The belated city wall that protected all this lasted until the eighteenth century, when most of it was demolished as London expanded. Only recently has it re-emerged as an intermittent feature of the modern City, miraculously appearing from within the fabric of later buildings, and in basements, as the City centre has fallen prey to a new wave of developers. A long stretch was discovered when a wartime bomb badly damaged the medieval church of St Alphege, which had been built right up against the wall. You can see it today, set in a garden among the ruins of the church, near the modern road that calls itself London Wall.

Londoners still navigate by the wall: Houndsditch is the street that follows the line of the defensive ditch running north-east; London Wall is a main east-west thoroughfare; and some of the Roman gates are represented by medieval roads called Aldgate, Bishopsgate, Ludgate Hill and Newgate. The west gate of the Roman fort has been preserved in the basement of a new building on London Wall near the Museum of London. Visitors can see the foundations of the northern tower of the gate just as they were discovered. The tower contained the guardroom and access to the sentry walk along the top of the wall.

It is not at all clear why London suddenly needed a wall. Again the historical record is silent, but historians tend to connect the event with the civil war in the late second century when the Governor of Britain, Decimus Clodius Albinus, claimed the throne of the entire Roman Empire. He wore the purple – the sign of imperial rank – for four years in the early 190s and in a period of turmoil may have felt the need to protect his capital and power base when he campaigned with the British army in Gaul. Albinus's reign came to an end near Lyons in AD 197 during a battle with his rival Septimius Severus, who then invaded Britain and chose to spend several years there.

It may have been the Emperor Severus who injected life back into the capital as a result of new campaigns of conquest in the north of Britain. In any event London in the third century was once again endowed with fine public buildings, a mighty wall and a new and even grander quayside.

The houses of the third century reflected London's regained prestige. Peter Marsden, excavating near Billingsgate, recorded details of a substantial building with two wings. Some of the rooms had hypocaust heating for their mosaic floors, and parallel to the east wing the house had its own bath, comprising three rooms with different temperatures. Dozens of fine mosaic pavements have been found during the past century, many of them now on display at the British Museum and the Museum of London. The evidence suggests that London in the third century could have had as many as a hundred substantial stone houses within its walls. With their gardens – there were still large tracts of "dark earth" – London must have resembled a walled estate for the wealthy.

One indication of wealth was in the Temple of Mithras, discovered in the Walbrook Valley by Professor W.F. Grimes in 1954. He had won permission from the insurance company Legal and General to explore the site on which construction of a large office block was soon to start. He had put a trench across the ancient stream-bed of the Walbrook and by chance hit upon a small Roman temple which had been built about AD 240 and dedicated to the god Mithras. Originally the Persian god of heavenly light, Mithras is believed to have insisted on a high moral code; important among his followers were military men, merchants and officials. What the adherents of the cult of Mithras did in private is still a mystery, but water, fire and sacrifice probably played a part.

The building itself went almost unnoticed by the public until the excavation began to produce the exquisite statuary that was probably on display in the temple. The newspapers, not usually entranced by London's archaeology, focused on the novelty of finding the paraphernalia of a mysterious eastern cult where twentieth-century clerks and typists pursued a much less exotic daily ritual. The public swarmed to see the excavations – one day there was a mile-long queue – and under such a blaze of publicity the insurance company agreed to give the archaeologists extra time and to re-erect the temple a short distance away in the windswept and sterile courtyard of their nondescript new office block at 11 Queen Victoria Street. Legal and General missed a wonderful opportunity to preserve the temple where it was found by incorporating it into their basement car park. Instead, it sits on a plinth on the car-park roof.

The temple's design is quite like that of a miniature Christian church, only 18 metres (60 feet) long and 8 metres (26 feet) wide with aisles and a row of columns on either side of a tiny nave. There

The head of Mithras, god of heavenly light, carved in Italian marble, found buried in the floor of the temple. The surface of the marble showed signs of having been burnt when it was first excavated, suggesting that fire might have been used in the ritual worship of the god.

Head of Serapis, Egyptian god of the underworld, with a corn measure on his head. With Mercury, whose head was also found in the temple, Serapis helped to guide the departed spirits on their last journey. A life-sized disembodied marble hand of Mithras was found along with the head of the god.

was a rounded apse at the west end and a well to one side of the raised sanctuary. In its original position by the stream the building was probably part of a private house.

The temple gradually went out of use during the fourth century and, according to the excavator, it deteriorated into a bit of a shambles towards the end of its days. Professor Grimes also suggested that the damage to the statues, and the attempt to hide them, may have resulted from Christian desecration after the empire officially espoused Christianity during Constantine's reign in the AD 330s. Historians now think that it is more likely that Mithras lost favour with Londoners who, some time in the fourth century, buried the statues in preparation for the arrival of another pantheon of gods. Grimes and his workmen found the marble head of Mithras, the heads of Minerva and the Egyptian god of the underworld Serapis, and they can be seen today as a group in the Museum of London.

When Grimes saved the Temple of Mithras he was Professor of Archaeology at London University and Honorary Director of the Roman and Medieval London Excavation Council. This was a private organization set up by the Society of Antiquaries, because at that time the Corporation of London took no responsibility for the rescue, or the recording, of any antiquities found in the City. They were pleased, however, to receive any antiquities that came the way of the Guildhall's collection, begun in the middle of the nineteenth century. The best that the immensely wealthy Corporation of London could manage for archaeology was a donation of £550 over fifteen years to the independently run excavation committee. The Corporation's Guildhall Library also employed one, or sometimes two, "excavations assistants" to collect finds for the museum section of the library.

When Ivor Noel Hume was hired by the Corporation in 1949 to do that job, he described his beat as stretching from one end of the City to the other, and across the river to Southwark. His tools consisted of such items as he could carry on a London red bus –

This round silver box containing an insert that might have been used for straining or infusing is the most mysterious find. It was found in a hole in the wall where it had perhaps been hidden deliberately. The decoration in relief depicts many animals, including an elephant, snake, lion, hippopotamus, deer and wild boar. One part of the decoration has been interpreted as griffins trying to tear open boxes that look like coffins. This is a unique object that has baffled all the experts.

A group of four mother goddesses from the Temple of Mithras.

there was no van or car provided – and the finds when they were plentiful "were carried through the streets to Guildhall on one's back in hundredweight coal sacks, or if the builders were helpful, in a wheelbarrow borrowed from the site."

Developers were not always helpful; Noel Hume confided to me that once when he was working at the bottom of a Roman well the builders began deliberately to tip rubble down on him. Very often the developers had no time in their schedule for any investigation of the archaeology and all the excavations assistant could do was to watch from the sidelines as mechanical grabs hauled up Roman remains. "Rarely was it possible to do more than photograph the destruction and to salvage individual objects as they spilled out of the loosened and dropped silt."

One of Noel Hume's successors, Peter Marsden, who joined the staff of the Guildhall Museum in 1959, suffered the same sort of frustration: "The years up to 1972 now seem like a bad dream, with missed opportunities and the ruthless destruction of large parts of Roman London. For example, to see an elaborately decorated

A Roman riverside wall in Upper Thames Street. Built between AD 255 and 370, its existence was only confirmed in 1974 when this stretch was discovered. The wall, 2.4 metres (7 feet 10 inches) wide, stood on the foundations of timber piles and chalk seen here.

Roman mosaic pavement destroyed without being able to uncover and record it is a tragic experience. In fact it will never be known how much potential knowledge was lost forever. For a very long time the buried city of Roman London was in desperate need for scholars to discover its history, but there was very little official help."

Despite such handicaps much was done. And with the Corporation's change of heart in 1972, when the City fathers agreed to the setting up of a well-funded Department of Urban Archaeology, most developers began to co-operate, with the result that even when Roman remains were destroyed, a proper record was made for the future.

During the course of the third century AD, the wealthy family and their friends who sought solace in the Temple of Mithras had to face an increasingly tense time in terms of security. They felt sufficiently vulnerable to build another wall along the river between the future sites of the Tower of London in the east and Blackfriars Bridge in the west.

The existence of that additional wall, begun in the late third century, was only confirmed in 1974 when excavations revealed a long collapsed stretch of it containing all sorts of large pieces of masonry from a demolished triumphal arch. There were enough blocks of masonry from the riverside wall and other sites nearby to reconstruct the top of the arch on paper. One of only a handful of arches to have been found in Britain, it measured 7.5 metres (25 feet) in width and was at least 8-9 metres (26-29 feet) high. The pieces of decorated stone show that it displayed life-size carvings of deities, including Minerva and Hercules; in a carved frieze along the top of the arch were seven deities representing the days of the week. It was a major discovery, for a better understanding both of the architecture of the City and of its subsequent struggle to survive.

The jumpy atmosphere of the late third century is reflected in the number of hoards of coins that have turned up all over the City. Raids by Saxon pirates had reached such a stage that the government constructed a string of forts along the east and south coasts – from the Wash to Portsmouth – to protect coastal communities from attack. The official in charge of this new line of defence was called the Count of the Saxon Shore. From bases like that in Dover, the Roman fleet patrolled the coastline and no doubt some of its vessels were regular visitors to the Port of London. The fourth-century Roman writer Vegetius described a very sophisticated naval presence "scouting vessels attached to the battle cruisers" and setting off on a search-and-destroy mission with "sails and rigging...painted a dark sea-blue colour so that ships do not give themselves away. Even the wax they use to caulk their vessels is dyed."

Tension must have been high when a certain Carausius, the Count of the Saxon Shore, declared himself Emperor of Roman Britain. He was popular enough with the army to rule for about six years, but like several other British usurpers who followed him he was murdered, in this case by his successor Allectus. The rebellion was finally put down by the true emperor's general Constantius

Chlorus, who invaded Britain in AD 295. That event won London a mention from the diarists of the time, because of an unexpected siege of the city. Frankish mercenaries employed by Allectus decided to sack London and were well into their task when a flotilla of Roman warships arrived in the Thames. The fourth-century writer Eumenius tells us that "the ships reached London, found survivors of the barbarian mercenaries plundering the city, and, when these began to seek flight, landed and slew them in the streets."

Britain was again reunited with the Roman Empire and a gold medallion was struck to commemorate the occasion. Made in Trier, the medallion was found in Arras, France, in 1922, amongst a hoard

The "Trier medallion", struck to celebrate the reuniting of Britain with the Roman Empire in the late third century.

of Roman jewellery. One side has the bearded portrait of Constantius Chlorus and the other a scene depicting a woman kneeling at a city gate, welcoming a Roman officer mounted on a horse. In the foreground is a Roman warship.

Such references to London are rare at this period, and there is no clear story to be deduced from the archaeological record either. We must be content for the time being with fragments of information gleaned from both: the great forum on top of St Peter's Hill was levelled in about AD 300; what was probably the governor's palace at Cannon Street became dilapidated at about the same time. The other 'palace', across the river at Southwark, was partly demolished, but London was also the seat of a Christian bishop – there is a documentary record of the bishop of the newly established Christian Church attending the Council of Arles in AD 314.

Further into the fourth century archaeologists have recorded the final days of the Temple of Mithras, between AD 341 and 346, at about the same time that the city made a big effort to improve its defences. At least twenty bastions – D-shaped towers – were added to the outside of the walls to provide a platform for catapults. Stone stolen from the amphitheatre may have gone into the towers, of which one foundation can be seen in the basement of Emperor House in Vine Street. Although London itself was hardly a thriving, confident capital at this time, the villa estates in the countryside around the city appear to have flourished. There is no sign of abandonment and indeed there is a reference to a fleet of 600 ships that was needed to carry British grain to the Lower Rhine in AD 359.

In the latter part of the century, however, the province's troubles deepened, reflecting the barbarian challenge to the authority of Rome on the Continent. When the Picts (peoples from north of Hadrian's Wall) and the Scots (the Roman name for the Irish) attacked the north in AD 360 the Emperor Julian sent troops who dealt successfully with the problem, but seven years later we read that Britain was invaded by a "conspiracy" of Picts, Scots, Saxons and Franks. More reinforcements had to be sent by the emperor under the control of Count Theodosius, who used London as his base, and order was restored in AD 369. But an increasingly restless British army rebelled in 382; the soldiers elected their own "emperor", Magnus Maximus, who collected all the British-based troops he could and crossed the Channel. He gained control of the western provinces on the Continent, and, having killed the legitimate emperor Gratian, held on to power until 388.

In Britain what was left of the army fought on against barbarian attacks by sea and land, but the empire, officially split into east and west in 395, suffered a serious setback in 407-9. Large numbers of Barbarian troops had penetrated into Gaul and Spain; communications between Rome and Britain were seriously weakened. The army in Britain then elected three leaders in quick succession: Marcus, Gratian and Constantine. The first two ruled a matter of months each and were both murdered, but Constantine, elected in 407, survived for three years. Like Magnus Maximus before him he set up a mint in London. Deciding perhaps that the main threat to

Britain was from chaos on the Continent, he declared himself Western Emperor and led an expeditionary force across the Channel to fight the barbarian intrusion.

Constantine is thought to have left Britain short of troops for its own defence and, as barbarian pressure increased around the British coasts, the Romano-British administration decided to drop its allegiance to Constantine the usurper. According to the Roman writer Zosimus, "The Barbarians beyond the Rhine, attacking in force, reduced the inhabitants of Britain and some of the Celtic tribes to the point where they were obliged to throw off Roman rule...expelled their Roman rulers and set up their own governments as far as lay within their power."

It appears that in AD 409 the Romano-British ruling classes staged a coup, dismissed Constantine's officials and immediately appealed to the legitimate emperor, Honorius, for help. Zosimus tells us that "Honorius wrote letters to the cities of Britain bidding them to take precautions on their own behalf." In AD 410, the Visigoth leader Alaric, who had many times before laid siege to Rome, finally took the city. The empire stumbled towards destruction, and Roman Britain faced the future alone.

Chapter 2
Lundenwic 410–1066

THE **ROMAN ADMINISTRATION** may have left London in AD 410, but for most people in Roman Britain it was business as usual. The roads were probably not crowded with Romans trying to reach the Channel ports; the province did not suddenly stop. No doubt the people who took control of the towns, including London, expected the trouble on the Continent to blow over and to welcome back the legitimate emperor's administration with the army in due course. But this is all speculation on our part.

There are few documents about the collapse of the empire as they relate to Roman Britain, and only through exploring the archaeological record is any more information likely to be added. The story differs from place to place, according to what has survived in the ground, and in London the evidence of post-colonial existence is thin.

We can, however, look north for an analogy, along Watling Street, or Edgware Road as we know it today, to Roman Britain's third largest town – Verulamium, the modern St Albans. There, two large town houses were built about AD 380 and one was lived in long enough to have had its mosaics repaired. Later, in about 430, a drying plant for corn was installed on top of one of the mosaics, and some time between 425 and 450 a water pipe was laid across the site. It is convincing evidence that Roman know-how was still being applied. At Cirencester, the worn floor of the forum was still being swept up to about 430, and at Silchester archaeologists have found jewellery and glass made in the fifth century.

One very clear indication of the continuity of Romano-British life in Verulamium at this time is the story of Germanus, Bishop of Auxerre, who, with another priest called Lupus, arrived in the town in AD 429. They were sent from the Church in Gaul to deal with a split in the British Church over the Pelagian heresy, which, among other departures from the Church's teaching, did not accept the doctrine of original sin. Constantius, the author of *The Life of Germanus*, written in the fifth century, describes the sect's leaders as "gleaming with their riches, brilliantly clothed, and surrounded by much flattery". St Germanus, we are told, successfully refuted the heresy during a public meeting and went on to heal the blind daughter of a man who exercised "the power of a Tribune".

That account certainly sounds as if some vestige of Roman authority was still in place. To round off his mission Germanus then appointed himself leader of an army which must have included many barbarian mercenaries, baptised them all and went on to do battle with a "fierce host" of Picts and Scots. Lying in wait for the enemy the two priests led a call of "Alleluia" that reverberated around the hills, whereupon "the enemy forces were struck with terror and fear [and] fled in all directions."

Another glimpse of post-colonial trauma comes from the British priest known to us as Gildas. Writing in the 550s about "the fall of Britain", he talks of "loathsome hordes of Picts and Scots" swarming across the sea: "Once they learned of the Romans' departure and their refusal to return, more confident than ever, they seized from its inhabitants the whole northern part of the country as far as the [Hadrian's] wall."

Gildas had a very poor opinion of the British defenders, whom he said were reluctant to fight. British sin, and massacres by barbarians, feature throughout Gildas's text, which also includes the only incident that can be closely dated in the twilight of Roman Britain. Gildas tell us that yet another appeal was made to the Roman authorities: "To Aetius, consul for the third time come the groans of the Britons...the barbarians drive us into the sea; the sea drives us to the barbarians; between these two means of death we are either killed or drowned." Aetius was the western empire's commander in chief and his third consulship, we know from Roman records, began in 446. But the Romans, beset with barbarian problems of their own, could do nothing.

Gildas gives us the impression that Britain was once more becoming a country broken up into various strongholds and ruled by local "kings". He never mentions London, but earthworks in the London area may denote some boundaries of the regional potentates: Grimes Ditch, built in pre-Roman times, may well have been reused at this time, and another bank and ditch on the east side of the Cray Valley may have marked a boundary between communities in London and Kent. Some of the Iron Age hill forts in the southwest of Britain were certainly occupied again, but the only fifth- or early sixth-century post-colonial Roman town to be identified is Wroxeter near Shrewsbury – the most westerly Roman town in Britain. There, archaeologists excavating over a wide area, and trowelling away only a millimetre ($^1/_{25}$ inch)'s depth at a time, were able to plot the position of wooden houses and public buildings laid out like a Roman town among the ruins of Roman masonry buildings. Although there are no signs yet of such rebuilding in London, archaeologists believe that some occupation persisted in the form of a religious precinct. There may also have been a seat of secular power for some unknown magnate carrying on the struggle against barbarian intrusions.

The most tangible evidence of London fading out in the early fifth century comes from a Roman town house in Billingsgate, with its own bath house. A hoard of 273 copper coins was found in the villa's east wing, and as it included the Emperor Honorius's coins, it must have been hidden sometime after AD 395. As the building staggered and fell through desertion and neglect, the coins were dislodged and spilled over the rubble-strewn floors before the tiled roof finally collapsed. Archaeologists in the 1960s found the coins where they had lain undisturbed for more than 1,600 years.

The villa's hypocaust in the east wing still had the ash in its stoke hole from the last time it was used, and a shard of pottery, imported from Palestine, suggested that people may still have been living there in the early 400s. Peter Marsden also found rubbish that might have been left by squatters; he thinks that the eventual collapse of the building may have driven them out. The ruins of the bath section with its hypocaust are still preserved in the basement of a modern office building on Upper Thames Street.

There is a poignant postscript to the villa's history from a much earlier visitor than the archaeologists. Well after it had been overwhelmed by dereliction, someone clambering through the roofless ruin dropped a small round metal brooch – a so-called saucer brooch made for a fifth-century Saxon.

The Anglo-Saxon Chronicle, a group of early writings brought together in the ninth century, has no doubts about the end of post-imperial British power. "In the year of our Lord 449...the Angles or Saxons came to Britain at the invitation of King Vortigern in three long ships." The Romano-British had decided to follow the familiar Roman recruitment pattern of hiring mercenary troops to deal with the Picts and the Scots. The famous barbarian brothers Horsa and Hengist led the group, and Gildas blamed Vortigern, whom he described as a tyrant, for what happened. "On the orders of that ill-fated tyrant they first fixed their terrible claws in the eastern part of the island as if intent upon fighting for the country, but in fact to attack it."

The Venerable Bede, England's first historian, writing in the eighth century, adds the Jutes to the list of invaders and tells us that they settled in Kent, the Saxons in the south-west and the Angles in the north-east. *The Chronicle* lists battle after battle, including a decisive one in 457: "In this year Hengst and Aesc fought against the Britons at a place which is called Crecganford [Crayford in Kent] and there slew four thousand men; and the Britons then forsook Kent and fled to London in great terror." It looks as if London's walls were still useful as a refuge even if, as the archaeological record suggests, there were very few people living there. Bede, who drew on the early annals of *The Anglo-Saxon Chronicle* for much of his history, was right about the origins of the new settlers, though there is considerable controversy among modern historians about the numbers of immigrants involved.

There are few mentions of London during the "missing centuries" of AD 400 to 600. The impression left by the few surviving documentary references is that the Romano-British Christians were pushed back into Wales, where it is now thought that vestiges of Roman civilization persisted into medieval times. Cornwall in the far south-west was another haven. Some Britons even crossed the sea to Gaul and settled in Brittany; the rest were either taken as slaves or quickly absorbed into the new Anglo-Saxon kingdoms.

London, with its walls still standing, was most likely a seat of power for the rulers of the East Saxons, but there is nothing in the archaeology to confirm or refute this view. In fact the layers of dark earth that began to cover large areas of the city in the second half of the second century were to remain undisturbed for several hundred years. What then are we to make of Bede's reference to the London of the early 600s as "a trading centre for many nations who visit it by land and sea"?

Historians and archaeologists, puzzled by the discrepancy, have searched the documents and sifted the archaeological evidence again and again. True, there were Saxon settlements in a ring around London from as early as the late fourth century. There were also what were thought to be Saxon farmsteads in the Westminster area, but within the old Roman walls the dark earth lay undisturbed until Alfred the Great reoccupied the city in 886. Nevertheless Bede was right; London was a great trading centre between AD 600 and 900. Bede's London has been discovered, not within the walls, but between the Fleet River valley and Westminster – a straggling settlement along the north bank of the Thames with the Strand as its main street.

Martin Biddle and Alan Vince, two archaeologists with a deep knowledge of Anglo-Saxon England, were the first to suggest this location for "mid-Saxon" London. They had independently reached the same conclusion by looking closely at patterns of stray finds of Saxon objects during the past three centuries: coins, pieces of pottery, a grave at Trafalgar Square and a building discovered in Whitehall. In the past such finds were summarized as belonging to isolated farmsteads along the road to the walled city. But since the 1985 excavation of the Jubilee Market building in Covent Garden, Biddle and Vince have been proved right.

That site in Covent Garden yielded the post holes and beam slots of wooden buildings in an area dotted with rubbish pits containing animal bones, loom weights, oyster shells and eighth-century pottery. There was slag from a furnace in which bronze was made. Other sites along the Strand and around Trafalgar Square produced timber-lined wells, glimpses of gravelled roads and an extensive gravel quarry under the site of the new extension to the National Gallery. In Maiden Lane, Covent Garden, an earthwork that might have been a defensive ditch was plotted, while down the steep bank beyond the Strand, archaeologists found the Saxon river-bank which had been revetted and planked to form a quay. It all added up to compelling evidence of a substantial town.

The boats that moored alongside, or were drawn up on the sandy shore at low tide, brought mill stones and wine jars from the Rhineland. Pottery made in France was also found in rubbish pits; such things as grape and fig seeds showed that foodstuffs were imported; exports might have included carved bone objects and wool – if not cloth. The large number of loom weights found suggested weaving on an industrial scale. Bede mentions Frisian slave traders operating in London in the seventh century, but the sound of manacles has not yet been heard in the archaeological record.

In many ways Lundenwic, as it is called in documents of the seventh to ninth centuries, is a larger mirror image of the Saxon town that preceded medieval Southampton, Hamwic. As much of that site today remains uncluttered by modern buildings, so more than fifty large-scale excavations have been possible, making Hamwic perhaps the most extensively studied Dark Age town in Western Europe. The trade connections reached across the English Channel and the North Sea to Dark Age towns in what are now Denmark, Germany and France. Hamwic, Lundenwic, Ipswich (on the east coast of England) and Eoforwic (Anglo-Saxon York) were all part of a network of manufacturing and trading towns. The imported goods show up in the Hamwic excavations today, along-side the remnants of small industries that were turning out a wide range of objects made of bone, horn, wool and metal.

As Saxon London grew it probably developed into a twin city, with the spiritual and temporal authorities residing within the Roman walls, while the merchants and the rest got on with their business along the Strand. By the beginning of the sixth century, Anglo-Saxon England had shaken down into a patchwork of more or less stable kingdoms, with Mercia seeming to box and cox with Kent for control of London.

The Kentish king Ethelbert, who had married a Frankish Christian princess from Paris, was the first of the pagan kings be christened. He allowed St Augustine into his kingdom, where he preached his first sermon on English soil in AD 597. Augustine, sent by Rome to re-establish Christianity in England, set up his mission in the small church in Canterbury (St Martin's), which the queen and her Frankish chaplain used. Four years later Pope

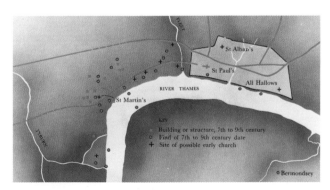

Map of Middle Saxon London, showing Saxon occupation along the Strand between AD 600 and 900.

Map of Anglo-Saxon kingdoms in the seventh to ninth centuries.

Gregory appointed Augustine archbishop of all the southern English. That included London and, according to Bede, the old city received its mitre in AD 604 when "King Ethelbert built a church dedicated to the holy apostle Paul in the city of London." Surely it must have been within the walls. Although no evidence has yet been found, it is possible that its ruins sit on top of the first Romano-British church in a layer cake of different churches, topped by the decorative present-day St Paul's.

The material culture of some of the early English kings gives the lie to the idea that they were a primitive people. As we have seen, the Anglo-Saxons were in close touch with the Christian Frankish kingdom and were also trading with pagan countries further north. But until the discovery of an Anglian king's ship burial on the east coast, at Sutton Hoo in Suffolk, the quality of their craftsmanship was greatly underestimated. The grave is almost certainly that of Redwald, who died and was buried in his longship in

opposite:
A page of Bede's Ecclesiastical History of the English People, *completed in 731. The works of Saxon scholars were greatly sought after in the so-called Dark Ages. Bede, who produced a small library of books in Latin on parchment in his scriptorium at Jarrow, was considered in his lifetime to be "the most learned man in Europe".*

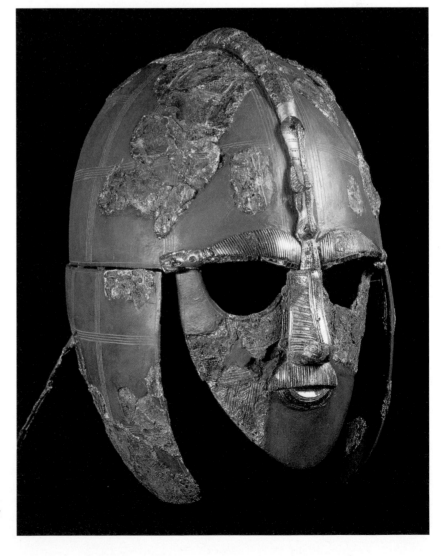

Redwald's helmet from Sutton Hoo. Reconstructed from fragments, it is made mostly of iron, but decorated with bronze, silver wires and gilt.

either 624 or 625. Curiously, though, there was no body. It had completely decomposed and the only evidence that it had ever been present came from chemical traces in the soil consistent with it having been a grave. As for the boat, it wasn't there either. The timber had rotted away, along with the iron nails. But because of careful excavation archaeologists could define the imprint of the planks in the soft, sandy soil and were able to take a plaster cast from which the ship was reconstructed. It can be seen today at the National Maritime Museum in Greenwich.

Buried with Redwald was an astounding treasure, which is displayed on the first floor of the British Museum. Redwald was one of the English kings whom Bede tells us was baptised. This accounts for the items of Christian silver in the grave, but everything else about that ship burial was pure pagan. Redwald was keeping his options open! Bede also records that Ethelbert's son Eadbald was just as ambiguous about his adherence to the church; he shocked the faithful by taking his father's second wife as his own. "However, this apostate king did not escape the scourge of god's punishment; for he was subject to frequent fits of insanity and possessed by an evil spirit." The King of the East Saxons also fell out with the Church and in AD 616, according to Bede, the Bishop of London was driven out of St Paul's and had to flee to France.

During the seventh and eight centuries references to London are sparse. The city is mentioned in some charters concerning trade and by the 640s gold coins marked with the word "Londuni" – the first coins to be minted in England since the Romans left - may well have been produced in London. There is no doubt, however, that large numbers of silver pennies minted in London were in circulation in England, and on the Continent, in the eighth century.

The greatest of all the seventh- and eighth-century Anglo-Saxon kings was Offa (757-796), whose Mercian kingdom at times held sway over most of England. Offa built the great dyke that still survives in the landscape as a barrier between England and Wales, and from the few letters that have survived it is clear that he was in close touch with Charlemagne and his burgeoning empire across the North Sea. Not only was trade carefully controlled by agreement between the two kings, but Charlemagne also welcomed Anglo-Saxon scholars to his court. When he was crowned Emperor of the Western Roman Empire in AD 800, it was to the English scholar Alcuin that he turned for advice and learning. Alcuin gathered around him a group of scholars – some of them drawn from his own monastery at York – and for more than twenty years was Charlemagne's chief advisor on the Church and on dealings with the English kings.

Anglo-Saxon kings lived a peripatetic life, dividing their time between palaces throughout their kingdoms. Some of these wooden halls and outhouses have been discovered in recent years, but no trace of Offa's palace has as yet turned up in the excavations in London. Its most likely location is within the old Roman fort area of Cripplegate and one clue comes from the excavation of a Saxon church in Wood Street. Professor Grimes, excavating after the Second World War, came across the foundations of a church that may be contemporary with Offa. The church of St Alban is only tiny and could have been built at any time in the middle to late Saxon period. But there is a tradition that Offa had a palace in London and that St Alban's was the palace chapel. Thomas Walsingham, the medieval chronicler, certainly believed that. And the tiny stone church does sit right in the middle of the fort – the traditional location of Offa's palace. Offa is also credited with founding or refounding the monastery at Westminster on Thorney Island, where the River Tyburn flowed into the Thames – a site that would evolve as a royal mausoleum, and later as the seat of government.

The City of London, although rich in late Saxon fragments of buildings on archaeological sites, is irritatingly short of upstanding Saxon buildings of any period, while the rest of England is overflowing with them – just over 400 can claim Saxon lineage. They are mainly churches whose original Saxon work survives as architectural features among centuries of alterations. You can, however, come across complete Saxon church towers, with their distinctive quoin stones and reused Roman masonry, or, as in the case of Bede's church at Jarrow, an entire surviving chancel. East Anglia is stiff with Anglo-Saxon churches, some of which were discovered in recent years under nineteenth-century cladding deemed to be "improvement" or restoration. The best piece of Saxon architecture above ground that the City of London can offer us is part of a church that goes by two names – All Hallows Barking and All Hallows by the Tower – probably founded in AD 675 by Erkenwald, Bishop of London.

Until December 1940, when the church was bombed, its Saxon origins were hidden. The blast demolished most of the nave and revealed the arch where the organ had stood along its south wall. It also brought to light some pieces of a Saxon stone cross that had been built into a medieval pillar, and the fragments of stone, with their design intact, are now part of a comprehensive display of artefacts in the crypt. There is a case full of Roman finds: bowls, bone hairpins, metal keys, pottery lamps and an outstanding collection of silver gilt plate, dating from 1626. Near the entrance there is a section of Roman pavement, part of which visitors have to walk across. But a modern chapel at the end of the crypt, with a gold-painted cement ceiling, fits uncomfortably into the medieval rough stone walls and arches.

The crypt of St Bride's Church, just off Fleet Street, also claims to have Saxon origins. These were discovered in the 1950s during the rebuilding of the Wren church following wartime bomb damage. The crypt, which had been sealed for centuries, was excavated by Professor Grimes, who recorded a series of earlier churches. There was certainly a Roman building on the site – the Roman pavement is preserved and on display – and some historians have made a connection between St Bridget, the sixth-century saint from Kildare, and the Fleet Street church. The skeleton of a Roman woman who may have been given a Christian burial has persuaded the Church authorities that Christian worship on this site goes back to the very origins of the Romano-British Church. Today's archaeologists, however, say that the evidence is not conclusive.

As for the Saxon church, of which there are the remains of stone foundations, there is more agreement on the date: eleventh century. And since the apse cuts through older burials there must have been an earlier church on the site. These layers of London's history, along with the remains of foundations of a Norman church, are topped by the post-war recreation of Wren's outstanding building, and in particular the 'wedding cake' steeple (which survived the war), which has been described as a madrigal in stone.

It was not until the time of Alfred the Great (the second half of the ninth century) that Lundenwic and Londinium began to come together again as one city, renamed Lundenburg. We have the Danes to thank for that. England in the eighth and ninth centuries was once again a target of barbarian attack, this time from the Vikings. In longboats, launched from the fjords of Norway and the estuaries of the Baltic, Viking warriors raided communities all around the British Isles. The first recorded incident was in AD 793 at the famous monastery of Lindisfarne, on an island off the northeast coast of England. Alcuin described the monastic church as "splattered with blood of the priests of god". Bede's monastery was attacked during the following year, and, as word spread in Scandinavia that English and Irish churches were stacked with portable riches, more Danes and Norsemen took to their longboats.

London, vulnerable at the tidal head of the Thames, was hit in AD 842 in a raid that a chronicler described as the "great slaughter". A hoard of silver coins, found at the Temple, just off Fleet Street, may have been buried at that time. Another reference we have for London is dated 851. Then we learn that no fewer than 350 ships came to plunder the city, and Canterbury as well.

Four years later, the Danes, emboldened by their success at hit-and-run raids, changed their tactics. "In this year, the heathen for the first time wintered in Sheppy [on the Kent coast]." That was to be the pattern – continuing campaigns as if they were an army of occupation. The denouement began with the arrival of "the great heathen army", which landed in AD 865. The locals were cowed into giving them horses and, according to *The Anglo-Saxon Chronicle*, "made peace with them". The heathen host then marched across Mercia into East Anglia and "over ran the whole kingdom".

The Danes were well on the way to subjugating the rest of Anglo-Saxon England when Alfred the Great strode into the story, having succeeded his brother as King of Wessex in AD 871. It took seven years for him to turn the military situation around. *The Chronicle* tells us that he fought a major battle with the Vikings at Edington in Wiltshire, where "he destroyed the Viking army with great slaughter, and pursued those who fled as far as the stronghold, hacking them down." Even more remarkably, he negotiated a truce with the Viking king Guthrum, who agreed "to accept Christianity and to receive baptism at King Alfred's hand".

Alfred, having become his enemy's godfather, agreed to the division of England between the Danes and the English. The Thames was to be the line between Alfred's Anglo-Saxon kingdom and the area to the east and north known as "Danelaw", where most of the Danish settlers were to be found. Alfred had won time for the survival of Anglo-Saxon England.

He used this breathing space to fortify the country – to establish a network of "burhs", or fortified towns, across his territory – but it was not until 886 that he finally dislodged the Danish occupiers of London. That same year, the Vikings sailed up the Seine and raided well into France.

Alfred set about reorganizing London, while thoughtfully leaving a little evidence in the ground for archaeologists to consider. As

The Saxon arch at All Hallows by the Tower (also known as All Hallows Barking), showing re-used Roman tiles. Bomb blasts in 1940 demolished a wall that had concealed the seventh-century arch.

Lundenwic was abandoned, he redesigned London within the walls, using the thirty or so burhs in other parts of the country as his model. Southwark is also included in Alfred's list of burhs, to protect the river crossing. According to an Anglo-Saxon "civil service" document called the Burghal Hidgage, the townspeople and the inhabitants of the villages around were responsible for the defence of these new settlements.

Alfred's strategy was tested in AD 892 when another great Danish army, reinforced by settlers from the Danelaw area, tried to take over Wessex. The defensive burhs held, and in the comparatively peaceful years ahead Alfred was able to spend time on becoming a man of letters. He ordered his judges to learn Latin or resign, and, according to his biographer, Bishop Asser, embarked on the study of Latin himself so that he could translate into English "some of the books that may be necessary for all men to know". English as a language of learning had arrived!

Alfred did not have to build a defensive wall around London, but in his time the city evolved as a network of streets laid out on a grid system. The Roman walls and gates continued in use and some streets had gravelled surfaces. Like the first buildings of Roman London over eight centuries before, the houses were made of wood.

Although the Anglo-Saxon layers in London were largely dug away to make room for nineteenth-century basements, just over

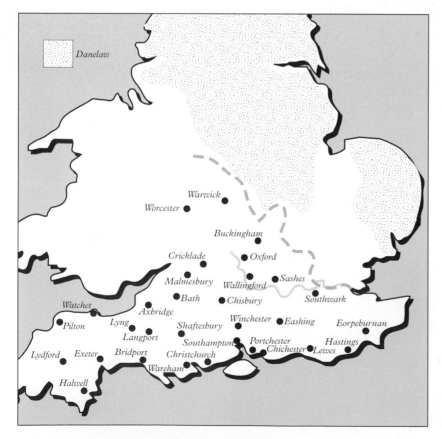

Alfred established at least thirty-three burhs; some, like London and Porchester Castle, were old Roman forts or walled towns. Others were villages which he replanned with a grid of streets surrounded by high earthen ramparts; plots of land were offered to attract settlers, who in return had an obligation to defend the burh.

forty different sites spanning the tenth and eleventh centuries have been located. Most of them were rectangular houses, built of timber above the ground. They had a central hearth made of baked clay, and from carbonized seeds we know that rushes were spread over the floor. Fragments of broken pottery, caught in the rushes, were periodically bundled up and dumped into pits at the back of the houses. Archaeologists examining these pits in recent years have been able to identify a wide variety of objects: lamps, cooking pots, a wooden ladle and plenty of pitchers and beakers. Wine was apparently imported in wooden barrels which were later used to line the many wells that have been found near houses.

The cellars discovered under some buildings were as deep as 2.3 metres (7 feet 6 inches); wooden steps leading down to the cellar floor were found in one instance, but there is no evidence of anything more than one-storey houses above those basements, and

A page from the Liber Pastoralis *of St Gregory the Great, translated from the Latin into Old English by "Alfred, King of England". He translated a number of works from the Latin and remains one of the few British monarchs to have distinguished himself as a writer.*

no stone foundations have been found in houses, in spite of all the Roman masonry that must still have been lying around. That, for some reason, was reserved for churches.

Alfred is credited with establishing the harbour known as Queenhithe on the Thames, still clearly marked on the large-scale maps of London as a bite out of the embankment between Southwark and Blackfriars Bridges. A road inside the wall, following its line, is believed to be another of his works, and some of the repairs to the Roman wall that you can see at St Alphege are thought to be of Saxon date.

The "Alfred Jewel". Found in Devon, it is inscribed in Latin with the words "Alfred ordered me to be made". It is one of the few objects associated with the king that have survived and may have been the ornate top of a book mark. It is now on display in the Ashmolean Museum in Oxford.

Alfred's son and grandson continued the fight against the Danes and by the late 920s the latter, Athelstan (924-940), could style himself on his coinage "King of All Britain". The Danelaw areas had been brought under Anglo-Saxon control, along with the surrender of Celtic kings in Wales and Scotland. London, however, was not yet a capital city. The kingdom was governed by a court that rarely rested in one place for any length of time. Decrees were issued after "Witans" (Parliaments) were held at the traditional palaces of the Anglo-Saxon rulers all over the kingdom. The system of government, borrowed from Charlemagne's empire, required county courts in the shires to read out the king's latest writ. By the middle of the tenth century the shires had been divided into "hundreds", which had their own local courts to deal with theft and violence; it is often forgotten that the Anglo-Saxon shire boundaries were hardly changed until the reorganization of local government as recently as 1974. London had its own "portreeve", or royal official, responsible for collecting taxes, and, at the "folkmoot" beside St Paul's Cathedral, the bishop and the royal official would convey the king's wishes to the assembled crowd.

Anglo-Saxon charters show that trade was important for London. A document at the end of the tenth century lists some of the items on which duty might be payable on the quayside at Billingsgate: silks, ivory, gold, wine and oil. For the return voyage merchants might have negotiated prices for the export of wool and cloth, fine metalwork and coin, and agricultural products. In peace time the Danish merchants were encouraged to come to London by the Anglo-Saxon kings because of their extensive trade routes. The Vikings had turned to trading ventures on a grand scale with towns such as Hederby on the Baltic, Dublin and Jorvik (Viking York). Their network of connections extended throughout Europe and east along the river systems to the Black Sea and beyond.

King Edgar's reign (959-975) might be described as the Anglo-Saxons' golden age. Viking pirates were kept at bay by the Royal Navy, established by Alfred many reigns before, and Edgar reformed the English monasteries and his Christian centres of learning exchanged views with such famous abbeys in France as Cluny. His legislators poured out sensible statutes; literature and art flourished.

But the Viking threat had not disappeared – the Danish royal family coveted England – and when Edgar died his unfortunate son Ethelred (978-1014) found himself in the front line of England's defence. "Ethelred the Unready" is a byword in English history for inadequate kingship. In fact the nickname is better translated as "the uncounselled"; it is a pun on Ethelred, which means "good counsel". Perhaps unfairly, Ethelred's reputation as an incompetent and treacherous king persists. He stands accused by his detractors of paying a high price for peace in the form of "Danegeld" – the English silver that was paid out to deter the waves of Danish armies over a period of thirty-six years.

The first attack of this new phase of Danish aggression, in 980, was recorded in a matter-of-fact style by *The Anglo-Saxon Chronicle*:

"In the same year Southampton was ravished by a pirate host and most of the citizens slain or taken prisoner." It was a familiar pattern year after year: attack, or threats, or both, followed by larger and larger sums of money in exchange for a short-lived peace. In 994 Swein, King of Denmark, and the Norwegian king Olaf Tyrggvason, "came to London with 94 ships, and kept up an unceasing attack on the city, and purposed, moreover, to set it on fire."

The citizens beat off the attack and the Scandinavian host rampaged off across the country doing so much "unspeakable damage" that Ethelred and his counsellors agreed to send to them, offering tribute and supplies, if they would desist from their harrying. The substantial sum of £16,000 changed hands. Even larger sums were demanded as the years went by: the last payment to Swein's son, King Canute (1016-35), was £72,000, plus an additional £10,500 from the citizens of London.

Some of that silver coin has been discovered by archaeologists in Scandinavia, where at least 50,000 English silver pennies, minted between 980 and 1050, have turned up in hoards. There is no doubt that this represents only a fraction of what must have crossed the North Sea during the long years of Danish assault.

The wealth of London that attracted Viking raiders came from international trade, which, by the year 1000, had become immensely important both to England and to London. With a cosmopolitan population and a well-organized royal system of exploiting the merchants who brought their ships into the Thames, the king's coffers benefited greatly. A glimpse of London's port in action comes from the recollections of the Icelandic poet Gunnlaug when he visited the court of Ethelred in 1001: "If a small ship came to Billingsgate, one half-penny was to be paid a toll; if a larger ship with sails, one penny

Alfred's London. Archaeologists have shown that many of London's medieval streets date from the ninth and tenth centuries. Pudding Lane and Lovett Lane to the east of London Bridge are two such medieval ways to the river-bank.

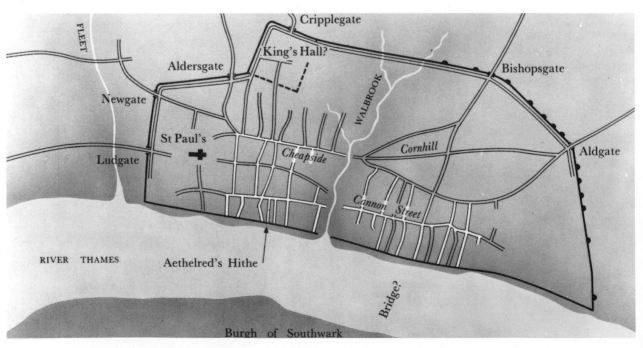

was paid. On three days of the week toll for cloth is paid, on Sunday, Tuesday, and Thursday...men of Rouen who came with wine of blubber fish paid a duty of six shillings for a large ship and 5% of the fish."

In 1002 Ethelred made an alliance that was to change the course of English history. He married Emma, a Norman princess. Whether or not Ethelred received much military or diplomatic help from the Duchy of Normandy is not recorded, but we know that he was concerned about Viking ships taking shelter and provisions in ports there – the duchy had been founded by an earlier wave of Vikings at the beginning of the tenth century. But the Danish attacks did not stop. In 1013 Swein returned with his army, determined to take England, and after a long siege of London Ethelred was forced to flee the country. The next year Swein died and was

St Clement Danes in the Strand: traditionally the church of the Danish community that settled in the area in the ninth century. According to John Stow's sixteenth-century Survey of London, a Danish king and other Danes were buried there. The picture shows the church after extensive wartime bomb damage, which has since been painstakingly repaired.

succeeded by his son Canute, who had then to face not only Ethelred but his new ally in the person of another Olaf – a later Norwegian king, the future St Olaf.

By this time, the year 1014, the Danes were in command of London's defences and, as Ethelred and Olaf approached the city with their invasion fleet, the defenders on London Bridge rained down missiles on the ships. Then, in the words of the thirteenth-century *Norse Sagas*, the ships rowed up and under the bridge "and tied ropes around the supporting posts, and rowed downstream as hard as they could. The posts were dragged along the bottom until they were loosened from under the bridge. As an armed host stood thickly on the bridge and there was a great weight of stone and weapons on it, and the posts beneath were broken, the bridge fell with so many of the men into the river; the others fled into the city or Southwark."

Ethelred and Olaf had won London, but a year later, in 1016, Ethelred died, throwing the kingdom into political disarray. His son, Edmund Ironside, was proclaimed as his successor by the council in London, while in other parts of England Canute was declared king. One of the battles which were fought that year to determine the leadership was another siege of London, in which Canute's fleet was once again stopped at London Bridge. In order to proceed up river they "dug a great channel on the south bank and dragged their ships to the west side of the bridge". That unlikely story has been given more credence since archaeologists, excavating a site in Southwark, came across a ditch which may well have been a section of Canute's siege canal.

Edmund Ironside escaped from London, but, after a valiant attempt to wrest the initiative from the Danes, lost the battle for England and agreed to a division of the country. Edmund died suddenly in November 1016, and, weary of war, the English offered Canute the whole of the kingdom.

Apart from such fragments of historical record, London's Danish period is mainly reflected in the names of several churches that seem to honour the saintly King Olaf, who won great admiration from Londoners when he stormed the city with Ethelred in 1014 after dismantling the bridge in such a memorable way. Six churches were dedicated to the sanctified Norwegian king including St Olave's, Hart Street, All Hallows Staining with St Katherine Coleman, St Mary Magdalene with St Olave's, St John's and St Luke's, Bermondsey (close to the Southwark end of the bridge), and the tower of St Olave Jewry. Some medieval fragments in these buildings survive, but today only the names link the churches to Danish London.

St Clement Danes at the Fleet Street end of the Strand also has strong associations with London's medieval Danish community. In his sixteenth-century *Survey of London*, John Stow says that the Danish King Harold and other Danes were buried there. Adding a snippet more information, he says that King Harold had been buried at Westminster, but that Canute's son "commanded the body of

Harold to be digged out of the earth, and thrown into the Thames, where it was by a fisherman taken up and buried in this [St Clement Danes] churchyard".

There is little chance of establishing the facts, as the church-yard has disappeared under modern buildings in Portugal Street. But it is recorded that a wooden church was replaced in the early eleventh century and that the remains of the medieval tower were incorporated into the Wren church. They can still be seen, having survived the 1941 bomb which gutted the rest of the church. Rebuilt in 1957, and now the London church of the Royal Air Force, the only original Wren furnishing is the wooden hexagonal pulpit that the famous carver Grinling Gibbons is believed to have made in the 1680s.

On the accession of Canute, the surviving Anglo-Saxon princes, including the future King Edward the Confessor, crossed the English Channel and went into exile in their mother's birthplace – Normandy. Canute, with a flourish of diplomatic acumen, per-suaded the ex-queen Emma to marry him, despite his existing marriage, or liaison, with an English noblewoman called Aelfgifu who had borne him two sons. For the next twenty years Canute, although spending most of his time in Denmark, led England through a period of peace and prosperity. But, as we have seen, remarkably few objects survive to remind us of that Danish period, or indeed of the many years of Danish rule in London when Ethelred was in exile.

When Canute died in 1035 there was a contest for the throne between his sons by both wives. Two sons who became king died in quick succession, and in 1042 the throne was offered to Emma and Ethelred's son Edward – an unmarried and pious prince who had spent much of his life at the court of the Duke of Normandy.

Edward the Confessor's indelible mark on London was the move that established London once and for all as a twin city. In his

A scene from the Bayeux Tapestry showing Edward the Confessor's funeral procession approaching the newly finished Westminster Abbey.

piety he decided to build a palace alongside the long-established monastery of St Peter on Thorney Island at Westminster, and with the palace, of which nothing survives, went an ambitious scheme to rebuild the old Saxon monastery. The style of Edward's new church and monastic complex would have been familiar to the Normans who were to follow him: a solid nave with great round columns and curved, ornately carved arches. As with the palace no trace of the church survives above ground, but excavations beneath the floor have made it possible to produce a ground plan of the building: cruciform in shape; a nave with six double bays; twin towers over the transepts; the whole building bigger than any contemporary church in Normandy.

The closest you can get to Edward's Benedictine monastery is through a door in Westminster Abbey marked Chapel of the Pyx. It is part of a small "discreet" museum that crouches among the arches of the undercroft of the old monastery dormitory. The outer walls, the vaulted ceiling, some of the arches that spring from circular columns in the middle of the undercroft, have been dated to the second half of the eleventh century.

When the Confessor died on 5 January 1066 – a matter of weeks after the abbey was finished – there was no son to succeed him. But in Normandy his cousin William declared that Edward had promised him the throne. This proposition was contested in England by the most powerful of the earls, Harold of Wessex, who claimed that the dying Edward had conferred the mantle of kingship on him. Harold was quickly crowned at Westminster Abbey and the stage was set for another abrupt turn in the fortunes of London.

Chapter 3

"This Noble City" –
Norman London 1066-1200

THIS WAS A FATAL DAY for England, a melancholy havoc of our dear country brought about by its passing under the domination of new lords."

The day was 14 October 1066, the day of the Battle of Hastings. William of Malmesbury, the medieval chronicler, reflecting on the changes wrought by that battle, blamed the English king, Harold, and the Saxon army for giving William the Conqueror an easy victory in a single encounter. But the odds were against the newly anointed monarch. Harold was beset by two claimants to his throne: the Norwegian king, Harald Hardrada, and William, Duke of Normandy, both of whom began preparations for an invasion almost immediately after Edward the Confessor died.

Harald Hardrada struck first. He landed an army on the north coast of England and took possession of the old Viking stronghold of York. Harold, in London, responded by immediately marching his army north, surprising the Norsemen outside the city and beating them at the Battle of Stamford Bridge.

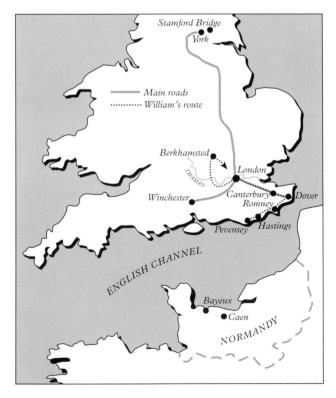

Map of England and Normandy in 1066, showing key points in the events of that momentous year and William's circuitous march to London.

Then it was the Normans' turn to catch the Saxons on the hop. Only three days after Stamford Bridge, William, encouraged by the Pope in his invasion, was also blessed with a fair wind that propelled his 400 ships and 8-10,000 men across the English Channel to an unopposed landfall on Pevensey beach. The battle-weary English had then to march at full pelt down more than half the length of the country, gathering reinforcements as they passed through London on their way to Hastings, where the Norman army waited. The chronicle of Florence of Worcester tells us that only about one third of the English forces were in position by the beginning of the battle, and we know from other contemporary accounts that the tactics of the Norman cavalry tipped the balance. The battle ended as the sky rained with arrows; the eleventh-century Bayeux Tapestry makes it appear that one hit King Harold in the eye, and all English resistance ebbed away. The contemporary chronicler William of Poitiers recorded that "the blood-stained battle ground was covered with the flower of youth and nobility of England."

William turned towards London. The towns of Romney, Dover, Canterbury and Winchester all submitted as he burnt and pillaged his way across Hampshire and Kent. Ensconced in Edward the Confessor's palace at Westminster, William, according to Guy, Bishop of Amiens, laid siege to London: "He built siege-engines and made moles and iron horns of battering rams for the destruction of the city; then he thundered forth menaces and threatened war and vengeance, swearing that, given time, he would destroy the walls, raze the bastions to the ground and bring down the proud tower in rubble."

But having failed to force his way across London Bridge William marched in a circle through Surrey and Hampshire and pitched camp at Berkhamsted, where, in the words of *The Anglo-Saxon Chronicle*, he was met by "all the best men of London who submitted from force of circumstances, but only when the depredation was complete". All that remained was to anoint William as king during a ceremony in Westminster Abbey which took place on Christmas Day 1066.

The Norman takeover heralded the end of the English aristocracy. Weakened by the double bloodshed of 1066, the Anglo-Saxon establishment, after several ill-fated attempts at insurrection, was quickly replaced by Normans from across the Channel. Within a generation English names disappeared from lists of the landholding classes as they accepted lower status or went into exile. Scotland was a favourite destination and even the court of the Byzantine emperor became a haven for members of the Anglo-Saxon royal family.

Londoners, however, appear to have received different treatment from William. While English influence waned in most other parts of the kingdom, an analysis of the names of prominent people in London a generation later shows that it remained predominantly an English city. London's trade, wealth and influence, not to mention its formidable walls, persuaded William to do a separate deal with its citizens, who were granted their privileges in writing soon after the coronation: "William the king greets William, Bishop of London, and Gosfrith the portreeve, and all the burgesses of London friendly. I give you to know that I will that you be worthy of all the laws you were worthy of in the time of King Edward. And I will that every child shall be his father's heir after his father's day, and I will not suffer any man to do you wrong. God yield you."

Written in English, William I's charter to the City of London contains the oldest known impression of the Conqueror's seal.

The people of London may have submitted, but to keep control, and to guard against the continuing Danish threat, William had three castles built by 1100: one, later known as Baynard's Castle, between Ludgate and the river; Montfichet's Castle, near St Paul's Cathedral; and the Tower of London. It is thought that Baynard's Castle was associated with one of the Conqueror's knights, Ralph Baignard, whose seat was at Little Dunmow in Essex. By the early thirteenth century the castle had gone out of use and it was swallowed up when the Black Friars built their monastery in 1275. The same fate appears to have befallen the second fortress – a tower built by a certain William de Munfichet.

The Tower of London, however, became not only a royal residence, but also one of the most powerful fortresses in the country and the seat of successive Norman portreeves, or sheriffs. The Tower first made use of the angle of the Roman city walls at the eastern end, by the river, and excavations have revealed the riverside Roman wall and the repairs that the Normans made to it. The heart of the castle that still dominates the eastern skyline of London – the White Tower, as it became known after Henry III had it whitewashed in the thirteenth century – began to rise in the late 1070s. All over England Norman "motte and bailey" castles (earthen walls and ditches surrounding a central mound with fortifications on top) sprang up in towns and at strategic points. But, as William Fitz Stephen observed, the Tower was in a league by itself. "On the East stands the Palatine Citadel, exceeding great and strong, whose walls and bailey rise from very deep foundations, their mortar being mixed with the blood of beasts."

The locals hardly needed reminding who was boss; the English idea of a fortress was a decayed Roman fort or the earthen banks surrounding Alfred's burhs. This new design was four storeys high with walls over 4.5 metres (15 feet) thick at its base and narrowing to just over 3 metres (a mere 11 feet) at the top. From the battlements it was a 27 metre (90 foot) drop to the courtyard below. The Tower's only entrance was 4.5 metres (15 feet) above the ground, up a wooden staircase that could easily be jettisoned in an emergency. Inside, the ground floor was used as a store room and dungeon; a spiral staircase led to the first floor and quarters for soldiers and servants; the banqueting hall and the chapel – the most perfectly preserved Norman church in England – shared the second floor, while above, the Norman kings had their bedrooms and council chamber.

Sixteenth-century plan of the Tower of London, showing it much as it would have looked in Norman times, though the clusters of smaller buildings are later.

A True and Exact Draught of the TOWER LIBERTIES, survey'd in the Year 1597 by *GULIELMUS HAIWARD* and *J. GASCOYNE*.

Over the centuries the Tower has been the home of kings, a prison, a mint and an armoury; it is still a garrison guarded by Beefeaters in ceremonial dress, and regular troops under the command of the Governor of the Tower. Every night at ten o'clock the Chief Yeoman Warder, wearing a red cloak and Tudor bonnet, and carrying a lantern, calls out, "An escort for the Keys." Four soldiers from the garrison then escort him, holding a great bunch of keys in his hand, to the entrance gate, which is duly locked for the night. The Chief Warder continues to the Bloody Tower, where a sentry challenges the group, and the ceremony ends with the cry, "God preserve Queen Elizabeth, Amen."

The additions to the Tower that have marked almost every reign since that of William the Conqueror have preserved examples of English architectural history through a timespan of almost a thousand years. But the White Tower itself has remained remarkably unchanged from the fortress that left the Anglo-Saxon Londoners awestruck over 900 years ago. Within its walls most of the accretions of the Middle Ages still stand; there is also a superb row of half-timbered Elizabethan houses, one of which is the governor's residence; early nineteenth-century buildings constructed for the military occupy one of the courtyards; and the recently vacated jewel house owes its bunker-like design to the 1960s.

The Tower is a vivid expression of the impact of the Normans on Anglo-Saxon England. But although more modest versions of the motte and bailey castle peppered the kingdom in their hundreds, giving the Normans a military grip on the landscape, there was no question of the country being flooded with settlers. At any one time there were probably never more than 10,000 Normans in England – a tiny proportion of an estimated population of no more than two and a half million. The English simply buckled under a regime that bristled with armour, redistributed most of the land in favour of the new Norman overlords, and gave control of the Church to foreign prelates.

Those bishops were just as tough on the English clergy as the secular authorities were on the old aristocracy and, in the words of William of Malmesbury, "England had become a residence for foreigners and the property of aliens. There is no English Earl, no bishop nor abbot; strangers all, they prey upon the riches and the vitals of England." Particularly intimidating for the God-fearing population was the Normans' attitude to English saints and the relics of the English Church. Saints' tombs were opened and relics subjected to the test of fire. If the bones did not burn they were considered to be genuine and worth venerating. Many failed the test.

William's policy towards any sign of English resistance was to move in and crush it with a ruthlessness that made even his admirers uncomfortable. "Wholesale massacre" was how one Norman monk described his king's campaign to put down a rising in the North of England in 1068-70. In 1086 William instructed his barons and Anglo-Saxon "civil servants" to conduct a census. The Domesday Survey of the English shires took his officials into every village, manor and town throughout the kingdom. The "Domesday

Book" – two volumes packed with details of land holding, agricultural equipment, numbers of people and animals – was completed in an amazingly short time, an indication of the quality of the Saxon royal government machine inherited by the Normans. Inexplicably London was omitted, but the Public Record Office in Chancery Lane has the two original books, the vellum leaves rebound in the 1980s, on permanent display.

William probably never saw the finished report. Having ruled England for twenty-one years, achieving comparative peace in the last years of his reign, he died on campaign in Nantes in 1087, while laying siege to the town and putting it to the torch.

The Tower of London, begun in the last years of William the Conqueror's reign. Still a royal palace, it has also served successive monarchs as a mint, prison, armoury, treasure house, royal observatory and menagerie. Henry III kept leopards and an elephant there. When he was given a white polar bear in 1252 the Sheriffs of London were ordered to pay fourpence a day for its upkeep and to provide a long chain and cord that would enable it to go fishing in the Thames. In 1835 the menagerie was closed, leaving only the famous ravens to carry on the tradition.

The new Jewel House, opened in 1994, contains an exhibition about the coronation ceremony as well as displaying crowns, sceptres, orbs, vestments and swords of state, many of which have been used for centuries in the coronation of the monarch.

opposite:
The Tower, with London Bridge and the City behind, as seen by an unknown illuminator working around 1500. Although highly stylized, it is regarded as the earliest representation of London in existence.

The Conqueror's successor, his second son, William II (Rufus, 1087-1100), was just as ruthless as his father but also distinguished himself as a builder. Westminster Hall was his inspiration – perhaps the biggest hall in Europe at the time, 73 metres (240 feet) long and almost 26 metres (67 feet 6 inches) wide. The Anglo-Saxon chronicler grumbled that 1097 was a bad year for the harvest and one in which men from many shires, "in full filling their labour service to the city of London", were oppressed both in building the wall around the Tower and in the construction of the king's hall at Westminster. Everyone was greatly impressed by the size of the hall when the king held his court there for the first time in 1099 – although Rufus is supposed to have remarked that it was "too big for a chamber and not big enough for a hall". In any event its dimensions have not changed. The lower part of the walls are still as they

Westminster Hall. Commissioned by William Rufus in 1097, it is the only surviving building of the Norman Palace of Westminster. The carved timber hammer-beam roof is the earliest example in existence: begun in Richard II's reign, it was completed after his death, in 1401.

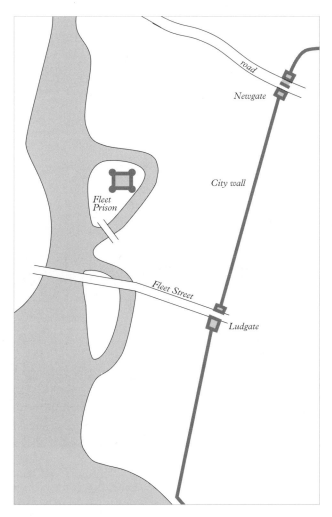

Excavation of the upstream island in the Fleet River, under what is today Ludgate Circus, shows that the Normans used it to build a prison. There was a prison on this site until 1846, when the infamous debtors' prison was demolished.

were, but the internal aisles were removed when the present magnificent hammer-beam roof – described as the finest timber-roof building in Europe – was completed in 1401.

We now know that William Rufus must also have built the Fleet Prison in the late 1080s. Famous as a landmark and for its reputation as a debtors' prison, it lasted in one form or another on the same site until 1846. But its origins could only be guessed at until excavations begun in 1988 produced some remarkable new evidence. As we have seen, the piles for a Roman bridge were found on one of the islands discovered in the Fleet River valley under what is today Ludgate Circus. In the eleventh century another bridge was built in exactly the same place, using the southern island as a stepping stone for its support; some of its timbers have been found and dated to about the time of the Norman Conquest. The Normans then built a prison on the upstream island. A square, stone building measuring 12.5 metres by 10.5 metres (41 feet by 34 feet) inside, with a turret at each corner, it must have looked like a smaller version of the White Tower.

The two bound volumes of the Domesday Survey, Great and Little Domesday, completed in 1086.

Excavations directed by Dr William McCann of the Museum of London over a period of several years have shown that, by the middle of the thirteenth century, the natural channel around the prison had been largely filled in, leaving an artificial moat about 3.5 metres (8 feet 6 inches) wide. Further construction went on on the site and by the middle of the sixteenth century the moat had become no more than a drain surrounded by other buildings, including what may have been a tannery. The first documentary mention of the prison concerns a warden and his stipend in 1130, during the reign of William the Conqueror's youngest son, Henry I.

The King's Prison of Fleet and the three castles that kept a watchful eye on London were soon joined by new monastic institutions complete with massive abbeys and priories in or just outside the Norman city. The same monastic advance was happening throughout the kingdom; by the end of the twelfth century about 600 such bastions of various monastic persuasions had taken root alongside the existing old Anglo-Saxon monasteries. We have no reason to doubt Fitz Stephen's observations: "There are both in London and the suburbs thirteen greater conventual churches and 126 lesser parochial churches." Indeed, the earliest panoramas of London show the skyline punctured with the spires of churches tightly packed into the city. Many of them were tiny, hardly more than the private chapels of wealthy citizens that had evolved into parish churches. Others, such as St Mary le Bow, Cheapside, were bigger. St Mary le Bow has a fine crypt dating back to the eleventh century, part of which is now used as a restaurant.

The twelfth century was also an age in which charity flourished and, in the suburbs outside the gates, the great and the good founded leper hospitals. Henry I's queen, Edith-Matilda, the last surviving member of the Anglo-Saxon royal family, founded the first leper hospital at St Giles in the Fields, on the site of the existing parish church, near the corner of Charing Cross Road and Oxford Street. A huge number of the Norman and later medieval churches were lost in the Great Fire of 1666, but over forty, most of them rebuilt by Wren, survive and the sites of many more are known. Occasionally you come across a patch of unloved-looking ground, perhaps surrounded by iron railings, which on closer inspection reveals a worn inscription or a plaque to a pre-fire church – preserved for posterity, but using as little real estate as possible, at the time of a nineteenth-century office expansion. But in the twelfth and thirteenth centuries the noise and the dust, scaffolding swarming with workmen, and the rumbling of carts laden with stone must have been as disruptive to city life as the redevelopment boom of recent decades.

The monasteries planted in London swallowed up prodigious quantities of land. Like small walled towns in themselves, they each housed a large community of religious and lay people, whose life was centred on a church of cathedral-like proportions. Excavations of the eleventh-century Cluniac monastery founded by William Rufus at Bermondsey, on the other side of London Bridge, showed the foundations of a church that was 94 metres (310 feet) long, about two-thirds the size of Westminster Abbey.

Perhaps the biggest twelfth-century landowner in the city was the Holy Trinity Priory. Another institution founded by Edith-Matilda, its plan survived in great detail among documents of the 1590s that belonged to Elizabeth I's Lord Treasurer, Lord Burghley. More architectural features of the buildings themselves were recorded in 1800, when an antiquary noticed ancient timbers and masonry in a later building that was being demolished after a fire. Such clues, and the results of recent excavations of the foundations and part of a wall of the side chapel, have enabled archaeologists to reconstruct the priory on paper.

Two fragments of the priory complex survive *in situ* above ground. One is the lower part of the tower of St Katherine Cree, built at the turn of the fourteenth and fifteenth centuries. The original church, of which nothing survives, was started in about 1280, when the Priory of Holy Trinity decided to build a chapel for ordinary parishioners in the graveyard of the priory church. What we see today on Leadenhall Street is a church started in 1628 in a "gap" between the architectural giants Inigo Jones and Christopher Wren – a rare period for London churches. It is unusual in that there is no division between the chancel and the nave; the spectacular plaster ceiling is decorated with beautifully carved and painted bosses depicting the arms of seventeen City livery companies. However, the need to build offices in the aisles to cope with the church's role as a Guild Church for Finance spoils the interior.

St Katherine Cree's garden behind the church, with a fountain and an eighteenth-century sundial, is on a patch of land that is all that remains of the medieval priory churchyard. The other fragment of the main priory church, a thirteenth-century arch, is preserved in a nearby office building.

Two of London's famous hospitals were founded at this time. St Thomas's was inspired by Thomas Becket, or perhaps even founded by him. Becket, Henry II's Archbishop of Canterbury, was a Londoner, the son of a Norman merchant. The famous hospital was across London Bridge in Southwark, and today occupies a prime riverside site further west, opposite the Houses of Parliament.

St Bart's Hospital buildings date from the eighteenth century, but the religious side of the twelfth-century foundation still functions as a parish church in a part of the original priory. Hard to spot from the road, it is one of London's best kept medieval secrets. Fitz Stephen says of the Smithfield area, "There is a much frequented show of fine horses for sale." According to his description a variety of other livestock and agricultural goods was sold at Smithfield in the 4 hectare (10 acre) market to which cattle were still being driven until the middle of the nineteenth century. As a meat market, Smithfield has chalked up about one thousand years of continuity and every day it is still full of lorries and meat traders.

Just across the square from the eighteenth-century buildings of St Bart's Hospital, there is an ornate arch with a half-timbered gatehouse above. Go through, and what looks like a modest parish church lies ahead. The interior, however, is a breathtaking surprise: you can still see the crossing and the choir of a monumental Norman church, with characteristic Romanesque arches and sturdy round columns sweeping towards an apsidal, or semi-circular, east end. This was the centre of a priory founded by a Londoner called Rahere who has been variously described as a court jester, a minstrel, a wealthy royal clerk or just an Augustinian canon. On a journey to Rome he fell ill with malaria and made a vow to build a priory church and a hospital if the good Lord would restore him to health and see him home again. A vision of St Bartholomew then appeared and directed Rahere to start work at Smithfield, where part of the medieval priory church and a heavily restored nearby hospital chapel called St Bartholomew the Less still stand.

St Bartholomew the Great was untouched by the Great Fire of 1666, but like so many other medieval buildings in London it succumbed to war damage – in this case during the First World War! In 1916 a bomb from a Zeppelin raid landed nearby; the blast tore off some tiles on the facade of the gatehouse, unexpectedly revealing a half-timbered house, dated to 1559, which restorers returned to its original condition, or very like it, in 1932. The priory building had already suffered greatly during Henry VIII's dissolution of the monasteries. After the priory's new owner, Sir Richard Rich, had pulled down the whole length of the nave, local people managed to persuade him to spare the choir, or chancel, as it was used for a parish church. But the rest of the building was either demolished or fell into a ruinous state. The resurrection of what was left, begun in 1819, took more than a century and today, although heavily restored, the choir is a precious survival of Norman London.

Another great Norman enterprise was the new cathedral of St Paul. Records at the cathedral point to the possibility that Rahere had been a canon of St Paul's in the early years of the twelfth century when the new Norman church was under construction. *The Anglo-Saxon Chronicle* records that the old Saxon church – at least the third building on the site – was gutted in the fire of 1087. "Before autumn, the holy church of St Paul, the episcopal see of London was burnt down, as well as many other churches and the largest and fairest part of the whole city."

The Norman building went up slowly and was extended twice during the twelfth and thirteenth centuries. In 1315 the spire was

Wenceslaus Hollar was a Czech engraver brought to England by the Earl of Arundel, a great patron of the arts, to draw views of London. This representation of Old St Paul's Cathedral dates from 1656. The 178 metre (489 foot) spire was struck by lightning in 1561 and not replaced.

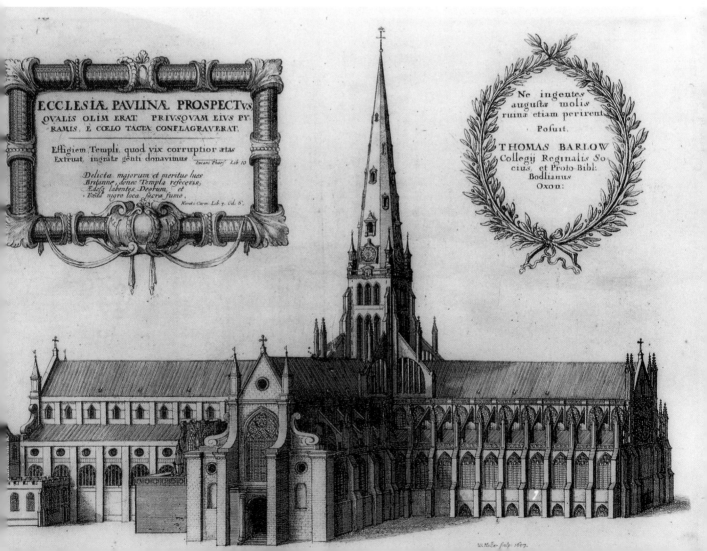

renewed to make it tower 149 metres (489 feet) over the city. At 178 metres (585 feet) long, it was one of the biggest cathedrals in England and the focal point for London life. Streets around the cathedral today mark the line of its thirteenth-century walled precinct: Creed Lane, Ave Maria Lane, Paternoster Row, Old Change and Carter Lane. The chapter house was surrounded by a two-tiered cloister of which some remains can still be seen in the garden on the south side of the seventeenth-century Wren nave.

The bishop's palace was also in the precinct, along with the free-standing bell tower known as the Jesus Bell. It summoned the citizens to a compulsory "folkmoot", the ancient assembly and court for Londoners, which met three times a year in the churchyard around a lead-covered wooden pulpit called St Paul's Cross. Beyond the precinct, which was walled in 1284 to keep out robbers, the cathedral's land-holding extended to property all over the city, as well as to large estates in Essex and Middlesex, and the castle and town of Bishop's Stortford in Hertfordshire.

One of Fitz Stephen's allusions to this part of the city concerns what is still one of London's best known boys' schools, St Paul's. Fitz Stephen thought it was "Famous" even in the twelfth century: "On holy days the masters of the schools assemble their scholars at the churches whose feast day it is. The scholars dispute, some in demonstrative rhetoric, others in dialectic...some are exercised in disputation for the purpose of display which is but a wrestling bout of wit, but others that they may establish the truth for the sake of perfection."

Norman masons, busy for over a century rebuilding royal and ecclesiastical London, also built stone houses for well-to-do merchants and officials. Fitz Stephen tells us that "almost all the bishops, abbots, and nobles of England are, as it were, citizens and townsmen of London, having their town houses when in London on business." But very little of those houses survives. Recent excavations have been disappointing and for evidence about such buildings we must turn to the records of nineteenth-century antiquaries. A square Norman undercroft, which may have been built at street level in the twelfth century, was found in Gracechurch Street. The arches and columns were faithfully drawn and the Roman bricks in the structure noted (the house happened to have been built above the Roman Forum).

The underground remains of another, much bigger stone house were found in 1830 in Southwark. It was just such a house as Fitz Stephen mentioned – the town house of the Prior of Lewes in Sussex, perhaps first built for the Earls de Warenne. Its undercroft was just over 12 metres (40 feet) long with a barrel-vaulted roof supported by columns with carved capitals; the doorways used stone imported from the quarries of Caen in Normandy. Roadworks associated with the coming of the railways dealt that piece of London's heritage a fatal blow.

One surviving Norman undercroft is in Mark Lane in the City. Its origins are uncertain, though we know that it was called the Chapel of St James and is first mentioned in the late twelfth century

NAVIS ECCLESIÆ CATHEDRALIS S. PAVLI. PROSPECTVS INTERIOR.

Sit rediviva mater Ecclesia et pereant Sacrilegi: ut navis Ecclesiæ temporum fluctibus immersura, salutaribus Dei auspiciis conservetur. Maiorum pietatem, imitando, mirentur posteri, ut stupenda hæc Basilica antiquitus fundata et iamiam collapsura, tanquam iterum Religionis Christianæ Monumentum in æternum sustineatur.

The Norman nave of Old St Paul's, by Hollar (1656). Most of the stone work probably dates from after a fire in 1136.

as being at Cripplegate on the Wall. After the dissolution of the monasteries it was sold to a cloth worker who passed it on to his livery company. Then in 1872 the company moved it across the city to a site near their hall where, with their permission, it can be approached through a church tower – the only part left of "All Hallows Staining".

Alas, no Norman house survives in its entirety in London, but there must have been many that looked like the twelfth-century house at Boothby Pagnell, Lincolnshire, now maintained by the government-sponsored agency English Heritage.

"To this city, from every nation that is under heaven, merchants rejoice to bring their trade in ship." Fitz Stephen went on to list some of the goods that flowed into London in the twelfth century. "Gold from Arabia" was top of his list, followed by incense and palm oil from the Near East; "fine gems from Nile, from China crimson silks". Excavations in 1980-82 showed that the medieval Port of London was busy. Wharves had been built on both sides of the bridge as landowners extended their property on reclaimed land, just as the Romans and the Saxons had done before them.

We know that the port was the centre of the wine trade from Gascony after Henry of Anjou (later Henry II) married the land-rich Eleanor of Aquitaine in 1152. Eleanor brought with her dowry vast estates in the south-west of France, an area that includes Bordeaux and the Dordogne. The Gascon wine arrived at a part of the London waterfront that is still called Vintners Place, a lane just west of Southwark Bridge. "Moreover there is in London upon the river's bank, amid the wine that is sold from ships and wind cellars, a public cook house." Fitz Stephen mentions that the menu included "coarser fish for the poor, the more delicate for the rich" and, reminding us that London, with about 25-30,000 people by the end of the twelfth century, included many foreigners, he adds, "However great the infinitude of knights or foreigners that enter the city or are about to leave it, at what ever hour of the day or night, that the former may not fast too long nor the latter depart without their dinner...."

A Norman house at Boothby Pagnell, Lincolnshire. It is a fine example of a twelfth-century building that clearly shows the undercroft beneath the main house.

In the documents of the time we read about merchants from Bordeaux, Rouen, Arras and Ypres; the latter two connected with the booming wool trade. Supplying the clothmakers of Flanders with English wool grown on the burgeoning monastic estates was one of the richer trades centred on the Port of London. Some of the wool merchants became rich enough to lend money to the king. By the late twelfth century craft and trade guilds were playing an increasingly important part in London's mercantile life, and in its social life, too. They were organized around a craft or a trade – the Pipe Rolls of 1179-80, records that were kept rolled like a pipe at the Exchequer, mention nineteen guilds, including bakers, fishmongers, saddlers and goldsmiths. Boys of fourteen could start a seven-year apprenticeship to gain the freedom of the guild, which gave them the right to set up in business on their own or to work for another master craftsman.

The guild's power was considerable. It set wages and prices and operated the medieval equivalent of a trading standards inspectorate. And woe betide anyone who stepped out of line. A baker, for example, found to be cheating on the weight of his bread, might be dragged through the streets with an offending loaf tied around his neck. Fear of such a fate led to the invention of the "baker's dozen" – selling thirteen loaves for the price of twelve.

The guilds were inextricably bound up with a local church – some even had their own chapel – and would stage religious plays called "mysteries". The Dyers, first mentioned in 1188, have as their official title "The Wardens and Commonalty of the Mistery of

Dyers of the City of London", and the Bakers started off as the "Fraternity or Guylde of Our Lady and St Clement". Great feasts in their halls with the members dressed in the "livery" of the guild were, and still are, a necessary part of life. In the spirit of mutual benefit the guild would also help members who became ill or who fell on hard times.

German merchants were also well established in London by the twelfth century. "The guild hall of the men of Cologne" is first mentioned in 1170 and on their site, now covered by Cannon Street Station, their hall came to be known as "the Steelyard" of the merchants of the Hanseatic League. The name steelyard derives from a

Stiliard

kind of medieval scales, and in the Museum of London there is an example that was found during the excavation of the site.

The German trading compound, some of whose buildings could still be seen before the coming of the railway, included a council chamber, a wine tavern, the master's house, merchants' houses and warehouses. Ships that tied up at the Steelyard's own jetty

The seventeenth-century reach of the Thames in Hollar's view of London, showing the Steelyard with its jetty, houses and stores.

brought barrels of hock; silver and gold cups; spices and wax; linen from Constantinople; and coats of mail from Regensburg.

Stone buildings of Norman London, or at least their foundations, are what archaeologists expect to find, but it is rare to find any remains of the ordinary timber and clay houses in which most of the population lived. A corner of Norman London, with floors, partitions and walls of wooden houses still visible, came as a great surprise to the archaeologists working under Guildhall Yard. The Norman remains are on the same site as the recently discovered Roman amphitheatre, but in an area that has never been disturbed by modern development.

This glimpse of eleventh-century architecture appears as a lane with a row of houses on either side. The property boundaries are marked with stakes driven into the ground; on one side of the lane the houses have walls made out of oak planks, while on the other they are of the more modest "wattle and daub" construction. Wood experts have identified the "wattle" as oak, with small oak branches and twigs intertwined with uprights to produce walls not unlike hurdles. Mud and yellowish brick earth would have been used to complete the wall. The houses have hearths, and floors made of either wooden chips or beaten earth. There are oyster shells everywhere, useful wooden objects such as bowls and cups, pins made of bone, plenty of William I coins, and a Norman carved bone gaming piece with a square dice to go with it.

To one side of the houses archaeologists came across a graveyard. It was almost directly below the present church of St Lawrence Jewry, which is part of the Guildhall complex. The simple coffins were made of oak and in the case of one burial at least some part of the clothes in which the body was wrapped survive.

Just as remarkable was a tree found in that Saxo-Norman churchyard, at least 3 metres (10 feet) below the ground. It was so well preserved that I could even see how its branches had been chopped and reduced to a stump.

There are still years of study ahead before archaeologists will have a definitive report, but it looks as if they have solved one enduring mystery: the whereabouts of the first London Guildhall mentioned in documents in the 1130s. Sticking out from the side of the excavation, some 3 metres (10 feet) below the surface, was a series of buttresses that could only be from a substantial building that lies underneath the existing one. There are, however, no plans to demolish the fifteenth-century Guildhall of London to prove the hypothesis!

Two religious organizations that influenced London life in the twelfth century were the "military orders". The Knights Templar and the Knights of the Order of St John of Jerusalem belonged to international monastic groups dedicated to the ideals of crusading. The Templars or Knights of the Temple, in white tunics with red crosses, and the "Hospitallers", in black habits decorated with white eight-pointed crosses, apparently found riding into battle on war horses perfectly compatible with their monastic vows of poverty, chastity and obedience. They were a curious mixture of warrior and monk: men, and in the Hospitallers' case nuns as well, who answered only to the Pope.

Both organizations operated throughout the medieval Christian world, from the west coast of Ireland through France and Italy to the desert borders of Christendom in Palestine and Syria. The knights in their great castles became the backbone of the Crusader armies in the East. And with their network of priory headquarters all over Europe, controlling thousands of agricultural estates, the military orders contributed both men and money to the defence of the Holy Land. The Templars, who took their name from the Temple Mount in Jerusalem, were brought to England by Henry I in the aftermath of the First Crusade, which had captured the imagination of the whole Christian world.

They set up first at Holborn and built a round church; then in 1162 the "New Temple" rose on a large tract of land between Fleet Street and the river. In 1159 Henry II also granted the Templars land on the east bank of the River Fleet, where Blackfriars is today: "a place on the Flete next Castle Baynard and all the course of the water of the Flete to make a mill there; and a messuage [dwelling-house] on the Flete by this bridge of the Flete". The Templars took the opportunity to reclaim a lot of land along both banks, ushering in a trend that would lead to the Fleet River becoming little more

The Romanesque west door of the Temple Church. Started in 1160, it was consecrated on 10 February 1185 by Heraclius, Patriarch of Jerusalem.

than a narrow open drain. On the east bank the Templars reclaimed no less than 20 metres (65 feet) by rebuilding the waterfront from the lower island to the confluence of the Fleet and the Thames, where they established a mill. Parts of what was probably the mill pond survived – a stone tank and masonry culverts – and nearby a large oval oven, completely lined and floored, with pieces of pottery, where the grain would have been dried before milling. The excavation also uncovered the remains of three other buildings that the knights probably let as tenements, and in the yard of one, where the base of a circular stone staircase survived, archaeologists found a three-seater lavatory made from a long oak plank.

The wet soil along the river bank also preserved an oak wagon axle which had later been used as part of a drain. A leather scabbard, medieval pottery, including a unique complete green-glazed jar of the thirteenth century, came from a well, and in a rubbish pit archaeologists found a well-preserved pair of medieval window shutters that must have been an everyday fitting on medieval London houses. Made of oak, the carved recesses for hinges were clearly visible, as were the nail holes. Nothing like this has come to light before and no doubt their survival is due to their having been thrown away and used to line the sides of the pit.

This part of the Templars' estate cannot be seen above ground as it was all demolished in 1308 and "the ancient timbers and tiles" sold for forty shillings. But an important Templar building does still exist in one of the Inns of Court off Fleet Street – the only survivor of a monastic complex that included a hall of priests, a cloister and a hall of knights.

The Temple Church is especially interesting as it marks the transition between the Romanesque and the Early English styles. The rounded Norman arch of the west door shares the architectural splendour with the pointed arches and slender marble columns of the round nave. But bolted on to the round nave is a later, much larger, rectangular choir: built about 1220 and designed with three aisles of equal height, it is one of the earliest examples of English Gothic. In the north-west wall are the slit windows of the penitentiary cell where the Grand Preceptor of Ireland starved to death for breaking the rule of the Temple. When the church was restored in 1950 a crypt full of bones and coffins was discovered under the south aisle of the choir. Historians believe that they may have found the treasury of the Order.

The Templars' legendary wealth helped to cause their downfall in 1308. The Order handled huge sums of money which it moved between Europe and the East as funds flowed in from donations and profits from their estates. Strapped for cash, the French king, Philip "the Fair", arrested the leaders of the Templars in Paris and seized their treasure for his own use. The knights in London, also accused of sodomy, heresy and blasphemy, were imprisoned in the Tower, and the Pope officially suppressed the order in 1312. The Hospitallers were given all the Templar properties, which they lost, along with all their own lands, at the time of the dissolution of the monasteries in the 1530s. The Temple Church has survived as the chapel belonging to the lawyers of the Inner and Middle Temple, who for hundreds of years have occupied much of the area that the Templars once controlled.

"There are also round about London in the Suburbs most excellent wells...among these Holywell, Clerkenwell and Saint Clement's Well are most famous and are visited by thicker throngs and greater multitudes of students from the schools and the young men of the city who go out to take the air".

With the permission of the London Borough of Islington, Fitz Stephen's "Clerkenwell" can still be seen at 14-16 Farringdon Lane. It is a pity that the great chronicler of London did not mention the Knights of St John at Clerkenwell while he was waxing lyrical about the suburbs. Like the ill-fated Templars, the Hospitallers blended

Effigies of medieval knights in the aisles of the round nave of the Temple Church. They include William Marshal, Earl of Pembroke, and the figure of de Ros – the effigy that was least damaged by the collapse of the burning roof during the German Blitz of 1941.

the savagery of war with charitable aims, but their original mission was to care for the sick. They were in Jerusalem a few years before the Crusaders took the city in 1099, and had established a hospital to care for Christian pilgrims who visited the city in large numbers even before the Crusaders arrived. The Hospitallers' castles and squadrons of cavalry in Palestine and Syria were added to the Order in the twelfth century, and some time in the 1140s a rich Anglo-Norman knight gave the Order 10 acres (4 hectares) of land in Clerkenwell on which to establish their English priory.

Finding a big chunk of the priory on St John Street today comes as a delightful surprise. It looks like one of London's medieval gates – a wide arch, supported by two four-storey towers, over the street. But we know that no City gate survived London's eighteenth-century expansion. The imposing early sixteenth-century gate was the priory's main entrance, saved from demolition in 1845 because of the tenacity of a local antiquary, W.P. Griffith. Under the arch there is a fine vaulted ceiling with a central boss carved with the Lamb of God – its Hospitaller flag is missing. Other bosses have the arms of the medieval Order: a white cross on a red background.

This gate would have seen young knights from all over England pass on their way to and from the Holy Land. Usually sons of gentry families, they would go out to the East to work in the Order's hospital in Jerusalem. Medieval reports of the hospital talk about 2,000 beds: a staff of surgeons and physicians cared for patients, all of whom had a bed to themselves! There was even an obstetric ward for women who produced babies in the middle of their pilgrimage. The Hospitaller knights themselves visited the sick and saw to it that they were served with meat three times a week and white bread to speed their convalescence.

The crypt of the Priory Church of St John – the only twelfth-century building of the priory now surviving.

There were never very many fully professed knights from the priories in Europe; only a few hundred at any one time. And as they took on more responsibility for the defence of the Crusader states they emerged as an officer corps commanding mercenary troops and squadrons of heavily armed knights – the medieval equivalent of the modern Saracen tank. The knights saw action in castles such as Crac des Chevaliers in Syria or Belvoir Castle, perched on the edge

A knight in the military dress of the Order of St John. The original fresco is in Siena Cathedral; this copy can be seen in the Church of the Order of St John in Clerkenwell.

of the Jordan Valley; later, when the Order moved its headquarters to Rhodes and Malta, they became commanders of galleys prowling the eastern Mediterranean in search of Muslim prizes.

The priory at Clerkenwell was a substantial establishment in itself and, through its income from many rural estates grouped into "commanderies" and rents from London properties, helped to fund the Hospitaller "empire" in the East. The surviving St John's Gate is only a fragment of what was there. Recent excavations in the Clerkenwell area have confirmed that the priory walls enclosed many buildings. A sixteenth-century inventory indicates a great hall, over 30 metres (100 feet) long, a counting house, the armoury, the priests' dormitory, the yeomen's dormitory, the wardrobe, the Lord Prior's chamber, a parlour, the distillery and brewery, and the kitchen. There was a school house, a fish pond and a garden, a slaughter house and an orchard. It was like a sizeable village surrounded by its own wall on the edge of the city. One of the recent discoveries made by archaeologists is that St John's Gate was the entrance to the inner enclosure – the religious and administrative area – and that the priory had an outer wall in which there would have been other gates. A priory graveyard was also discovered in the early 1990s. One of the graves was that of a young woman who died in childbirth; the tiny bones of the foetus were breech on and trapped by a very small pelvis. An examination of the mother's bones showed that she had had rickets, but how that tragic pregnant girl came to be buried in the priory will always remain a mystery.

The crypt of the Hospitallers' priory church, the Grand Priory Church of St John, is the only twelfth-century building left on the site. The earliest part is the western end, where there are three bays of rib-vaulted ceiling that are Norman. The rest of the crypt, built about 1185, has pointed vaulting, indicative of the architectural transition towards the English Gothic style. A sixteenth-century alabaster effigy of a knight from the Order's priory in Castille is a reminder of the international nature of the Hospitallers. In the North Chapel, William Weston, Prior of England at the time of the dissolution, is represented in a cadaverous sculpture that once graced his tomb. His heart gave out on the day that Parliament passed Henry VIII's act of dissolution of the monasteries.

London had been transformed by the arrival of the Normans. It had become the kingdom's biggest city. Its first mayor, Henry Fitz Ailwin, had been elected in 1189, and a sophisticated and effective form of self-government for London was emerging; royal government at Westminster had also become more efficient under Archbishop Hubert Walter in the 1190s, while Richard I was being a Crusader in the East and later a political prisoner in Austria. Monumental and pleasing private and public buildings graced the streets of the city; and, with the Norman ruling class controlling large estates from the Scottish border to the foothills of the Pyrenees, the trade that followed brought wealth and power to London. No wonder the Anglo-Norman Fitz Stephen glowed with pride as he looked around towards the end of the twelfth century: "Among the noble cities of the world that are celebrated by Fame, the City of London, seat of the Monarchy of England, is one that spreads its fame wider, sends its wares further, and lifts its head higher than all the others."

Chapter 4
London's High Middle Ages 1200-1485

ENRY II, THE FIRST PLANTAGENET KING, died in 1189 after a lifetime of internecine feuding with his family and war with France. His empire was bequeathed to his eldest surviving son, who became Richard I (the Lionheart) and might accurately be described as England's absentee king. After his coronation at Westminster Abbey in 1189 he rarely set foot on English soil, except to raise money for his famous crusade to Palestine. Richard died besieging a castle in France in 1199 and when his duplicitous brother John succeeded to the throne much of the Plantagenets' continental lands were lost to the French; the English baronial rebellion forced Magna Carta on the king at Runnymede, near Windsor, in 1215; and a year later the hapless John almost lost his kingdom during a French invasion. The barons of London, who had closed the city gates against the royal forces, welcomed the French as allies in what had become a full-scale civil war.

John died on campaign in 1216 and the civil war died with him. The French withdrew and the barons accepted John's infant son Henry as their future king. His regent, the Earl of Pembroke, William Marshall, whose effigy lies in the nave of the Temple Church, ruled until Henry III assumed the throne in 1232. Like his father, Henry pursued continental wars that drained the royal coffers, but he literally emptied them pursuing another passion: architecture. Castles and great houses grew in expensive profusion across the kingdom while Henry made plans for his greatest and most costly project: the rebuilding of Edward the Confessor's Westminster Abbey, begun in 1245. Henry made up for his lack of political judgement with an impeccable eye for architecture, painting and sculpture.

His vision of a new abbey church included a mausoleum to replace the loss of the Plantagenets' Fontevrault Abbey in the Loire Valley, where a number of Henry's ancestors, including Henry II and Richard I, lie. Westminster Abbey was to take on that role, but with a decidedly French architectural accent. In no other English church did vaulted ceilings soar to the height of the abbey's 31 metres (103 feet). The walls seem almost to be transparent, so tall and so wide are the windows compared with those of any other church in England from the thirteenth century. Flying buttresses made this lofty design workable: tiers of arching stones that are in themselves a striking architectural feature. Five radiating chapels at the east end are also reminiscent of the great French cathedrals at Rheims, Amiens and Paris.

Henry III's gilded effigy in the chapel of Edward the Confessor, Westminster Abbey. The king's heart was buried separately at the Abbey of Fontevrault, Anjou.

The entire country seemed to be galvanized into producing the new building. The Clerk of the King's Works recorded that two hundred boatloads of stone were delivered in five weeks in 1246; Caen stone cost £5.12.0 a boatload, while Kentish rag stone (from which most of the Roman wall had been built) came out at only £4.12.3 for fourteen loads. Other quarries were in Reigate, Surrey, and Corfe, Dorset, while forests in Essex and Kent produced oak in large quantities. Lead for the roof came from mines in Derbyshire and the accounts record an added cost: £9.10.0 for the salvage of a cargo of lead that went to the bottom of the sea off Great Yarmouth.

Only a short section of the nave had been finished by 1272 when Henry III died and work had to stop. He had spent the amazing sum of about £45,000 on his pet project – the equivalent of scores of millions of pounds at today's prices. The rest of the work had to wait for almost a century until the master mason Henry Yevele started building again in 1375. To the wonderment of architectural historians, Yevele resisted the temptation to leave his own mark on the nave and carried on with the original design. You can only just see the join in the nave at the sixth bay from the east where the window design is slightly different in detail. But many more centuries of master masons and famous architects were to have a hand in the building before its west towers, designed by Sir Christopher Wren and built by Nicholas Hawksmoor, added the final touch of symmetry in 1745.

The centrepiece of Henry's new abbey church was the shrine to the Saxon saint, Edward the Confessor, whose great abbey was to have such a profound effect on the development of the "twin" city of

London. The east end, with its ambulatory (semi-circular walkway behind the altar) and radiating chapels, was designed around the Confessor's shrine, which took Henry's craftsmen some twenty years to complete. "Picked goldsmiths from London", according to the thirteenth-century chronicler Matthew Paris, fashioned the shrine, which was "of purest gold and precious stones". The casket that contained the saint's bones was covered in jewels and adorned with golden images of kings and saints; and beneath, the ornate marble base had niches in which pilgrims and the sick could crouch. Most such medieval shrines were swept away in their entirety during the dissolution of the monasteries and the later desecration of shrines under Edward VI, but fortunately the base of the Confessor's shrine has survived. The mosaic pattern – similar to that of the thirteenth-century pavement of the presbytery – is still clear. You can read some of the letters of blue glass on a gold background above the niches, recording that the work was done by "Peter Civis Romanus, to the orders of King Henry III".

The curious-looking construction that now sits on the marble base dates from the Catholic Queen Mary's attempt to reinstate the shrine in 1557, but it gives no hint of the jewelled magnificence of the medieval original. The Confessor's chapel is ringed with tombs of medieval kings and queens: Henry III's son Edward I, the first king to be crowned in the new church built by his father, lies there in a plain stone tomb chest along with a more elaborate casket of his beloved first wife, Eleanor of Castille. When she died in 1290 Edward had tall stone crosses, adorned with carved figures of the queen, erected at every place the funeral cortege stopped on the journey from Nottinghamshire, where Eleanor had died. The cross in the forecourt of Charing Cross Station is a copy of the last one to have been erected.

The thirteenth-century carved marble base of Edward the Confessor's shrine in Westminster Abbey. The double-tiered wooden shrine on top dates from the sixteenth century.

Henry III's new abbey church, conceived as a royal mausoleum, was begun in 1245; the west towers, designed by Christopher Wren, were not completed until 1745.

Edward III also lies near his wife, Philippa of Hainault, in a tomb built by the celebrated Henry Yevele; Richard II and his queen, Anne of Bohemia, share a tomb with effigies that once held hands until they were damaged. Anne died in the Palace of Sheen, on the outskirts on London, in Surrey, and the heartbroken king not only abandoned and cursed the palace, but demolished it.

With its back to the screen that divides the Confessor's chapel from the altar in the sanctuary is the carved oak coronation chair. It was made for Edward I, and has built into the seat the ancient Stone of Scone which Edward seized from the Scottish kings in 1296. The theft of the stone still rankles with some Scots, but since the early fourteenth century all but three of the English monarchs have been anointed and crowned sitting in the solid-looking Gothic chair with the mystical stone secured by iron clamps.

Edward III lies in an altar tomb of Purbeck marble with niches around its sides to hold images of his fourteen children by Philippa. On her death bed, according to the medieval chronicler Froissart, the queen took the king's hand and pleaded that "when it should please god to call you hence, you will not choose any other sepulchure than mine, and that you will lie beside me in the cloister at Westminster". Every year on St Edward's Day, 13 October, the secular hordes who normally shuffle through this sacred part of the abbey give way to the revival of a medieval custom: a small band of modern pilgrims offer prayers to the saint and remember Henry III, whose gilded effigy shares a corner of the Confessor's chapel.

Henry's royal mausoleum must be judged a success by the number of monuments to English kings and queens that have been squeezed into its aisles and chapels. Almost the whole history of the monarchy is in the carved effigies and inscriptions above their caskets, along with courtiers, warriors, poets and tycoons of every age. The church looks cluttered as a result, but who would deny a place to the monuments to James I's children: Princess Sophia, alive for only three days and shown lying in a cradle, and Princess Mary, aged two years, carved in a reclining position on a small altar. In another "innocents' corner" there are the bones of two small children found in the Tower of London in the seventeenth century and moved to the abbey on the command of Charles II in 1674; the remains were thought to be those of the boy king Edward V and his brother Richard, allegedly murdered by their uncle Richard of Gloucester (later Richard III), in 1483.

Perhaps the simplest and most moving of the modern monuments is that of an unknown soldier whose remains were brought from a World War I battlefield in France and placed beneath a marble slab from Belgium, at the west end of the nave.

The abbey's special status as royal treasury and mausoleum protected it from the worst ravages of the dissolution. Not only have many of the medieval monastic buildings survived but, as we discovered earlier, there are areas of the cloisters that date back to the Norman monastery. Sated with history and architecture, a visitor could be forgiven for missing the eleventh-century Pyx Chamber in the undercroft at the end of the east cloister. It is not officially part of the responsibility of the modern Dean and Chapter, which has charge of the rest of the abbey. Pyx Chamber, beneath the library, was a strongroom and part of the royal treasury, the place where the standard pieces for the kingdom's coinage were kept in large "pyx" chests. At the "trial of the Pyx", coinage in circulation was tested by independent goldsmiths in front of a large jury to confirm that the coins were as pure as the standard laid down. The "trial of the Pyx" is still an annual event, but these days it is held in the Hall of the Goldsmiths in the City. The Pyx Chamber, commandeered by the Crown at the time of the dissolution and never given back to the Dean and Chapter, is now a separate museum run by English Heritage. It still contains some of the coin and bullion iron-bound boxes, but the two largest medieval ones, too big to pass through the door, must have been constructed in the chamber. Two parts of the furnishings that have never moved are an altar and a piscina which were installed when the undercroft served as a sacristy (store room for vestments and sacred objects) in the mid thirteenth century.

The room next to the Pyx Chamber – the continuation of the eleventh-century undercroft – has a small museum between the cylindrical columns, run by the Dean and Chapter. The most compelling items are the effigies of kings and queens that were carried on top of their coffins during funeral processions; after the burial, the effigies remained on show and became the property of the abbey. Edward III's death mask is the earliest (1377) – it is a wood carving covered with a thin coat of plaster. Among the others are a painted wooden head of Richard II's queen, Anne of Bohemia (died 1394), and the modelled head of Henry VII, who died in 1509, having added his stunningly beautiful Tudor chapel – of which we shall hear more in the next chapter – to the abbey's architectural heritage.

The entrance to Henry III's thirteenth-century Chapter House is also off the east cloister. Another part of the monastic precinct retained by the Crown in the sixteenth century, it was used as a store for the Exchequer's mass of documents, including the Domesday Book; a new wooden floor was laid and a gallery was added for extra storage space. Everything was cleared out in the mid nineteenth century when the Public Record Office was established in Chancery Lane, and, for the first time in several hundred years, the full beauty of the building could be appreciated. It had been badly neglected and Sir Gilbert Scott is said to have made a sympathetic restoration so that its appearance today is very like "the incomparable Chapter House" that the chronicler Matthew Paris saw in the early 1250s.

It is a daring piece of design: a central cluster of slender marble columns appears to be the only support for a web of ribs and arches that in turn supports the eight vaults of the ceiling. The monks, when they were deliberating, sat on the stone benches with painted niches behind – a little of the medieval painting can still be seen – while the six great windows that measured 12 metres by 6 metres (40 by 20 feet) flooded the chamber with light. The glazing is modern, but the floor is another of London's medieval treasures, one of the biggest spreads of tiles of the period to survive in any English building. Each tile was fired with different shades of clay and is a work of art in itself. Henry's arms, comprising leopards, wyverns and centaurs, are interspersed with scenes from palace life, including musicians performing and the queen shown hunting with a falcon on her wrist.

The daily affairs of the abbey were discussed here, but the Chapter House also played a unique role in nurturing one of England's most important national institutions – the House of Commons. The Commons began meeting in this almost circular chamber in the fourteenth century and for forty years endured the barbed remarks of monks who objected to the members' noise and wear and tear on the Chapter House's decorative floor. The monks' refectory, since destroyed, was another meeting place for the burgesses and knights of the Commons, but in the sixteenth century a permanent chamber was assigned for their debates in the nearby Palace of Westminster.

William the Conqueror suffered a setback when he wanted to improve or extend the old Saxon palace at Westminster. Goscelin, a Norman monk of Canterbury, recorded that fourteen ships out of a fleet of fifteen loaded with Caen stone bound for Westminster foundered in the English Channel. The earliest tangible evidence of a Norman palace is in the walls of William Rufus's Westminster Hall, but it was not until John's reign (1199-1216) that Westminster could claim to be the seat of government. By that time the main

Henry III's Chapter House at Westminster Abbey. Completed in the 1250s, it later became the first meeting place of the House of Commons.

treasury of the English Exchequer had been moved from Winchester, and by the fourteenth century the royal courts, and all the machinery of medieval government, had taken root in the precincts of the Palace of Westminster, or nearby.

Among the buildings there were the royal apartments and the "White Chamber" or House of Lords. The King's Great Chamber, another of Henry III's lavish projects, was the centre of decision-making. A large room some 26 metres (80 feet) long, and known for centuries as "the Painted Chamber", it was covered from floor to

A tile from the floor of the Chapter House at Westminster Abbey. It is one of the best preserved medieval tiled floors in England.

ceiling in murals by the best artists in the kingdom. An Irish friar, on his way to the Holy Land in 1332, was clearly impressed: "Near the Abbey stands the celebrated palace of the kings of England, in which is that famous chamber on whose walls all the war like scenes of the bible are painted with wonderful skill, and explained by a complete series of texts, beautifully written in French." The king also slept among his works of art in a bed painted green with gold stars, from which he could look through a window into St Stephen's Chapel and see the altar.

The kings lived side by side with Parliament in Westminster Palace until Henry VIII decided to abandon the rambling old palace and make a new start in Whitehall, for which he had grandiose plans. At the time of the Reformation in the sixteenth century, the rectangular St Stephen's Chapel was turned into the House of Commons – the members simply moved into the pews left vacant by the departed clerics. The modern House is laid out in the same way as the chapel, with members on opposite benches hurling heated arguments across the floor or deferring to Madam or Mr Speaker sitting where the altar used to be. Parliamentarians sometimes wonder if the familiar confrontational debating style would have developed such a cutting edge had the chamber been modelled on the lofty roundness of the Commons' first meeting place – the Chapter House.

Drawings of the Painted Chamber were made in the first quarter of the nineteenth century as layers of accretions came off the walls during renovations, revealing some of the paintings that had been covered since the Reformation 300 years earlier. The drawings were done just in time. On an October night in 1834, an overheated palace furnace set light to the buildings and the entire place was gutted by the morning. Antiquarians also recorded details of what was left of the buildings and noted that the undercroft of St Stephen's Chapel had survived the fire. Restored as a private chapel for members of both Houses in the nineteenth century, it lies beneath the modern House of Commons.

Another architectural survival from the old palace is a heavily restored sixteenth-century gallery with attractive fan vaulting, between the chapel and the Great Hall; it escaped destruction from both the 1834 fire and the fire bombs of the Second World War, as did Westminster Hall with its glorious timber roof, carved for Richard II by Hugh Herland at the end of the fourteenth century.

A new wave of ecclesiastical building hit London in the thirteenth century as various orders of friars arrived and set up monastic houses: Blackfriars (Dominicans); Greyfriars (Franciscans); Whitefriars (Carmelites); Austin Friars (Augustinans); Carthusians, and the Crossed or Crutched Friars. Most of these orders have left their names on the modern street maps because they, like the twelfth-century monasteries before them, acquired land within or just outside the city walls to build their conventual churches and monastic complexes. Redevelopment projects have turned up remains of some of their buildings on such sites as 1-9 Whitefriars Street, between Fleet Street and Tudor Street. In 1988 a late medieval undercroft was preserved intact by underpinning with a concrete raft and hoisting the crypt clear of the site with a view to restoring it in the basement of the new building. The Whitefriars precinct lay on the river-bank, where excavators discovered that the friars had reclaimed no less than 61 metres (200 feet) of further land from the river.

Most details of a medieval friary, however, have come from the site of the old Blackfriars monastery behind Blackfriars Station, between Upper Thames Street and Ludgate Hill. The excavation, at 10 Friar Street and 69 Carter Lane, was in the middle of a precinct that the Archbishop of Canterbury, himself a Dominican, acquired for the Blackfriars in 1275. The site included those two fortresses erected by the Norman kings on the western side of the city, Montfichet's Tower and Baynard's Castle, which by this time had fallen into disuse. And such was the influence of the Blackfriars that the king allowed them to extend the city wall around two sides of the priory. An 18 metre (60 foot) stretch of the medieval wall, surviving to the height of 2.8 metres (9 feet) and with three turrets, was found under Pilgrim Street and is now preserved in the basement of 100 New Bridge Street.

A great conventual church arranged around two cloisters was the main focus of the priory for the 400 monks who lived there in its heyday. Not unlike a royal palace in size and appointments, the monastery was often used by the king to accommodate foreign ambassadors; the Privy Council and Parliament sometimes met in the Great Hall, and the monastery was also a useful venue for political and religious discussions. Edward I's Queen Eleanor was a benefactress of the priory, and it is believed that, when she died in 1290, her heart was placed in a tomb in the choir of the great church. During excavations in 1988 foundations for the prior's lodgings were found, as was part of a wall of the Chapter House, and a cemetery showing evidence of fifty-eight burials. A total of 300 worked stones from windows, doors, vaults, ribs and shafts was also recovered and from their study reconstruction drawings of the buildings can be made. Perhaps the most spectacular find was in the undercroft of the Provincial's Hall: a 3 metre (10 foot) high window that was largely intact and is now destined for display in the new building.

The Blackfriars monastery was only one of a string of large houses established along the waterfront from the city walls to Westminster, some of which London's first antiquarian, John Stow (1525-1605), named: "Somerset House; Essex House; Arundel House; Bedford or Russel House." Savoy Palace, on the site of the plush present-day Savoy Hotel, took its name from Peter, Count of Savoy: Henry III had given it to him in 1246 at an annual rent of three barbed arrows. By 1361 it belonged to John of Gaunt, Edward III's third son, and it was there that Geoffrey Chaucer married Philippa Swynford, John of Gaunt's sister-in-law. Put to the torch in the Peasants' Revolt in 1381, it was later used as a hospital, a barracks and a school. Most of the old hospital buildings were cleared to build Waterloo Bridge in the early nineteenth century and the only remaining relic of the site is the Queen's Chapel of the Savoy, in a little square behind the hotel. The chapel, much restored and repaired, dates from the early sixteenth century and is one of the few royal chapels in London whose clergy are appointed by the Queen.

Across the river at Southwark the Bishop of Winchester's medieval palace has been partially excavated. There is no evidence of the bishop's medieval brothels, or of his Clink prison for prostitutes who broke the rules, but underground are the Roman remains we discovered in Chapter 1 and some 9 metres (30 feet) above the ground an exciting and evocative find was made: one of the windows in the bishop's Great Hall, still *in situ*. Parts of the fourteenth-century walls, complete with a magnificent rose window, had been incorporated into a nineteenth-century riverside warehouse, in a canny move to trim construction costs! The rose window, a unique design, was restored in 1972.

Southwark had always been a lively place because of its situation at the end of London Bridge – the only bridge in the city until the eighteenth century – which, according to Stow, "seemeth more like a continual street than a bridge". He described the great con-

A window of the thirteenth-century undercroft of the Blackfriars' Provincial Hall. The window, largely intact, was 3 metres (10 feet) high and is preserved in the basement of the new building on the site.

struction as having houses on either side with a drawbridge and "arches made of squared stone, of height 60 feet, and in breadth 30 feet". This first stone bridge was begun by Peter, vicar of St Mary Colechurch, at the east end of Cheapside, in 1176. It replaced the various Roman bridges, of which we know practically nothing, and several Anglo-Saxon and Norman crossings that are just as mysterious in their detail.

Archaeologists had a hint of the first stone bridge when, excavating at Fennings Wharf in Southwark, they came across a field of wooden piles that had once protected one of the piers of the bridge from the Thames current. It was exactly on the alignment of Peter de Colechurch's Norman bridge and, when it was studied by dendrochronologists (scientists specializing in dating wood by tree rings), a late twelfth-century construction date emerged. An added bonus to this important find was an even earlier timber pile at a lower depth. Dated to the eleventh century, it may have belonged to the protective "starling" of the first wooden Norman bridge.

"London Bridge is falling down", a rhyme still known to most English children, reflects an aspect of life that must have been familiar to Londoners over two millennia; fire was the greatest hazard (as shown by excavated burnt debris in the streets on both banks of the river), but warfare, dereliction and weather also took their toll. Even Peter's innovative nineteen stone arches did not solve the problem. On a July evening in 1212, only four years after the bridge's completion, a fire in Southwark attracted flocks of sightseers to its southern end. Sparks blown across the river ignited some buildings at the London end, cutting off the sightseers' return. But according to Stow the Southwark end of the bridge also caught fire "so that the people thronging themselves between two fires, did nothing else but expect present death." Seafarers, fishermen and boatmen went to their rescue in small craft and ships, "into which the multitude so unadvisedly rushed, that the ships being drowned, they all perished." The bridge was inevitably a hazard to those who made use of it – it was also ideal for jousting in the early days, before houses appeared on it – and "shooting" the white water through the narrow arches could be just as dangerous. The winter of 1282 cracked apart the masonry and five arches tumbled into the Thames.

The bridge survived many such vicissitudes and, by the seventeenth century, had evolved into something like a linear small town. Visitors marvelled: "A beautiful long bridge with quite splendid handsome and well built houses which are occupied by merchants of consequence." That German visitor also noted at least thirty rotting traitorous heads on spikes over the bridge's towered gateway – a gruesome custom that persisted until the Restoration of the monarchy in the seventeenth century.

Crossing the bridge must have been an ordeal at peak times. The houses and shops on either side, three to seven storeys high, left a carriageway less than 4 metres (about 12 feet) wide; pedestrians, animals and wheeled traffic made slow progress among the clutter of stalls selling a complete range of high-street produce. It was recorded in 1358 that there were 138 shops on the bridge contributing to its upkeep. Pilgrims from all over England also swelled the numbers, because Peter de Colechurch had built a little chapel to the martyred Thomas Becket right in the middle of the bridge. From the records there seems to have been no trouble in attracting funds for the maintenance of the bridge: one will of the period left "to the poor 20; to London bridge 100 marks". Such bequests were common. Indeed, Robert Large, a mercer who had served as mayor in the early part of the fifteenth century, also left money to bridge the Walbrook, which must still have flowed through the City. Even more generous was the benefactor, unnamed by Stow, who left the rents of all the houses in a street called Pater Noster Row "to the maintenance of London Bridge".

The Dutch engraver Nicholas Visscher's view of London Bridge dated 1616 shows the houses that merchants in the Middle Ages found so desirable. One mansion, Nonsuch House, which John Stow greatly admired, was four storeys high. It was a Renaissance design, painted in bright colours, with onion-shaped domes on slender towers at each corner. Pre-fabricated in Holland and shipped to London, where it was "pegged" together without the use of iron nails, this remarkable building, along with all the others, was demolished in 1758 and the bridge strengthened. Since then two more bridges have been built: Sir John Rennie's five arches of stone in 1823-31, and the present 1967-72 pre-stressed concrete cantilevers that form just three spans. Rennie's bridge was snapped up by Lake Havasu City, Arizona for $2,460,000 (it was widely rumoured at the time that they thought they were buying the more eye-catching Tower Bridge) and shipped across the Atlantic for re-erection over an artificial lake in the Arizona desert. One remarkable piece of continuity in the story is the role of the Bridge House Estates – the medieval foundation set up to maintain Old London Bridge. Its invested wealth still maintains the modern bridge and, coincidentally, is a major contributor to the cost of the Guildhall Yard excavations and the new art gallery that will contain the conserved remains of the Roman amphitheatre.

Some of the stones from Old London Bridge are in the churchyard of St Magnus the Martyr in Lower Thames Street, which until the nineteenth century nudged the abutment of the downstream side of the bridge. The church also received part of its income from the

Visscher's view of London, published in 1616.

bridge, in the form of a proportion of the alms given by travellers to the chapel of St Thomas Becket. Since the new bridges were built slightly upstream of the medieval alignment, a modern office block has filled the empty space, towering above St Magnus's spire, and obscuring the splendid eighteenth-century clock that used to be visible as people crossed into London. In the church, according to Stow, "Henry Yevele, freemason to Edward III, Richard II and Henry IV, who died in 1400; his monument yet remaineth." Sadly I could not find any trace of it, nor of the church's medieval origins. But its sumptuous carved baroque interior by an early twentieth-century restorer, within the Wren rebuilding, is a haven from the maelstrom of traffic along Lower Thames Street.

St Magnus the Martyr. The medieval church that once stood on this site received part of its income from the chapel on the bridge. This photograph was taken before a modern office block dwarfed the Wren spire.

Between the tenth and fifteenth centuries the river frontage advanced into the Thames by about 120 metres (400 feet), as Londoners, like the Romans before them, reclaimed land from the river foot by foot. As property boundaries advanced, so did lanes and alleys and, by the fourteenth century, the river-front between Billingsgate and Blackfriars was cut by dozens of narrow lanes that ended at quaysides for either private or commercial use. Only certain quays were authorized to handle foreign trade: Queenhithe, Steelyard, Billingsgate and the Custom House were the principal landing places.

Stow tells us that "every great ship landing there [at Billingsgate] paid for strandage two pence, every little ship with orelockes a penny, the lesser boat called a battle a half penny." Some of the "great" ships would have been the Venetian state galleys that docked regularly in London after the direct sea route to the Mediterranean had opened up in the fourteenth century. They would have arrived laden with spices and precious cloths and stayed for two to three months while they sold their cargo and loaded wool, cloth, hides, tin and pewter products.

The dues were collected at the Custom House, where in the 1370s Geoffrey Chaucer, the first writer to use only English for his works, held the position of Comptroller of Customs and Subsidies of Wools, Skins and Hides in the Port of London. Excavations in 1973 revealed the foundations of the counting house where the poet and courtier would have worked. Chaucer would also have collected dues on "sea coal" for the king, so called because it arrived from the mines in Newcastle by sea. Used both for industry and in the home, by the late thirteenth century coal was already the cause of complaints about the pollution in London!

Along the waterfront today, between the modern office blocks that crowd on to the river's edge, some of the lanes, no bigger than their medieval counterparts, are still in use. Occasionally barges load city refuse from a quay just upstream from Southwark Bridge and at low tide, with the barges stuck fast on the shingle, it is not uncommon to see "mudlarkers" in their wellington boots hoping to find a medieval coin or a pilgrim's badge dropped from a vessel's gangway centuries ago. Vintners Place, one of several lanes between Queen Street and Queenhithe, squeezes its way down to the riverside and ends in a cul-de-sac in front of a large modern building completed for the Vintners' Company in 1994.

The new Vintners' building, in sandstone with Grecian columns at the front, is an expression of how London's medieval livery companies can sustain their ancient customs while exploiting centuries-old real estate on the river-front. A document witnessing the deed that first connects this land to the wine trade was signed by John Chaucer, the poet's father, in 1352. It is one of the hall's many treasures in a collection that includes a fifteenth-century tapestry and a sixteenth-century funeral pall.

The main staircase in the Vintners' Hall, looking much as it did when it was built in the 1670s. The lion and the unicorn are original, though the heraldic shields they hold are post-war replicas. The portraits are of the late Duke of Gloucester and his duchess, Honorary Freemen of the Vintners' Society.

The present hall, which dates from 1667, after the Great Fire, claims to have one of the oldest surviving seventeenth-century rooms in London – the company's panelled court room. The main staircase, made in 1673, with its richly carved balustrades, is a fine example of the period. Stow records that the Vintners produced many Mayors of London, one of whom hosted a dinner for five kings at the hall in 1363: Edward III, John I of France, David II of Scotland, Peter de Lusignan of Cyprus and Waldemar of Denmark. On formal occasions the Vintners' Master and Wardens, dressed in gowns and wearing their badges of office, still drink the royal toast with five cheers rather than three. Stow gives us an insight into the importance and power of the City establishment in a story about Lombard wine merchants who were accused of adulterating wine: "When knowledge there of came to John Rainwell, Mayor of London, he in divers places in the city commanded the heads of butts and other vessels in the open streets to be broken, to the number of 150, so that the liquor running forth, passed through the city like a stream of rain water."

Livery companies like the Vintners' grew out of the twelfth-century trade and craft guilds – "livery" simply means the members' distinctive dress that differentiates them from other companies – and like many other City livery companies, the Vintners still play an active role in their trade. The company's inspectors, as in Edward III's time, have the right (under EC legislation) to examine stocks that merchants hold so that the origin of the wine can be guaranteed. The company also funds education and training in the industry and offers the qualification Master of Wine.

The most curious of all the company's activities is, however, "Swan Upping". The Vintners and the Dyers have always had the right to own swans on the Thames. All the rest of the swans belong to the Crown, and every July and August the cygnets must be given a mark of ownership. The Queen's swan marker, assisted by representatives of the two companies, sets off on a voyage along the river to count the swans and mark the cygnets: two nicks in the beak for the Vintners' swans and one for the Dyers'; the royal cygnets go unmarked.

Eight hundred years ago the Vintners' butts of wine stored in cellars along the waterfront would have been transported to the centre of the City through the web of streets and lanes that had started to appear in the ninth century. Bow Lane was probably the main route to the taverns and merchants' houses of Cheapside – medieval London's main market and shopping street (*Ceap* or *Chepe* was the old English word for market). The lane, according to Stow, was a centre for the hosiery trade, and runs off Cheapside by the side of St Mary le Bow. Today it is one of the few areas "within the walls" that feels like a living city: the buildings are mainly nineteenth century and there are still useful shops such as a butcher's. Clothes shops – modern versions of mercers' establishments – compete for floor space in the lane with winebars and pubs, and one of the narrow alleys that runs off Bow Lane has a tavern at its end.

The buildings may be comparatively modern, but Stow would still recognize many elements of the street plan around Cheapside. Excavations of several basements in Bow Lane, Cheapside, Milk Street and Ironmonger Lane have confirmed that property alignments were remarkably consistent from the mid thirteenth century through to the Great Fire in 1666. Some have not changed at all.

Archaeologists from the Museum of London found that the tenth-century Bow Lane was made of compacted Roman building rubble, and what began as a street about 9 metres (30 feet) wide in the ninth century had narrowed to about half that width by the end of the twelfth. In places it could have shrunk to as little as 2 metres (6 feet) as people invaded the street with gardens, walls and even extensions to the houses. By 1100 there were large timber cellars along the frontages of both sides of Bow Lane and later substantial stone houses began to appear among the shops and warehouses. In the late thirteenth century we know that at the top end of Bow Lane, alongside St Mary le Bow, a wealthy vintner, Osbert of Suffolk, owned a vaulted cellar which was probably a tavern. Known first as Cordwainers Street (Street of the Shoemakers), the lane went through several changes of name: it was called Hosier Lane in the thirteenth century when drapers (woollen cloth merchants) and mercers (dealers in linen, silks and other fine textiles) moved into the area, and by the time Stow described the ward of "Cordwainer", Hosier Lane had taken on its modern name, after the famous church that stands at the top of it.

Walking along Bow Lane today you can imagine two- and three-storey wooden buildings with porches and upper rooms or solars overhanging the street. At times the smell must have been dreadful; the lane was a convenient place to dump rubbish and even the entrails of slaughtered animals, which were left for roaming pigs to clear up. Some of the houses would have had refuse chutes from indoor privies running down the side of the building into a cess-pit. And after 1212, when the first Mayor of London, Henry Fitz Ailwin, tightened up the fire regulations, many houses would have had tiled roofs instead of reeds, rushes or stubble.

Well Yard, now renamed Well Court, is one alley off Bow Lane that Stow would have known. Building works between 1976 and 1980 gave archaeologists of the Museum of London an opportunity to trace the remains of houses from the 1250s to the mid fifteenth century. Walls, pavements, cellars and hearths revealed that this Bow Lane frontage was occupied by a row of houses with two gates that gave access to bigger houses behind. The entrance to Well Court marks one of those gates today, and with the help of historians working on a project called The Social and Economic Study of Medieval London, it is now possible not only to reconstruct some of the buildings on paper, but to know the names of the people who owned and rented the houses at various times.

The earliest rents went to Canterbury Cathedral Priory, from John son of Baldwin: thirty-nine shillings. Charters from the Corporation of London's archives show that at various times one property, for example, was in the hands of Robert Westmelne, citizen and "pepperer" of London; John de Essex, citizen and apothecary; Adam Staple, mercer and mayor in 1376-7. One John Bradlee and his servant Janyn rented one of the property's smaller tenements – a draper's shop and at least three other rooms. The way they left has a familiar ring about it. When the landlord inspected the property, he found fittings and fixtures missing: a wooden counter from a shop, a tiled pavement from a chamber, several partitions or screens, a cupboard of Eastland (Baltic) board from the parlour, plus a great deal of stone. Bradlee was already in prison for another crime, so his servant was ordered to replace the tiles and clean out the filth from the house. Drapers and mercers predominate in the list of tenants and it is clear that Bow Lane was full of desirable residences – just around the corner from Cheapside, the medieval equivalent of London's "golden mile".

Cheapside was more than just a market. It was a meeting place and ceremonial way where the City would turn out to welcome royalty or punish miscreants; Stow mentions hands severed, floggings and "divers executions" that took place around a fountain, known as the standard, outside St Mary le Bow. The main sources of water for Cheapside, however, were the little conduit near St Paul's and, at the east end of the street, "the great conduit of sweet water, conveyed by pipes of lead underground from Paddington" which was built about 1285. Wine was substituted for water on festive occasions, such as the arrival of Edward I's bride, Eleanor of Castille. Cheapside was chosen as the site of another Eleanor Cross, erected by the grief-stricken Edward on the death of his queen. Its three storeys of inscriptions and statuary can be identified in the drawing of 1638 that depicts Marie de Medici in Cheapside on a visit to her daughter, Charles I's queen, Henrietta Maria.

By 1200 shops in Cheapside formed a continuous row; the plots of land, frequently subdivided, were 6-9 metres (20-30 feet) wide and divided again into shop fronts that could be as narrow as 2 metres (6 feet). Under the shops there were vaulted cellars, like the one excavated in Bow Lane with low, street-level windows, and between the shops and taverns passage-ways led to larger plots behind, where traders set up bazaars with stalls and chests against high stone party walls. The great market of Cheapside spilled over into side streets such as Bow Lane, Milk Street and Ironmonger Lane, where excavations indicate that the shops were bigger and probably used for manufacturing and processing as well. The street names tell their own story: Bread Street for bakers; goldsmiths in Goldsmiths' Row; fishmongers in Friday Street; money-lending Jews in Old Jewry; poulterers in Poultry; dairymen in Milk Street. Saddles were made at the western end of Cheapside and on the north side cutlers made their knives and scissors, while mercers and drapers had their shops in the market's central area. The rumbustious nature of the street in the Middle Ages was aptly portrayed by Chaucer in the "Cook's Tale":

> There was a prentice living in our town,
> Worked in the victualling trade and he was brown,
> At every wedding he would sing and hop
> and he preferred the tavern to the shop.
> Whenever an pageant or procession
> Came down Cheapside, goodbye to his profession.
> He'd leap out of the shop to see the sight
> And join the dance and not come back that night!

Chaucer's cook must also have been in the crowd that went to see the jousting in Cheapside, when, according to Stow, "the stone pavement [was] covered with sand, that the horses might not slide." But on the occasion of the Black Prince's birthday, the wooden stand for the ladies crashed to the ground, "and such as were underneath were grievously hurt." Stow says that Queen Philippa successfully pleaded with the king (Edward III) to forgive his carpenters: "After which time the king caused a shed to be strongly made of stone, for himself, the Queen, and other estates to stand on, and there to behold the joustings."

That royal "shed" was built alongside St Mary le Bow and, when Wren rebuilt the church after the Great Fire, he added a balcony to the tower to commemorate the traumatic collapse of the stand in 1330. Wren's monumental tower, his grandest in the city, is built out from the church because he discovered a solid stretch of Roman road on which to build the foundations. Although the church was burnt out in 1941, the tower, with its outstanding steeple, survived and the famous "Bow Bells" (to be a true Cockney you must be born within the sound of them) rang out their "oranges and lemons" rhyme again in December 1961.

Thomas Becket was born in Cheapside, in a house on the corner of Ironmonger Lane. After his murder in Canterbury in 1170, the house became part of a hospital, inspired by the Crusades, called St Thomas of Acon (Acre). Part of the hospital was bought by the Mercers' Company, whose charters go back to 1394, and in the early sixteenth century they built a hall. The Mercers acquired the whole site after the dissolution of the monasteries. They provided the money to set up St Paul's School, and their investment income

Wagon and Tun decorative piece made in 1554, part of the Mercers' magnificent plate collection. It has a clockwork motor which can still propel the tun (wine barrel) along a smooth surface.

continues to support both the boys' and the girls' schools. The Mercers' second hall, built after the Great Fire, served as the first home of the Bank of England in 1694 and was also used by the East India Company as its headquarters in 1702. That hall succumbed to bombing raids in the 1940s, but some of the panelling was saved and incorporated into the new hall, which is part of the modern office block called Becket House. Excavations on the site in 1958 turned up a beautiful life-size recumbent statue of Christ that may have come from the medieval hospital.

The lorry containing the Irish Republican Army bomb was parked outside the medieval church of St Ethelburga when it exploded on 24 April 1993. One wall was reduced to rubble, the remaining three were badly damaged and much of the furniture and objects inside were smashed into matchwood.

The hall today contains one of the most important City company collections: a set of spoons, once owned by the Mercers' most famous member, Sir Richard (Dick) Whittington; a late fifteenth-century cup and an array of sixteenth-century silver including a rare "college cup" – the earliest example of a type that was used in some of the Oxford colleges.

As for intact buildings that take us back beyond the nineteenth century, there are very few in this part of the City. The corner of

Wood Street and Cheapside, however, has a strong hint of the past amongst the banks and prestige office blocks: three narrow shops, two storeys high, are said to have been built by the parishioners of St Peter Westcheap – one of the thirty-four City churches that perished in the Great Fire, never to be rebuilt. Its churchyard survives in a truncated form, a somewhat sad little plot with iron railings, cheered up by a single leafy plane tree.

Historians can trace the existence of 107 churches, mainly within the city walls, by the fourteenth century. But few have come down to us in a form that preserves anything like the bulk of their medieval fabric – of the thirty-eight remaining after 1666 only three could be described as substantially medieval, or pre-fire: St Bartholomew's, St Andrew Undershaft and St Helen Bishopsgate. There were four such venerable buildings in the City until 1993, when St Ethelburga's in Bishopsgate took the full force of an IRA terrorist bomb and was left in such a ruinous state that it is unlikely that it will ever be rebuilt.

St Andrew Undershaft – another rare example of a pre-fire church that escaped both the Great Fire and the bombs of the Second World War – suffered in the same terrorist attack. It retains much of its sixteenth-century restoration (although many "improvements" were perpetrated on the building in the eighteenth and nineteenth centuries) and one of its attractions is the monument to John Stow, who was buried there in 1605. The marble effigy depicts him seated at a table, writing a book with a quill pen, and every year on the anniversary of his death London's Lord Mayor, attended by his sheriffs, replaces the quill pen and presents a copy of Stow's *Survey of London* to the writer of the best essay on the capital received that year. St Andrew Undershaft suffered two terrorist attacks within a year – ironically, when the second blast rocked the City in 1993, workmen were just putting the finishing touches to the repair to the windows and roof after the previous year's bomb.

Not more than a couple of minutes' walk away, St Helen Bishopsgate with St Martin Outwich was also damaged by both bombs and needed extensive repairs to the roof, windows and furnishings. The external south and west doors were blown off their hinges by the blast. Unlike St Ethelburga's the building remained sound; its fourteenth-century north aisle survives from the Benedictine nunnery founded on the site in 1205-15; because the nuns' chapel and parish church were side by side, and under the same roof, the building was spared in the dissolution of the monasteries. The interior of the "double nave" has so many original pre-fire features that it is sometimes called "the Westminster Abbey of the City". Sadly the City fathers of the 1960s and '70s, unmindful of a suitable setting for this architectural gem, sanctioned the building of nondescript towers of concrete office blocks that all but smother St Helen's with their blankness. Two medieval chapels survive in the south transept, and in the late fifteenth century the merchant and diplomat Sir John Crosby left money to build the present nave arcade. The church has fifteenth-century choir stalls, a seventeenth-century font and several early brasses. Crosby and his first wife are buried in the church, along with many other notables whose monuments help to recreate the spirit of medieval and Tudor London.

While Londoners were celebrating Edward III's victory at Crécy in 1346 (the first battle of the Hundred Years' War), a more potent enemy was moving towards the gates of the city – the Black Death. Rats had carried the disease west from Asia throughout the early years of the fourteenth century – it had reached the Mediterranean by 1347 – and from a ship from Gascony, which docked in Weymouth in Dorset, infected rats ran ashore. England was only just recovering from a terrible famine brought on by years of bad winters with storms and floods, in which large numbers had died or become seriously undernourished. Such a vulnerable population quickly fell victim to the disease which, in its most virulent form, could kill within two or three days. A Rochester monk, William of Dene, observed, "Men and women carried their own children on their shoulders to the church and threw them into a common pit."

The plague reached London in September 1348 and within two months the disease had spread through the rubbish-strewn streets and claimed thousands of victims. Graveyards were soon filled and plague pits had to be dug in different parts of London as families brought out their dead for hurried burial. Existing church-yards also accommodated plague victims: that of the Holy Trinity, in the grounds of a Cistercian abbey on the site of the old Royal Mint next to the Tower of London, archaeologists found three mass burial trenches containing the remains of 762 people who had died of the dread disease. Very few objects were buried with the bodies, which appeared to be densely but carefully laid out. In places the burials were five deep in layers with earth sealing each one. Only 230 bodies were in coffins; some were interred surrounded by charcoal, the significance of which is not yet understood. Many of the livery company records note the loss of office holders, and although no one can say for certain, it seems likely that up to half of London's population of 40-50,000 was wiped out. In Smithfield alone it is estimated that 10,000 victims were buried. The tragedy, however, spurred the king to proclaim that the mayor and sheriffs should exercise greater control over the slaughtering of animals, whose putrid blood often collected in pools along the streets.

A medieval market that has proved to have remarkable continuity is Leadenhall Market, at the corner of Gracechurch and Leadenhall Streets; it still sells eggs, butter, poultry and cheese as it did in the fourteenth century. The market enters London's history in 1195, when the Neville family of Essex built their town house, Ledene Hall, on the site. By 1321 we know that the courtyard was being used by out-of-town "foreigners" to sell poultry and, later, cheese and butter. The City Corporation took over the building and its traditional market in 1411, when Dick Whittington was mayor, and embarked on a large new development – a granary, chapel and school. The granary or Garner – to provide grain in times of poor harvests – was a monumental three-storey building with four ranges enclosing a rectangular courtyard some 60 metres (200 feet) long. The upper two floors, reached by spiral staircases in towers at each corner, were designed to store grain, while the ground floor was arcaded and included an entrance to the Garner's chapel. The adjoining school also used the chapel.

But this laudable civic enterprise never achieved its potential. The school faded away and the granary seems to have been used as a general warehouse for several organizations including, for a time, the East India Company. As a market, however, the Garner was a

The remarkable survival of the medieval "Garner" walls. Encased in a nineteenth–century office block, they were in places preserved to their full height of 11 metres (36 feet).

continuing success. It was rebuilt after the Great Fire and again in the nineteenth century, when a new development cleared the site, and the building we know today, roofed with cast-iron girders and glass, took shape. That historical perspective was shaken, however, when, in 1986, archaeologists had the opportunity to test the documentary record by excavating buildings on the edge of the present covered market.

On top of the foundations of the Roman basilica they found evidence of the original Ledene Hall and its fifteenth-century successor, the Garner, which, until then, everyone thought had been razed by nineteenth-century developers. During excavations of the foundations, 177 carved stones from doorways, arches and windows began to reveal important architectural details. It was a great surprise to find that one of the 1445 walls had survived – a wall that had been singed by the the Great Fire, threatened by nineteenth-century builders and shaken during the Blitz. The outside wall of the west range of the Garner had been encased in a Victorian office block, only to re-emerge, surviving to its full height of 11 metres (40 feet), when the nineteenth-century plaster was stripped off. This evidence, in addition to some nineteenth-century sketches, has made it possible to draw a more accurate picture of one of London's medieval public buildings on a site that has been a market for almost 700 years.

The master mason responsible for Ledene Hall, John Croxton, also built London's Guildhall. He started work in 1411 and took about thirty years to complete the 45 metres (150 feet) long hall, second in size only to Westminster Hall. It was not the first building to house the heart of London's government. As we have seen in the Guildhall Yard excavations, a wall has been found that was probably part of an earlier hall, and the west crypt of the present hall clearly belongs to a smaller building that pre-dates it. But why the building, away from the main commercial centres of medieval London, should have been built there at all is still a matter of conjecture. The name Aldermanbury, for the street outside and the nearby square, may, however, be a clue. It is an Anglo-Saxon name that means "the fortified residence of an Alderman" – a Saxon royal official. Historians have come to believe that that house probably occupied the site of the eastern gate of the Roman fort, which may have survived into the Dark Ages to be used as part of the palace of the Saxon kings. There are precedents for this in other European cities, and in London there is a persistent legend that makes the same claim.

If that were the case, the old Roman gate would have become the natural seat of power for the king's representative in charge of the City when Edward the Confessor moved his palace to Westminster. Archaeologists are still hoping that some sign of "Aldermanbury" will emerge in a future excavation to confirm that the location of today's Guildhall is more than just a geographical accident.

The election of the mayor and the aldermen who govern the City happens in much the same way today as it has done for over 800 years; once a year 132 "freemen", usually from the livery companies, stand for election in the City's twenty-six wards for a place on the Court of Common Council. The Lord Mayor, who is also elected once a year, presides over the council, which deals with most of the City Corporation's day-to-day affairs. The Court of Aldermen, whose members are appointed for life, now plays a smaller role in the government of the city and has evolved into a sort of "Upper House". The Lord Mayor, whose splendid Georgian Mansion House stands, significantly, opposite the Bank of England, takes precedence over everyone except the sovereign at any City function, and once a year reminds the citizens of his office by travelling in the golden coach that is kept for the other 364 days in the Museum of London.

The Guildhall suffered badly in the Great Fire and again in the Blitz, losing its roof on both occasions. The present one, with stone arches, was finished in 1953. But the medieval walls remained, along with most of their flamboyant marble monuments to merchants, mayors and military heroes, and much of what we see today is fifteenth-century masonry. The facade facing the yard, however (rebuilt after the Second World War), is from the imagination of the late eighteenth-century architect George Dance, and combines Gothic and classical themes. The main entrance, the porch with sturdy vaults for a ceiling, is very much how John Croxton would have left it.

Two other medieval halls, on a more modest scale, that help to conjure up an impression of a lost city, are close together at Holborn Bar. Barnard's Inn and Staple Inn were Inns of Chancery and, like the more resilient Inns of Court, provided accommodation and training for young men who wanted to enter the expanding legal system of the Middle Ages. They have not survived as part of London's legal establishment, having been absorbed by the four remaining Inns of Court: Grays Inn, Lincoln's Inn and the Inns of the Inner and Middle Temple.

Barnard's Inn, built in the late fourteenth or early fifteenth century, was reconstructed and repanelled in the Tudor style in the early sixteenth century, but much of that work had to be redone after the wreckage left by the Gordon Riots in 1780. Restoration was needed again in 1932, when the Mercers' Company, whose school by then occupied the site, provided the initiative and the money. The hall is one of the few ancient buildings that was not burnt out in the Great Fire, or hit during the Second World War, and as well as its roof the armorial arms of the Principals of Barnard's Inn, set into the tall windows, are there to be admired in all their sixteenth- and seventeenth-century colour. The hall is now let to Gresham College – an institution founded in 1597 by the former mercer and Lord Mayor Sir Thomas Gresham.

Staple Inn in Holborn, reached through an arch set into the facade of a row of Elizabethan houses, began as a wool warehouse in the late thirteenth or fourteenth century. It was an important centre for London's medieval wool trade, but by 1400 the hall and its surrounding buildings were being used by lawyers who set up the Inn of Chancery. That lasted until well into the nineteenth century, but the present hall, built in the sixteenth, was badly damaged during the Second World War and reconstructed in 1950. The architectural historian Nikolaus Pevsner does not exactly gush with admiration about the post-war hammer-beam roof, describing it as "odd" and "fanciful". However, the reconstruction of the roof is remarkable in that it was achieved using the one hammer beam that survived the bombing; it is the first beam a visitor sees on entering the hall, which is now let to the Institute of Actuaries.

The Guildhall was badly damaged in both the Great Fire and the Second World War. The fifteenth-century porch, however, still has its original vaults.

> This royal throne of kings, this Sceptr'd Isle,
> this earth of majesty, this seat of Mars,
> this other Eden, demi Paradise,
> this blessed plot, this earth, this realm, this England.

The Bard often took licence with factual history, but he cannot be faulted for the setting of that famous speech from the mouth of John of Gaunt as he lay dying in Ely Place. Despite its name Ely Place is indeed in London, in an elegant little street off Holborn Circus alongside Hatton Garden; it was built by the Bishops of Ely between 1286 and 1290, and John of Gaunt lived there after his own house, Savoy Palace, had been burned down during the Peasants' Revolt in 1381. What remains of the bishop's palace can still be visited.

The palace, one of scores of large town houses established by secular and ecclesiastical landowners during the Middle Ages, was built around a hall that was 22 metres (72 feet) long, 10 metres (32 feet) wide and 9 metres (30 feet) high; there was a large courtyard in front and a cloistered quadrangle behind, and, like the Ledene Hall, the house had its own large chapel. It was a palatial enough house for royalty frequently to make use of it. Before her wedding to Edward III in 1327, the fourteen-year-old Philippa of Hainault stayed there. Richard II was also a resident at one time and the wealthy bishops – their estates in Cambridgeshire were at the centre of England's wool trade – could afford to entertain lavishly. Who paid for Henry VIII's five-day banquet in 1531 is not recorded, but John Stow seemed shocked at the scale of it all, and at the expense: "Twenty four great beefs at twenty six shillings and eight pence a piece; one hundred fat muttons, two shillings and ten pence the piece; fifty one great veals at four shillings and eight pence the

The exterior of Crosby Hall, which preserves most if its original architectural features from the fifteenth century.

piece." The poultry order followed, with hundreds of birds of various kinds, including "pigeons thirty seven dozen at ten pence the dozen, swans fourteen dozen, larks three hundred and forty dozen at five pence the dozen, etc."

After Henry VIII's dissolution of the monasteries in the 1530s, Elizabeth I forced the Bishops of Ely to lease much of the property to one of her favourites, Sir Christopher Hatton, for ten pounds a year plus ten loads of hay and a rose picked at midsummer. The Great Fire spared the palace but it fell into a state of dereliction – the chapel crypt was used as a brewery at one stage – and after the death of the last Lord Hatton in 1772 the property reverted to the Crown. All the buildings except the chapel, which is dedicated to the Anglo-Saxon Saint Etheldreda, were demolished and in their place the row of houses we see today was built. St Etheldreda, Ely Place, is another of London's architectural gems tucked away in an eighteenth-century street behind imposing iron gates. The only part of the church visible from the street is the west end, which, like Westminster Abbey's walls, appears to be made only of glass and stone tracery. The stained glass is modern, having been restored at least twice. The roof was also destroyed by bombs or missiles during the 1940s, but the interior wall survived the attacks, as did the sturdy timber floor – another rare example of medieval carpentry.

The present-day diamond traders' street – and an area of several streets around it – took its name from the seventeenth- and eighteenth-century owners of Ely Place and attracted well-to-do families. Hatton Garden's connection with the diamond business is recent: some time during the first half of the nineteenth century some jewellers began working there, and since then it has become the centre of the trade in London. In an alley that connects Ely Place and Hatton Garden, a pub called the Mitre, the successor of a tavern that had been established for the servants of the palace, slakes the thirst of those in search of London's past. In the bar, a piece of cherry wood is said to have come from the tree that marked the boundary between the gardens of the bishop and Sir Christopher Hatton. St Etheldreda's was the first pre-Reformation church to revert to Catholicism, and for more than a hundred years, since the freehold of the church was acquired, mass has been celebrated according the Roman rite.

Ely Place was still surrounded by fields and gardens when Sir John Crosby built his town house within the walls in what is now called Crosby Square, between Bishopsgate and St Mary Axe. Sir John, one of medieval London's great and good, had made his money as a merchant dealing in wool and fine silks. He became a freeman of the Grocers' Company in 1452-4. He leased a house from the Prioress of St Helen's Nunnery for some years, but in 1466 took more land and expanded the house into a great mansion. Of the house Stow says: "Built of stone and timber, very large and beautiful, and the highest at that time in London".

Crosby's mansion, which was built around an outer and an inner courtyard, had as its central feature a 21 metre (69 foot) long hall. Semi-octagonal bay windows two storeys high overlooked the outer courtyard, while the interior, with a large fireplace at one end and perhaps a central hearth as well, would have been hung with richly embroidered tapestries. Like Ely Place, Crosby's great house was often at the centre of City and national events: Richard, Duke of Gloucester (later Richard III) was living at Crosby Hall in 1483 when he heard that the Princes in the Tower had been murdered; Shakespeare mentions the house several times in his *Richard III*; Sir Thomas More owned it in 1532; Sir Walter Raleigh stayed there; and, as with several other grand buildings in the City, the East India Company used it for a head office from 1621-38. The Great Fire missed the house and it survived demolition until as late as 1907. But wiser counsels must have prevailed concerning the hall. It was bought by the University and City Association of London and, a year later, moved stone by stone to a new site – Danvers Street in Chelsea. The ancient building with its original timber roof, now decorated in crimson, gold and green, once served as the refectory of the British Federation of University Women but is now privately owned.

Crosby Hall gives us a unique insight into the lifestyle of London's merchant princes, and a hint of their wealth and the commercial strength that underpinned the dominant trading position of medieval London. Sir John lived through the Wars of the Roses (so called because both sides chose the same emblem – a rose; red for the Lancastrians and white for the House of York). Richard of York, a descendant of Edward III's second son, Lionel, challenged the incompetent and unstable Lancastrian Henry VI, and, with noble families taking sides, fighting broke out in 1455. The decisive battle was at Tewkesbury in 1471, when the flower of Lancastrian nobility was trampled on the battlefield by the Yorkist king Edward IV. When he died suddenly in 1483 his young sons were incarcerated in the Tower by their uncle, Richard of Gloucester. The Princes in the Tower were never seen again and it is widely believed that ambitious Uncle Richard had them murdered. He took the throne as Richard III, but was forced to fight for his crown at the Battle of Bosworth in 1485. His challenger, Henry Tudor (another of Edward III's descendants, this time through John of Gaunt), is said to have slain him and plucked his crown from the thorn bush into which it had rolled. The long line of Plantagenets who had governed England since Henry II had ended. The new king, Henry VII, would found a new dynasty of Tudors to preside over London, which was poised to become one of biggest, wealthiest and most powerful cities in Europe.

Chapter 5
Tudor London 1485-1603

"EXHILARATING" is a word that architects reach for when trying to describe London's greatest architectural legacy of the early Tudors – the interior of Henry VII's chapel at Westminster Abbey. Contemporaries such as John Leland, the sixteenth-century antiquarian, thought that it was a "wonder of the world", and the authoritative, and usually more restrained, Nikolaus Pevsner says that it is "a superbly ingenious fantasy on the theme of fan vaulting". The interlocking radiating fans of finely carved stone that culminate in long slender pendants are indeed spectacular, as is the quality of the carving of the saints, who look down from their clerestory gallery of niches. Miraculously, ninety-five out of the 107 originals are still in place, as are the monuments of kings, queens and courtiers that surround the central tomb of Henry VII and his wife, Elizabeth of York.

Henry originally planned the chapel as a memorial to his step-great-uncle, Henry VI, but the latter's body remained at Windsor and the nephew decided to make the chapel a memorial to himself and his queen. Henry III's Lady Chapel had to be pulled down to make way for the Tudor "wonder", which was begun, according to the sixteenth-century chronicler Holinshed, "on the 24th daie of January [1503], a quarter of an hour afore three of the clocke at after noone of the same daie, the first stone of our Ladie Chapell within the monasterie of Westminster was laid...." The royal building accounts have not survived, but we know that Pietro Torrigiano, who learned his trade from the same master as Michelangelo, was the designer of the black marble tomb with its gilt bronze effigies of the royal couple. The carved frieze is decorated with medallions in copper gilt depicting the Virgin Mary and Henry's ten patron saints. The small altar containing precious relics such as the leg of St George and a piece of the True Cross, which used to stand at the foot of the tomb, was swept away by the Reformation.

The queen, who died first, was taken through the city to the abbey on an elaborately decorated hearse with her effigy dressed in royal robes. Eight ladies on white horses followed the hearse, which was met by the Abbots of Westminster and Bermondsey at Charing Cross, and escorted to the abbey. The wax effigy of the queen's head is one of those that have survived and is on display in the Westminster Abbey museum.

Henry was just as punctilious about his own funeral and what should happen after it. He wrote in his will that a specially recruited staff of clerics should say mass every day "perpetually for ever while

Henry VII's chapel, Westminster Abbey. Built between 1503 and 1512, its fan vaulting is a superb expression of Tudor Gothic design.

the world shall endure". It is ironic that his son, Henry VIII, not only finished building the chapel after his father died, but contrived to put an end to the monastic world in England during his violent and bitter dissolution of the monasteries.

Both Henrys were prodigious castle- and palace-builders, as we can see from documents held in the royal archives, the Public Record Office and the British Library. Most of their buildings have left some physical trace, but not all. Henry VII's Baynard Castle (built 1501) appears in the records, but until recently no one was quite sure where its remains might be found. Redevelopment of the waterfront downstream from Blackfriars Bridge, however, located Henry's castle, which he rebuilt, from an earlier mansion, for his main residence.

Stow described it as "not embattled, or strongly fortified castle-like, but far more beautiful and commodious for the entertainment of any prince of great estate". Excavations in 1972 and 1981 have yielded details of the shape of the lost palace, built around a rectangular courtyard. On the river-front there were two large octagonal towers at either end and a series of five smaller towers, including a water gate, between them.

The north wall of the palace was especially interesting: an excavation in 1974–5 uncovered a section of the Roman river wall, confirming for the first time that such a wall ever existed. The Tudor builders had also found it and used the massive blocks of carved masonry as foundations for the northern wall of the new palace.

Henry VIII, who had extended the castle by adding towers along the river to the west, gave Baynard's Castle to Catherine of Aragon in 1509; she used it until her divorce in 1533. Lady Jane Grey and Mary Tudor were both proclaimed queen there; Pepys in his diary mentions that Charles II visited, but all was lost in the Great Fire except for one turret, which was last recorded in the early eighteenth century.

Henry VII's stone-built palace and his extravagantly beautiful chapel were not, however, trendsetting buildings for Tudor London. The chapel was more the apogee of English Gothic grandeur – a building that marked the end of the Middle Ages. London's great stone edifices had already begun to contrast sharply with the warm glow of red brick that changed the appearance of the capital in the fifteenth and sixteenth centuries. Londoners had rediscovered what the Romans had known a thousand years before – that clay for good building material lay beneath their feet. London "brick earth" mixed with chalk or ash could be turned into bricks, on or near a building site, without the expense of hauling stone from Surrey, Kent or even Normandy. The trend began in the early fifteenth century with undercrofts and foundations; brick was even being used for tombs and, in the mid fifteenth century, about two million bricks were ordered for Eton College.

The Morton Tower, Lambeth Palace. Built between 1486 and 1501, it is one of the best examples of Tudor brickwork in London. Behind the imposing gate is a complex of buildings of all periods, and the site has served the Archbishops of Canterbury as their London home since 1197.

Lambeth Palace, the London home of the Archbishops of Canterbury since 1197, is a superb expression of that new and practical fashion. One of the most impressive and evocative brick buildings of the period, the gatehouse takes its name from the incumbent in Henry VII's time, John Morton. Parts of the five-storey towers that flank the gateway were knocked about by shrapnel during the Second World War but, unlike so many other historic buildings, the damage was only superficial. The gate opens, if you have an appointment, into a precinct that includes a medieval chapel crypt, a Tudor Great Hall and a nineteenth-century Bath-stone mansion with lashings of mock Tudor in its crenellated towers and tall windows.

The thirteenth-century chapel was twice destroyed and rebuilt: once by Cromwell's soldiers in the seventeenth century and again in the 1940s. But its crypt is original, the oldest part of the palace and the least "improved". It was the scene of the official hearing that led to the invalidation of Henry VIII's marriage to Anne Boleyn in 1536, but in later years it degenerated into a wine cellar and store room. Occasional flooding from the Thames over the centuries had half filled the crypt with silt, which was dug out in 1907, and since the latest restoration, in the 1980s, religious services are once again being held under its elegant vaults.

The tower that used to give access to a jetty on the Thames and the archbishop's barge – the so-called Lollard Tower – has a niche that you can still see in the rag-stone wall facing the river. The niche once held a statue of Thomas Becket which Thames boatmen used to acknowledge by doffing their caps in respect – until the statue was removed during Henry VIII's purge of the monastic houses. At the top of the fifteenth-century tower there is a small prison where it is believed that the followers of the Oxford philosopher John Wycliff, the Lollards, were held on charges of heresy. Their prison, reached by a spiral staircase, still has the iron rings in the walls that secured the supposed heretics.

The Great Hall, rebuilt in 1663 after Cromwell's troops had dismantled it and sold the stone, lost a section of its fine hammer-beam timber roof during the Second World War. The mending is invisible today, but an oak table in the hall still shows the scars of burning from the incendiary bombs that hit the building on 23 April 1941. Many books were lost from the palace library, which had been moved to the Great Hall in the nineteenth century. Founded in 1610, the library has one of the kingdom's most important collections of medieval manuscripts, archives and books: the ninth-century Mac Durnan Gospels; the beautifully illuminated eleventh-century Lambeth Bible; a Gutenburg Bible (one of the first to be printed with movable metal type at Mainz in the 1450s); six of Caxton's first printed books; Elizabeth I's prayer book; Francis Bacon's letters; a first edition of the King James Bible (much of which was written at Lambeth Palace in the early 1600s); and an important collection of documents from the time of the founding of the first colonies in North America. One fascinating item of Stuart memorabilia is a pair of leather gloves given to Bishop Juxton by

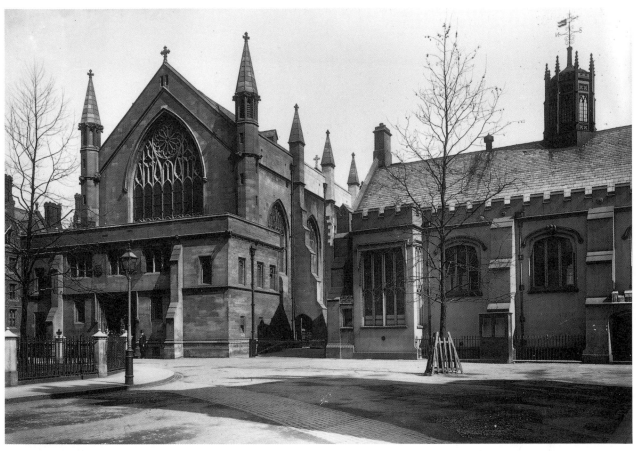

The seventeenth-century chapel and Old Hall of Lincoln's Inn.

Charles I on the scaffold in Whitehall, just before the king was executed in 1649.

The church to the side of the Lambeth Palace gatehouse, St Mary's, is not part of the archbishop's demesne but a former parish church whose nave is substantially fourteenth century. Made redundant in 1972, it was later taken over by the Museum of Garden History, which has planted a seventeenth-century garden in the churchyard. The idea centres around the grave of John Tradescant, who, as Charles I's gardener, was responsible for introducing many exotic plants to England. The Tradescants, of whom three generations are buried in the churchyard, were also great accumulators of "curiosities", and it was their collection of antiquities and other unusual objects that formed the nucleus of the Ashmolean Museum in Oxford.

The Tradescant sarcophagus has reliefs over all its sides depicting trees, a crocodile and a hydra-headed snake in a landscape that features several ancient-looking buildings. As if to underline the suitability of St Mary's new role, one of London's oldest trees flourishes alongside the archbishop's Great Hall: a large, straggling fig tree that Cardinal Pole is known to have planted in the sixteenth century.

The story of Jacob's Ladder, as depicted in the eleventh-century Lambeth Bible.

The survival of the medieval and Tudor buildings at Lambeth owes much to the continuity of the organization that built them. The same is true of historic buildings in the four Inns of Court – Lincoln's Inn, Gray's Inn, the Inner Temple and the Middle Temple. Here, senior barristers lectured the students, who were also taught history, music and dancing as preparation for moving in the circles of polite society.

The Inns at this time were London's equivalent of a university (which, until the early nineteenth century, the capital strangely lacked), and for more than six centuries the Inns have exercised their exclusive right to provide barristers to defend and prosecute cases in the English courts. Even today, students who graduate in law studies at universities must study for a further year at the Inns of Court Law School in London before they can be "called to the Bar", but membership of an Inn is also obligatory, and only students who have attended a qualifying number of dinners with "Benchers", senior members of the society, are eligible to take their final exams.

Although the Law College at Gray's Inn, organized and funded by all the Inns of Court, now has the responsibility for the formal education of barristers, the individual Inns still provide chambers for members and their apprentices, and organize debating sessions, scholarships and awards. Each Inn has an extensive library, a chapel and, as its focus, a Great Hall, preserving many of the traditions of the Middle Ages.

Within their leafy precincts these remarkable medieval institutions harbour some outstanding historic buildings, which, in the same way as buildings owned by the Church and the state, have been less susceptible than business empires to whims of taste and change. Lincoln's Inn, on the opposite side of Carey Street from the Royal Courts of Justice, looks like an Oxford or Cambridge college with its 4 hectares (11 acres) of gardens and quadrangles of mellow stone and brick buildings. The gatehouse (1518) on Chancery Lane, a smaller version of the Lambeth Palace gate, lets you into one of the oldest parts of the complex. The arms of the Earl of Lincoln, whose house was taken over by the Inn in the late twelfth or early thirteenth century, are above the gas lamp over the central arch. The Tudor arms, and those of Sir Thomas Lovell, are also featured above the original oak gate.

The quadrangle beyond the gate is all brick, except for the 1619-23 stone-faced chapel, which still has some of its original furnishings, including the communion rail and pews, but much of the stained glass had to be replaced after an air raid in 1915. Unusually, the chapel stands on pillars above an open undercroft where burials took place up to the middle of the nineteenth century; at one time the undercroft was known as a place where unwanted babies could be left in the knowledge that they would be cared for and often given the surname of Lincoln.

The Tudor buildings of "Old Square" lost their authenticity in a nineteenth-century rebuilding, but another Tudor court, reached through a narrow passage by the hall, offers brickwork dating from 1530 and stair turrets with original windows. It is here that you can get a good impression of what a great many large Tudor houses in London must have looked like. "Old Hall" is also Tudor, 1489–92, and built of brick, with a fifteenth-century style of timber roof. In 1624 two new windows were put in for more light, and the superbly carved early seventeenth-century screen was added to the furnishings. Another of the hall's treasures is Hogarth's painting of *St Paul before Felix*. Old Hall has been restored and rebuilt, but with few obvious changes, and was the centre of the Inn's social life until the nineteenth century, when the much bigger "New Hall" was built.

All the Inns have customs that date back many centuries; at Lincoln's Inn no one stands for the royal toast, because of a precedent established during a four-day visit by Charles II and his retinue in 1672. They had all become so "legless" during a dinner that the king granted the members of the Inn the privilege of drinking his health sitting down!

Gray's Inn, at the north end of Chancery Lane, boasts that "the ration of wine and port is more generous than any other Inn". This is not an inflated medieval claim, but, it seems, a modern marketing

Old Hall, Lincoln's Inn, dates from the reign of Henry VII. Built in 1490 and in need of repair by the 1920s, it was dismantled, all the stones numbered and the building re-erected. The numbers, still on the stones, are now part of Old Hall's heritage.

ploy to attract students in a newly competitive legal world. The Inn is known to have been founded about 600 years ago in a manor owned by Sir Reginald Le Grey, but, as with the other three Inns, none of its earliest records has survived. Gray's Inn suffered very badly during the Second World War: the hall, chapel and library were all destroyed and had to be rebuilt. The only significant building to have been spared was the seventeenth-century gatehouse into South Square.

The hall was an enormous loss, but its sturdy mid-sixteenth century walls remained upstanding and were used in the rebuilding of 1951. All the fittings and furnishings that had been moved to safety at the beginning of the war came back to the hall, which is now a replica of its pre-war condition. Its centrepiece, an Elizabethan carved screen, was also reinstated, with added historical credentials. It had the reputation of being an "Armada" screen – made from the wood of a wrecked or captured Spanish galleon. Many such claims are made for sixteenth-century screens but recent scientific analysis has confirmed the date of this one and the origin of the tree: Spain. Gray's Inn's Golden Age was Elizabethan: it was a time when legal education was expanding quickly; Shakespeare chose the Great Hall for the first performance of his *Comedy of Errors*; and many luminaries of the sixteenth and seventeenth centuries were members, including the courtier, statesman, philosopher and writer Francis Bacon, whose statue looks across South Square.

The Great Hall of the Middle Temple, one of the two Inns of Court that share the old Knights Templar estate along Fleet Street, is one of London's luckiest sixteenth-century buildings. While ancient buildings all around it were gutted during bombing raids in the 1940s, this lawyers' hall, though damaged, was reparable. Finished in the 1570s and officially opened, it is believed, by Elizabeth I, its double hammer-beam roof of oak is 30 metres (100 feet) long, just over 12 metres (40 feet) wide, almost 18 metres (60 feet) high and original in most respects. When a land mine exploded outside, on 15 October 1940, most of the east wall was reduced to rubble, leaving the magnificent roof still in place, but with only three walls to support it. Miraculously, only a few beams were damaged. Two pictures in the entrance porch show the gaping hole and the pile of rubble that landed on the floor of the hall. Later in the war, 140 incendiary bombs fell on buildings of the Middle Temple, including several on the hall, but the fires were brought under control and the roof was spared once again. Only the cupola had to be rebuilt.

Three of the hall's panelled walls carry rows of plaques with the arms of distinguished members of the Inn; the suits of armour that decorate the walls are Elizabethan, and, not to be outdone by Gray's Inn, Middle Temple Hall claims to have given Shakespeare the opportunity to perform his *Twelfth Night* in 1601. The 9 metre (30 foot) long high table, a gift from Elizabeth I, was made from a single oak felled in Windsor Park and floated down the Thames to the Middle Temple jetty. It weighs one and a half tons. The smaller table, called the "cup-board", is believed by the Benchers to have been made from a hatch cover of the *Golden Hind* after her circumnavigation of the globe in 1580. It is no coincidence that Sir Francis Drake, the piratical master of the ship, was a Middle Temple Master of the Bench, albeit a "social" member.

But for sheer Elizabethan elegance the carved oak screen at the other end of the hall can not be beaten in London. It caught the full fury of the flying rubble in 1940 and ended up in a thousand pieces scattered across the floor. Two hundred sackfuls were collected and the screen was defiantly put back together like a giant jigsaw puzzle. Today it survives as a spectacular piece of Elizabethan craftsmanship, made up of ornately carved panels, Roman Doric columns and a classical frieze above two round-headed doorways, while above a line of caryatids supports the topmost carved panel that reaches almost as high as the pendants of the hammer-beam roof.

The Benchers of the Middle Temple share this medieval Templar estate with that other Inn of Court, the Inner Temple. The two societies are distinguished by their motifs: a Pegasus for the Inner Temple and the Paschal Lamb for the Middle, and if you notice more lambs than winged horses carved and moulded on buildings and drainpipes, you have probably strayed into Middle Temple territory. The two Inns do, however, share the Templars' twelfth- and thirteenth-century round church (see Chapter 4), which was given to them by the Crown. But in keeping with their independence, the members of the two Inns sit as separate groups and face each other, like Members of Parliament in St Stephen's Chapel, across the aisle of the choir. The Inner Temple lost its hall during the Blitz, but attached to the neo-Georgian replacement there are two medieval rooms with vaulted ceilings that appear to date from the fourteenth century, one on top of the other. Both have rib vaults and the lower room is dominated by a large fireplace with an angel above, holding two shields dated to about 1500. Two blocked doorways complete the enigma.

The gateway leading into the Middle Temple from Fleet Street. The date, 1684, is still visible above it.

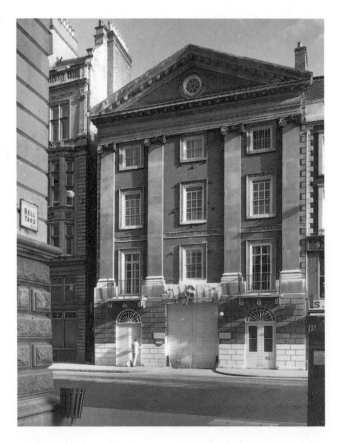

Both Inns, although they lost many thousands of books in the Blitz, still have valuable libraries, and their collections of sixteenth-century silver and gold plate, rarely seen except by members of the Inns on ceremonial occasions, are national treasures. Except for the Inner Temple gateway (1610–11) and the Wren buildings of King's Bench Walk (1677–8), almost everything else of that Inn is nineteenth century. The Middle Temple property, which begins on the west side of Middle Temple Lane, has a similar legacy, with the exception of the hall, the 1684 Middle Temple gateway into Fleet Street, New Court (1676), and numbers 1-3 in Middle Temple Lane, which were built in the 1690s.

New Court, with its fountain and mulberry trees, lies just to the west of the Middle Temple Hall and was designed by Christopher Wren, as was the "Little Gate" that marks the western limits of the Temple. And despite the many modern buildings forced on the societies since the Second World War, the lanes and

Elizabethan carved screen in the Middle Temple Hall.

courtyards of the Inns retain a special quality of the past. The literary associations range from Shakespeare to Dickens, and both Inns have had their share of Lord Chancellors, Prime Ministers, Archbishops and military heroes.

The Temple gardens, like the great swathes of grass and avenues of trees in Gray's and Lincoln's Inn, preserve ancient areas of open space that have defied the developers. The lawyers say that the emblems for the two sides in the Wars of the Roses (1455-85) were chosen in Middle Temple gardens: the red rose for the Lancastrians and the white for the Yorkists. More recently, the Inner Temple gardens first hosted the famous flower show which is now held annually in Chelsea. The gardens have almost doubled in length since the building of the Thames Embankment in the nineteenth century; and behind their ornamental gates they represent the last remaining gardens of the great medieval estates that once lined the Thames bank from Blackfriars to Westminster.

A Tudor stair turret of Bridewell Palace drawn during final demolition in 1803, after the building had served both as a hospital and as a prison.

The Tudor lawyers of the Inner and Middle Temple shared this stretch of the river with one of Henry VIII's London houses. Bridewell Palace (built 1515-23) has a story not unlike that of Baynard's Castle – no one had seen a sign of it for almost two centuries, and once again the opportunity to explore the area arose due to redevelopment, this time between St Bride's Church and the river.

Henry needed another palace because fires had wrecked both the royal apartments in the Tower and his Whitehall Palace. Stow says that Henry also wanted somewhere to accommodate the retinue of the Holy Roman Emperor Charles V when he visited London in 1522. The emperor stayed in the palatial monastery of the Blackfriars on the other side of the Fleet River and, according to

Stow, was given apartments in Bridewell for his nobles. A bridge was then needed over the Fleet to link the monastery and the palace – an innovation that did not apparently please Stow, who described it as "a breach in the wall of the city, and a bridge of timber over the Fleet Dike, betwixt Fleete bridge and Thames, directly over against the house of Bridle. Thus much for gates in the wall." Another description says that the bridge was at first-floor level and ran along the line of the later Apothecary Street; at just over 12 metres (40 feet) in length and hung with tapestries from end to end, it was long enough to have a midway chamber as a resting point.

Excavations at 1-3 Tudor Street and 9-11 Bridewell Place uncovered foundations of the two main courtyards that had been built on reclaimed land at the confluence of the Fleet and the Thames. Chalk piles had been laid first, and large brick-built arches used to carry the walls, also of brick. Only one horizontal surface survived the digging of nineteenth-century basements: an area of courtyard paving made of bricks set on end was found alongside the modern Bridewell Place. One of the most interesting discoveries was the foundations of a large external staircase in the entrance court.

Whitehall Palce, as it appeared in the reign of James II, towards the end of the seventeenth century.

Leading to the palace's most important rooms on the first floor, it must have been one of the earliest grand staircases designed for state occasions in England.

Another satisfying find was the foundation of a turret staircase, such as we saw at Lincoln's Inn, but for which there is documentary evidence. That polygonal stair turret is the one that was drawn in 1803 at the time of the demolition of the Tudor building. Bridewell became a City prison in the mid sixteenth century, when the old Fleet Prison was also rebuilt. The last vestige of its island site in the Fleet River – a dreadfully smelly moat – was filled in and a new brick prison constructed.

One of Henry VIII's palaces which has all but disappeared is Whitehall. Cardinal Wolsey knew it as York House, the London seat of the Archbishops of York, before Henry confiscated it in 1530. He expanded it to embrace all the land between Westminster and Charing Cross, built a tilting yard for tournaments, a cock pit and tennis courts. The public thoroughfare of Whitehall divided the palace, so Henry linked the two halves with a bridge that came to be known as the Holbein Gate, after the artist who painted it. The gate is no longer there, but a wall that belonged to the Great Close tennis court and Small Close tennis court does survive behind the nineteenth-century "old Treasury building", now the Cabinet Office. Pevsner dates it to about 1530: some 9 metres (30 feet) of the Tudor

The wine cellar under Whitehall Palace. Built for Cardinal Wolsey, it and the rest of what had been known as York House was commandeered by Henry VIII after Wolsey's fall from grace in 1530.

Revels, Edmund Tylney, lived in the priory and presided over her court entertainments: masques, feasts, tournaments and plays. The props and scenery were also kept in the priory, and from his office there the Master licensed plays, including many early Shakespearian productions.

The crypt of the priory church was used as a wine cellar by the seventeenth-century Cecil family and what was left of the church later became a Presbyterian chapel. Rebuilt in 1722-3, it was reconsecrated as a parish church in 1723. St John's Gate itself survived as a house, a coffee shop run by the family of William Hogarth, a printing works from which *The Gentleman's Magasine* was launched, and a public house evocatively named the "Old Jerusalem Tavern".

The monastery that caused Henry VIII most angst was Charterhouse at Smithfield. Unlike the residents of most establishments, the monks here resisted. It has to be said that, except for an uprising in one area in the North of England, Henry reaped his harvest of treasure with surprising ease, but at Charterhouse many monks were executed before the surrender was made.

There had been monks at Charterhouse since 1371, when it was founded by Sir Walter Manny, one of Edward III's courtiers and distinguished soldiers. He first rented 5 hectares (13 acres) from St Bartholomew's for a much-needed plague cemetery during the Black Death and went on to acquire more land on the northern edge of Smithfield Market. Henry Yevele, the master mason who finished the nave of Westminster Abbey and built the great hammer-beam roof that is still going strong in Westminster Hall, designed and built the Carthusians' Great Cloister at Charterhouse. The monks lived in individual cells arranged around a walled garden, where they led a mainly silent and austere life of prayer until 1535, when the prior, John Houghton, was executed for refusing to recognize Henry VIII as the supreme head of the Church in England.

Houghton and two other recalcitrant priors were dragged on a hurdle from the Tower to Tyburn, hanged and, while still alive, drawn and quartered. One of the prior's severed arms was nailed to the gate of Charterhouse as a warning to the rest of the community, but it took another three years and fifteen more martyred Charterhouse monks and lay brothers before the survivors gave up the struggle and left. The west window of nearby St Etheldreda's Church in Ely Place has a modern stained-glass depiction of the martyrdom of Houghton and the other two priors at Tyburn gallows (near where Marble Arch now stands).

Sir Richard North, a courtier dealing with the disposal of monastic properties, bought the site and demolished many of the medieval buildings, whose beams and stone were used to construct a modern mansion. It was grand enough for Queen Elizabeth to stay for five days in 1558 and to receive the homage of a string of nobles, and again in 1561 when she made a splendid royal progress through the City. Entertaining the royal court is said to have financially ruined North, who was obliged to sell the house to Thomas Howard, fourth Duke of Norfolk, in 1565. Norfolk continued to add to it, and what we see today is the legacy of both owners – the only surviving Tudor town house in Central London.

After several more owners and tenants the house was sold in 1611 to one of England's richest merchants, Thomas Sutton, whose great wealth was used to set up a school for forty-four poor boys and a hospital for eighty "gentlemen by descent, and in poverty". Charterhouse School moved to Surrey in the nineteenth century, but the gentlemen pensioners, called Brothers, still occupy the palatial rooms of North and Norfolk and a nineteenth-century range of buildings known as Pensioner's Court.

The gatehouse, with the original gate on which Prior Houghton's arm was nailed, and the row of eighteenth-century houses facing the grass of Charterhouse Square, belie the size of the site, which covers several acres of courtyards and buildings, including a chapel and the Great Hall where the Brothers take their meals. The complex took a battering during the Second World War, and, during reconstruction, archaeologists found the site of the medieval church and the grave of Sir Walter Manny, the founder of the monastery. It was made of brick and stone and contained a lead coffin in the shape of a man. Inside was a male skeleton and a seal of Pope Clement VI (1342-52), who is known from documentary sources to have issued Manny with permission to select a priest to deal with absolution and the remission of sins. That excavation also traced many of the medieval buildings of the monastery and identified worked stone and timber that had been reused for the sixteenth-century mansion.

More survives from the old Carthusian monastery than one might expect. The Lay Brothers' courtyard, now known as Wash House Court, was built at the beginning of the sixteenth century – a Tudor brick building – and is more or less intact, serving the hospital's administration. Even remains of the fourteenth-century Great Cloister can still be seen in the later cloister, where an arched doorway to a cell survives, along with a small hatch through which the monk received his food.

In 1990 the Museum of London excavated a site in nearby St Bart's Medical College and found the remains of five cells. They discovered that the Great Cloister wall was made of squared blocks of chalk with a second stage of rag stone and green sandstone. Each cell area, including the walled garden, was about 16.5 metres (54 feet) by 16 metres (52 feet) and the floor space of the cell itself about 7.5 metres (25 feet) square. Each cell had been divided into two small rooms and there might have been a floor above. A latrine was provided for each inmate and in one trench a length of lead pipe was recovered that would have led to a tap in a passage outside the cell door. A layer of red plaster suggests decoration and in one cell a tiled floor survived.

When Richard North built his Great Hall, with its hammer-beam roof carved with cherubs' heads, he used timbers and stone from the medieval church, and although the hall was untouched by the Great Fire, incendiary bombs set it alight during the 1940s. The flamboyantly carved Elizabethan oak screen bears the date 1571 and the carved Caen stone fireplace, put there in 1611 by Thomas Sutton, displays two stone cannon and powder kegs as a reminder to everyone that the self-made philanthropist was at one time Master of the Queen's Ordnance in the North.

The Great Chamber, hung with huge tapestries, said to have been the finest Elizabethan room in London before it was bombed, has been restored to its sixteenth-century self. This was the sort of room in which the increasingly self-confident Elizabethans would have discussed their expansion on many fronts: the success of the Tudor education system and the grammar schools that shaped such talents as Shakespeare's; the gradual weaning away of the population from Roman Catholicism; the great voyages of discovery and pillage that challenged the might of the Spanish and Portuguese empires: Frobisher's heroic voyage to the Arctic in 1576 in an attempt to find the North West Passage to China; Sir Francis Drake's circumnavigation of the world (1577–80); the setting up of companies of merchant adventurers to trade with the Baltic, West Africa and

One of the most imposing monuments in London: the tomb of Thomas Sutton in Charterhouse.

Turkey; Raleigh's first attempt to establish an English settlement in Virginia; and the founding of the mighty East India Company in 1599. In the Great Chamber at Charterhouse Lord Thomas Howard entertained Queen Elizabeth shortly before she died in 1603, and when James I stayed in Charterhouse a year later, he used the Great Chamber to create 133 new knights.

The monastery's chapter house survived to be used as a chapel by Thomas Sutton's school and hospital, but only after an additional aisle had been added. Sutton's tomb is spectacular: black and gold iron railings protecting a marble canopy supported by black marble columns. The effigy of the great man is in painted alabaster while above him is an inscription tablet supported by two knights. Above the inscription is a carving of a skull and an hour glass between two figures: Old Father Time and a child blowing bubbles!

An artist's reconstruction of the Rose Theatre after the 1592 extension, which is reckoned to have increased its capacity by 20-30 per cent.

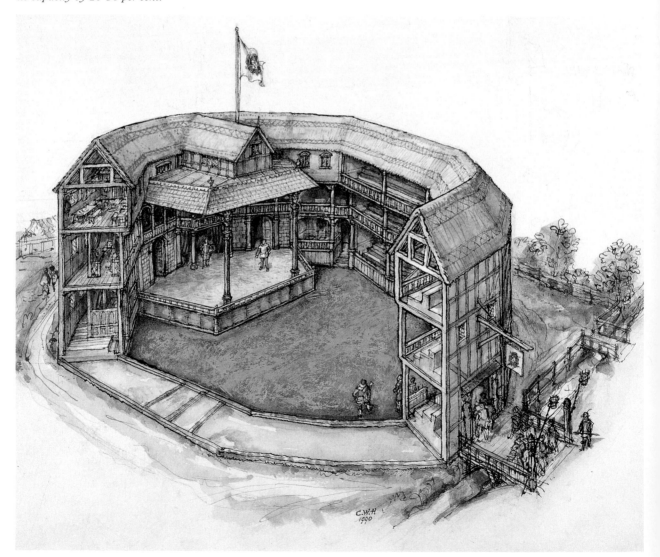

When Elizabethans looked for entertainment they turned across the water to Southwark, to a stretch of the south bank, opposite the City, where they could find bear baiting, cock fighting, bowling alleys, taverns, brothels – and theatres, including the Rose and Shakespeare's Globe. Playhouses like these saw the birth of the modern English theatre tradition.

But Bankside was equally famous for its whores, who were known as "the Winchester Geese", a reference to the fact that the brothel keepers all paid their rents to the Bishop of Winchester. The bishop's palace was on Bankside – the medieval rose window we looked at earlier is the only surviving part – and on his extensive riverside estate the "stews" had flourished since the twelfth century. Stow wrote about them, and of the regulations governing the trade drawn up in the reign of Henry II. He says that prostitutes were not to be held against their will by the "stew-holder"; that the rent for a room should not exceed fourteen pence; no trade on holidays; no nuns or married women; "no single woman to take money to lie with any man, but she lie with him all night till the morrow. No man be drawn or enticed into any stew-house. No stew-holder to keep any woman that hath the perilous infirmity of burning [venereal disease]...." The stews, which had to be inspected every week by the constables, were not allowed to hang their signs outside, so names such as the Boar's Head, the Cross Keys, the Gun, the Castle, the Crane and the Cardinal's Hat, had to be painted on the walls.

Sam Wanamaker's replica of the Globe as it appeared in April 1994. Tragically, the man who had put so much into this project died in 1993, just as his dream of reconstructing Shakespeare's theatre was becoming a reality.

The bishop's estate on Bankside was a "liberty", with its own powers and privileges outside the jurisdiction of the city. Law and order were administered by the bishop and his bailiffs, who saw to it that the troublemakers did some time in the bishop's prison, which Stow knew as "the Clinke". There is no sign of the prison now, but Clink Street, alongside the remains of the old palace, preserves a name that, throughout the English-speaking world, has become synonymous with prison. The Clink had a special section for the Winchester Geese and stew-holders who transgressed and, according to the Bankside historian E.J. Burford, the women endured torture and starvation during stints inside. At the end of a life often shortened by disease, the "Geese" were buried in an unconsecrated "plot of ground called the Single Woman's Church Yard, appointed for them far from the parish church". (A small museum dedicated to the prison in Clink Street occupies the basement of the nineteenth-century warehouse, built over the site of the bishop's palace.)

Some of the stews, however, were very plush establishments that provided a bath house, refreshments, suites of rooms for distinguished clients, and the services of beautiful and expensive courtesans. Elizabethan high frequented a brothel called the "Hollands Leaguer", set up in the grounds of an old manor house where it is said James I sometimes went with his courtiers.

The only upstanding building that E.J. Burford can identify with one of the stews is at 49 Bankside, in the last row of houses before the mountainous brick walls and chimney of the Bankside Power Station, completed in the 1950s. Burford believes that this eighteenth-century house is on the same site as the stew called the Cardinal's Hatte, which is first mentioned in 1361. Rebuilt more than once, it was still a brothel in the early seventeenth century, but a document of 1615 describes it as an inn. The present building, on top of the Tudor cellars, is dated to the early seventeenth century and carries the plaque, "Here lived Sir Christopher Wren during the building of St Paul's Cathedral. Here also in 1502 Catherine Infanta of Castile and Aragon, afterwards the Queen of Henry VIII took shelter on first landing in London." The mystery deepens, but the building is worth a visit for the experience of walking down Cardinal's Hat Alley, which runs alongside the house – perhaps the narrowest and most evocative of the Bankside lanes which once led in great profusion from the riverside to the revelry beyond.

Bankside's theatres may have had strong financial links with the brothels. According to Burford there are documents linking both Edward Alleyn, one of the theatrical stars of the day, and David Henslowe, the successful theatre owner and manager, with the ownership of, or financial interest in, several stew-houses. One of Henslowe's brothels was called "the Little Rose". Arriving in Bankside, where Puritan prejudices were less disruptive, this successful team built the Rose – the first theatre on Bankside – in 1587, and during its nineteen years as a playhouse presented many of Marlowe's plays and some of Shakespeare's.

The theatre, according to the records, gave its last performance in 1603 and was demolished by 1606. More than that nobody knew, until almost four centuries later, when, in 1988, excavation began on a site between Rose Alley and Southwark Bridge Road. No one knew what to expect, only that the office block for which foundations were being dug, might be near the suspected site of the Rose.

In a matter of weeks they found remains that could have been part of a Tudor theatre: structures that might have been the inner and outer walls of the theatre's galleries. But the developers, the Imry Development Corporation, wanted to move ahead quickly with the building and insisted on a time limit of two months for the archaeological investigation. In a blaze of publicity a new timetable was negotiated, giving the archaeologists another eight to ten weeks, during which time two thirds of the foundations and floor of the theatre were revealed.

The preservation was better than anyone had dared to hope. They found not a round theatre, as Shakespeare would have had us believe from his famous "within this wooden O" speech in the prologue to *Henry V*, but a many-sided building – an irregular polygon of thirteen or fourteen sides, about 22 metres (72 feet) across. There were two parallel walls made of chalk blocks, just over 3.5 metres (11 feet 6 inches) apart. The two walls would have supported the timber galleries that carried the seating, while the arena and the stage were open to the sky. The stage projected out into the arena, or courtyard, and probably had a solid wall of brick and timber. The floor of the yard, where people stood to watch the performance, was made of mortar, whose preservation was good enough to show the indentations where rainwater had dripped from the gallery above.

Less well defined was the rebuilding phase of 1592. Archaeologists found evidence of the outer wall and inner walls having been pushed back some 2.5 metres (8 feet) to increase the capacity of the theatre by about 20–30 per cent. At that time Henslowe had laid a new floor of compacted earth cinder and cracked hazelnut shells, one of which I remember picking up and studying with great solemnity when I visited the site in 1989. The new stage was probably covered, and in the layers of the new floor archaeologists found deposits of thatch and wooden shingle tiles – perhaps from the roof over the stage. For the first time it was possible to make a reconstruction of an Elizabethan theatre based on something more than a vague outline.

When the significance of the find and the financial implications became apparent (as in the case of the Roman Temple of Mithras some forty years earlier), the responsible authorities, property development companies and construction firms tried to minimize the unbudgeted extra costs. There was a strong lobby in favour of simply covering the remains and leaving them buried under concrete until the next stage of redevelopment in another age. However, the Rose today is buried under a layer of sand in a specially constructed basement of the new building – a double-storey space that was won by public pressure. On 30 April 1989 a "Save the Rose" campaign led by eminent actors, politicians, archaeologists and historians culminated in a candlelight vigil on the building site. The following day, an embarrassed government announced a grant of one million pounds to cover the cost of delays to the site's development, so that a new foundation preserving the Rose could be incorporated into the design of the building. The Rose Theatre Trust hopes to open an exhibition above the remains of the theatre, in the basement. But how the Elizabethan remains are to be displayed for posterity is still a matter for discussion and money.

As if finding the Rose on Bankside was not enough to digest, six months later, about 90 metres (100 yards) to the east, Shakespeare's own theatre was found. The Globe, in 1599, was the third theatre to have been built on Bankside. The Burbage family had first built it in 1576, in Shoreditch. But when the lease fell in Richard Burbage decided to find a new location for the family enterprise. He formed a syndicate to finance and run it with his brother and five actors, one of whom was William Shakespeare. Following the lead of the Rose, and the second theatre built on Bankside, the Swan, they chose to settle in the Bishop of Winchester's fun-loving "liberty". The actor-managers brought their own timber with them from the dismantled Shoreditch theatre and re-erected it between Park Street and what is now Southwark Bridge Road.

The redevelopment of the Courage Brewery site gave archaeologists their chance to rediscover Shakespeare's theatre but, unlike the Rose Theatre, only a fraction of the Globe was located. The rest is still under the nineteenth-century Anchor Terrace, alongside the new *Financial Times* building. The angles of the walls that could be seen indicate a polygon shape like that of the Rose, but how many sides it had is still uncertain. It may have been slightly bigger than the Rose, but more details can only be won from the site if the Terrace (which is a Grade II listed building) is demolished or very expensively propped up to allow archaeologists to dig under its massive concrete raft foundation.

The only standing building still in use with an undisputed claim to have stood on the Bankside of Shakespeare is Southwark Cathedral. As part of the fabric of the Priory of St Mary Overie (over the water), the church was built in 1106 by two Norman knights. Some features of that twelfth-century church can still be seen amongst the later medieval rebuilding and the nineteenth-century work. The Augustinian monks founded a hospital dedicated to St Thomas (still a going concern but resited at Lambeth) and continued their work until the reformation, when St Mary Overie was given to the parish of St Saviour. During the reign of the Catholic Queen Mary (1553–58) Protestants were tried and condemned to death in a consistory court set up in the retro choir; it survived the Civil War intact, but by the middle of the nineteenth century, after several earlier major repairs, the Bishop of Rochester, in whose diocese the church now was, campaigned for the building of a badly needed new nave. The foundation stone was laid by the Prince of Wales (later Edward VII) in 1890 and the splendid building we see today, abutting the medieval tower and transepts, was the result.

In the north aisle an effigy of one of England's early poets, John Gower (d. 1408), a friend of Geoffrey Chaucer, lies with his head resting on three of his best known works. A rare wooden effigy of a thirteenth-century knight is another treasured possession, along with several flamboyant tombs of Elizabethans. Every year on Shakespeare's birthday a special service is held to honour the Bard. His brother Edmund is buried somewhere in the church, along with the Jacobean dramatists John Fletcher and Philip Massinger, who share a grave. Philip Henslowe, of the Rose and other ventures not mentioned by the Dean and Chapter, is also buried in the church, having served his time as a respected churchwarden.

The Elizabethan theatre is alive again on Bankside. A replica of the Globe, based on documentary evidence and the structural remains of the Rose, has been built there. For the sake of perfection Sam Wanamaker, the American film director whose brainchild it was, hoped that the real Globe would be excavated before the rebuilding began. That has not happened, and, more sadly, the man who fought for twenty-five years to build a working replica of the Globe on Bankside died in 1993, just as his dream of a Shakespeare theatrical centre was becoming a reality.

One of the few clues to how Elizabethan London might have looked is in a courtyard off the Borough High Street in Southwark. The George Inn is the last of London's galleried coaching inns and,

The George Inn, Southwark, a galleried coaching inn of the type in which Tudor plays were performed before the first theatres were built in London. The present building was rebuilt in 1676 after a bad fire and occupies the site of an inn that existed in 1542.

although rebuilt after a fire in 1676, it gives a good impression of an earlier period. Until the Great Northern Railway decided to demolish two of its wings in 1881, the galleries were on three sides, giving actors a natural theatre in which to play. It is probably no coincidence that the reconstructed Globe, with its galleries around a central court, resembles the courtyard of Southwark's coaching inn.

Perhaps the best impression of an Elizabethan street can be gained in Holborn, where the facade of Staple Inn has been preserved. The inn, which has a reconstructed medieval hall in a courtyard behind, dates from the 1580s, but having been restored in 1886 and reconstructed in 1937 it cannot claim to be original except in the spirit of the Elizabethan age it brings to this part of London.

Throughout the Elizabethan period, London's population had been steadily building up, as merchants and aristocrats clenched their grip on the nation's trade and government. London merchants had, for example, about 68 per cent of England's cloth and wool trade, and no other town in England could match its spectacular growth. The centralization of power, the conspicuous consumption of the aristocrats, gentry and clerics in their town houses created jobs with higher wages, which in turn drew in large numbers of landless people from the provinces. Houses were subdivided, gardens built over and, in the aftermath of large monastic estates suddenly being released for private speculation in and around London during the 1530s, '40s and '50s, the economy was given an extra spurt. Waves of immigrants from the Netherlands, fleeing religious persecution, added to the swell, and London was bursting at its medieval seams.

The best estimates of the population that scholars can come up with show an astounding growth during the second half of the sixteenth century. In 1550 there were about 120,000 people living in the city and its suburbs, but by 1600 that number had grown to about 200,000. London, in the middle of another boom, was breaking out beyond its medieval boundaries, and was well along the way to becoming the largest city in Europe.

Chapter 6

Plague and Fire – the Seventeenth Century

J**AMES I**, who succeeded his distant cousin Elizabeth in 1603, harboured an ambition to change London. As extravagant as Elizabeth was frugal, he promulgated many new building regulations, wanting to be remembered as the king who "had found our citie and suburbs of London of stickes, and left them of bricke". He recognized the fire hazard in London, but despite his proclamation banning timber-framed houses, they continued to be built in the Elizabethan style. London, spilling out into its northern and eastern suburbscontinued to grow rapidly and the population reached about 375,000 by 1650.

Size had not altered the fact that London, at the beginning of the seventeenth century, was still like a medieval city: dirty, overcrowded, a warren of streets, lanes and alleys; four- to five-storey houses cheek by jowl, with upper floors jettied out over the street to take advantage of any extra square footage that might be added to their floor space. The only Jacobean half-timbered building to come down to us is the Inner Temple Gateway at No. 17 Fleet Street – a handsome, three-storey house with two gabled rooms at the top. Mullioned oriel windows on the first floor are overhung by a matching set on the second, and the round arched gateway of stone allows traffic through to the old Knights Templar estate.

The ceiling of Prince Henry's Room in the Strand. The Prince of Wales's motif in the centre (with the letters PH) led some experts to believe that the room once served as the prince's council chamber; it was, however, just a tavern named after him.

The gateway is one of the few surviving secular pre-fire build-ings and, until recently, was thought to have been the council chamber of James I's son Henry. The richly decorated plaster ceiling with the Prince of Wales's feathers as its central motif nurtured that idea, but the building has been unmasked as a seventeenth-century inn or tavern built in 1610 – the year that Henry became Prince of Wales. Perhaps it was simply a matter of a landlord's sense of poli-tical correctness to have commissioned such a handsome ceiling and renamed the tavern in the prince's honour!

Although the building has many original features, it should also be admired in the light of its chequered history. By the beginning of this century, when the London County Council acquired it, the facade had lost its bay windows and the timber beams had disap-peared under planks and paint; then the entire structure was moved about 3 metres (10 feet) to the south when Fleet Street was widened in 1904-6. Restoration returned No. 17 to its Jacobean style, leaving the ceiling intact, along with one wall of original panelling. The Corporation of London now maintains a museum of Samuel Pepys's possessions in Prince Henry's Room (the seventeenth-century courtier and diarist was born in Salisbury Court, off Fleet Street, near St Bride's Church), while the rest of the building is used by its traditional tenants from the Inner Temple.

Both King James and the Prince of Wales before his premature death in 1612 engaged the services of a cloth worker's son who had become England's first classical architect. Inigo Jones was baptized in one of the surviving medieval churches in Smithfield, St Bartholomew the Less, in 1573, and at the age of fourteen was apprenticed to a joiner in St Paul's churchyard. Few other details about his youth are known and we next hear of him working for the Danish court, having spent some years in Italy. There he had fallen under the spell of Palladio, whose Renaissance ideas and approach to classical architecture greatly impressed the young Jones. We know practically nothing of what he did in Italy and Denmark, but by 1605 he was back in London working for James's queen, Anne, sis-ter of the Danish king, as a "picture painter". That was the description given to designers of masques – an expertise that Jones had perhaps acquired while he was abroad. For Anne of Denmark he designed costumes and scenery in collaboration with the play-wright Ben Jonson – costly extravaganzas, sometimes funded by the livery companies, based on mythological or patriotic themes and using poetry, music and dance to create an evening of theatrical magic for the royal court.

Inigo Jones's architectural reputation was wrought after his sec-ond stint in Italy in 1613, when he was chosen by the Earl of Arundel to be part of his train in an official visit to Heidelberg, fol-lowed by a "Grand Tour" through the Renaissance cities of Italy. Arundel's interest in antiquities, and the prodigious number of crates full of statues and other objects he shipped back to Arundel House on the Thames, helped to develop a national taste for the Grand Tour, not to mention for the loot that could be acquired in the excavation of ancient sites. English country houses are still stuffed with such prizes. Inigo Jones was also interested in antiquities and wrote a book on Stonehenge, but, on his return from Italy in 1614, his career as an architect began to flourish. Queen Anne commissioned a palace in Greenwich – the Queen's House – that still stands surrounded by the parkland in which it was set by the "picture painter" who so profoundly influenced the architectural landscape of England.

Inigo Jones's name has been linked with another great house at Greenwich, Charlton House, which is acclaimed by architectural historians as the finest complete Jacobean mansion in the London area. The red-brick building, three storeys high and built above extensive cellars, has two parallel wings on either side of a huge hall that is the full width of the central area of the house. There are many original seventeenth-century features inside, including a fine

The Queen's House, Greenwich. Inigo Jones started it in 1616 for Anne of Denmark, consort of James I, and finished it for Charles I's queen, Henrietta Maria, in 1635. Sumptuously redecorated in the 1980s, it is now part of the National Maritime Museum.

The magnificent Tulip Staircase in the Queen's House.

Built in 1607-12 by Sir Adam Newton, tutor to the Prince of Wales, Charlton House is the finest complete Jacobean mansion within the London area. It was acquired by the Greenwich Borough Council in 1925.

plaster ceiling in the saloon and several impressive fireplaces, both wooden and marble. Jones's connection may lie in the summer house in the grounds. Its date – 1630 – and "a complete absence of Jacobean frills at such an early date" have led architectural historians to attribute it to the Palladian master.

The fire that burnt down the old Banqueting House in Whitehall, where so many of his masques were performed, gave Jones an opportunity to design its successor, which is still such a feature of Whitehall. Started in 1619, it is more like the nave of a great Renaissance cathedral than a venue for court masques and a grand salon for state occasions. What a shock it must have been to Londoners accustomed to the ubiquitous half-timbered Tudor and Elizabethan buildings! It looked even more like a temple or a basilica church when it was just finished because of the huge niche or apse at one end. That was changed soon after the building was completed and, according to architectural historian Sir John Summerson, "the Banqueting House is the poorer".

The effect of this building is stunning nevertheless. Its facade on to Whitehall is divided into seven bays by Ionic pillars and pilasters, while at the second-floor level the tall windows are flanked by Corinthian columns and pilasters. A balustrade hides the low-pitched roof. The interior, a geometrically perfect double cube that measures 33.5 by 16.75 by 16.75 metres (110 by 55 by 55 feet), is almost overwhelmed by the dazzlingly rich ceiling painted by Peter Paul Rubens. That was added after Charles I succeeded to the throne in 1625, and the theme, featuring the monarch's perceived benefits of the union of England and Scotland, is like the story of one of the king's masques: nine panels of allegory depicting the "wisdom" and "good government" of this debauched and corrupt king. The building itself even triumphed over the masques. By 1635, the Banqueting Hall was considered too precious to be used for such revelry and the masques were performed elsewhere.

It was from under that ceiling that, on the morning of 30 January 1649, Charles I walked to his place of execution in the final act of the English Civil War. Charles's relationship with his Parliament had been strained at the best of times by the king's high-handedness, his unshakable belief in the divine right of kings to rule as they chose, and his frequent demands for more money. His marriage to a Catholic princess, Henrietta Maria of France, outraged Protestant opinion, and when, in 1629, Parliament refused to vote more money to pursue wars with France and Spain, the king dismissed the Members of Parliament and took personal control of the kingdom.

The Royalists lost the Civil War that followed; the king was tried for treason and condemned to death by a court convened by a Parliament dominated by his victorious adversary, Oliver Cromwell. The scaffold, draped in black, was erected over Whitehall against the facade of the Banqueting Hall, and through a window on a stairwell annex (since demolished) Charles was led towards the executioner and a small group of courtiers and soldiers. He made a speech protesting his divine right to kingship, which few in the crowd below

The Banqueting House, Whitehall. Designed by Inigo Jones for James I in 1619, it introduced the Palladian style to England and thus marks a turning point in English architecture. The facade has changed very little since this engraving was made in about 1690.

could hear; he gave Bishop Juxton his rings and gloves, and, after taking off his coat, lay on the scaffold with his head on the block, waiting for the axeman's single blow.

During the ensuing Commonwealth period (1649-60), Cromwell used the Banqueting Hall to receive ambassadors, and the Rubens ceiling, well out of reach of Puritan zealots, survived those troubled years. After the Restoration of the monarchy Charles II used the Banqueting House for ceremonial occasions. The fire that raged through the Palace of Whitehall in 1698 mercifully spared Inigo Jones's masterpiece, so that the Jacobean addition is the only building left of that sprawling Tudor complex.

For the following two centuries the Banqueting House served as a royal chapel; then as a military museum from 1893 to 1964. It reverted to a place of ceremony and banqueting after restoration in the mid 1960s and is now regularly used by private and commercial organizations for grand functions. Its outward appearance has changed a little due to an eighteenth-century restoration of the facade, when the original three types of stone, each with a different colour and texture, were replaced by a uniform cladding of Portland stone.

The Queen's Chapel, St James's Palace. Built by Inigo Jones in 1623-7 for Charles I's queen, Henrietta Maria, it was a Catholic chapel and had a friary of Capuchins to serve it.

A smaller and less flamboyant building of Inigo Jones's is almost invisible because of its site and modest exterior. The Queen's Chapel does not look like a church where it stands at the end of St James's Street, alongside Marlborough House. The facade of cream-painted stucco, topped by a simple pediment, hides England's first classical church. It was started in 1623 as a chapel for the Infanta of Spain, whom James I had in mind as a wife for his younger son and heir, Charles. When that alliance fell apart building work stopped in sympathy, only to resume in 1626 after Henrietta Maria became Charles's queen. It was a Catholic chapel for a Catholic queen and was served by a friary of Capuchins in St James's Palace, of which the chapel was an integral part. The existing road to the Mall, whose heavy traffic today acts like a wall, was built between the chapel and the palace as early as 1809.

The interior of the Queen's Chapel, like that of the Banqueting House, is a double cube, and is modelled on a Roman temple which Palladio had restored in Italy. A striking feature is the window behind the altar, probably the first "Venetian" window in England, which has a round-topped central panel and two smaller rectangular panels on each side. The wooden panelling along the lower part of the walls dates from a later seventeenth-century restoration (c. 1662-80) when Charles II's queen, Catherine of Braganza, also a Catholic, worshipped there; Wren's hand can also be seen in the design of the organ gallery, the stalls and the lectern.

Inigo Jones was at the peak of his career as Surveyor to the King's Works at the time of London's first big expansion into what was to become known as the West End. He was, for example, deeply involved with the laying out of London's first square – Covent Garden. It takes its name from the "Convent" garden of

Westminster Abbey that had been acquired by Sir John Russel (later Earl of Bedford) in 1553, after the dissolution of the monasteries. The third earl built Bedford House on the south side of what is now Covent Garden, and by 1631 the fourth earl had won a licence to build as many "houses and buildings as fitt for the habitacons of gentlemen and men of ability" as he pleased. Inigo Jones was the architect, and once again his Italian experience was brought to bear on this novel piece of town planning for London.

Covent Garden, based on the piazza at Leghorn in Tuscany, had arcades around two sides of the square with houses opening on to them in the Italian way. Behind the houses were gardens and stables, and, on the west side of the square, Jones designed a church whose 18 metre (60 foot) wide portico is still an outstanding feature of the piazza. Mindful of the expense, the earl is supposed to have told Jones, "I would not have it much better than a barn." Jones's retort was equal to the challenge: "Well then, you shall have the handsomest barn in England." It is also unusual in that the portico

The portico of Inigo Jones's St Paul's Church, Covent Garden. Built in 1631-3, it is the last surviving original element of the Earl of Bedford's grand scheme for gracious town houses around London's first square.

as an entrance is a mere sham – the grand door from the square into St Paul's is false, and today, as in the seventeenth century, access is from the churchyard behind.

The portico is all that remains of Inigo Jones's grand scheme, and even that had to be rebuilt in 1795 after a fire gutted the church. It was faithfully reconstructed, and the only substantial alteration to its design was a nineteenth-century substitution of the arches for walls at both ends of the portico. The interior of the church has suffered from eighteenth- and nineteenth-century restoration and is dismissed by Summerson as "a neat but uninteresting Georgian box". Today it is known amongst theatricals as "the actors' church", and many distinguished and well-loved actors are remembered by monuments set into the walls.

Jones's arcades and houses have all gone. The "gentlemen and men of ability" for whom the square was built drifted away, when the Bedford estate started a fruit and flower market in Covent Garden, to the more fashionable squares further west; here the big landowners cashed in on the building boom to house London's burgeoning population.

The existing buildings of Covent Garden are mainly nineteenth century, although one range on the north-west side, built by the Duke of Bedford in the 1870s, was modelled on Inigo Jones's design. Its arcades and cafes give a more than tolerable impression of what was lost. The attractive market buildings in the square today date from the 1820s, but the fruit and flower market was moved to Nine Elms in Battersea in 1974, and the buildings in Covent Garden were restored as shops and restaurants. The result is a pleasing corner of London where developers in the late 1960s and early '70s had hoped to add high-rise office and housing blocks. They were thwarted by vociferous heritage groups and, more decisively, by the collapse of an overheated British economy in 1972.

The Covent Garden of the seventeenth century was just the beginning of a speculative building boom in the pastureland and fields on the western side of the City – the West End. To the horror of the lawyers behind their walls in Lincoln's Inn, William Newton, one of London's first developers, obtained a licence to build thirty-two houses in Lincolns Inn Fields. The whole area was not built upon – Inigo Jones presumably saw to that – but by 1658 there were houses

Hollar's view of Lincolns Inn Fields in the seventeenth century.

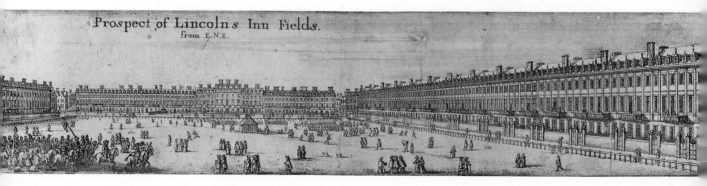

Prospect of Lincolns Inn Fields.
from E.N.E.

on three sides of the huge square which the fields had now become. Like Covent Garden, Lincolns Inn Fields attracted wealthy residents whose palatial houses saw the comings and goings of merchants, noble landowners and, at one time, Charles II's mistress, Nell Gwyn, whose bastard son, the future Duke of St Albans, was born in one of the houses.

Most of the earliest houses are on north side of the square, where Nos 1 and 2 are early eighteenth century and several others, including Nos 12 and 15, date from the 1790s and the 1740s. The three Georgian houses, Nos 13-14, belonged to the architect Sir John Soane and were left by him as a permanent museum for his extraordinarily rich collection of antiquities, paintings and books. A century after the Earl of Arundel and Inigo Jones collected statues in Italy, Soane epitomized a new generation of collectors by filling his house with seventeenth-century furniture, countless classical sculptures, the sarcophagus of the pharaoh Seti I (one of Soane's great treasures, which he bought from the early nineteenth-century adventurer Belzoni), the famous series of William Hogarth paintings of

Lindsey House, the only one of the original houses of Lincolns Inn Fields to have survived. Built in 1640, it is believed by most experts to have been designed by Inigo Jones.

1733 called *A Rake's Progress* which depict life in eighteenth-century London, and a large collection of architectural drawings by the Elizabethan John Thorpe. Other great architects' drawings, some by Christopher Wren and Robert Adam, are also in the collection, which fills every room, a number redecorated as Soane knew them before he died in 1837.

The one remaining original house in Lincolns Inn Fields, Lindsey House, No. 59-60, was built in 1640, on the western side of the Fields, and, in the opinion of most authorities, was designed by Inigo Jones himself. In its tall pediment windows, pilasters and pleasing symmetry, we can recognize the forerunners of elements of Georgian architecture which, in the eighteenth and nineteenth centuries, were to spread across cities as far apart as Dublin, Boston and Sydney.

The dining room in Sir John Soane's museum on the northside of Lincolns Inn Fields. Soane (1753-1837), the architect responsible for the Bank of England, lived in the house, which is packed with his important collection of antiquities, books and paintings.

Many houses in the two new London squares were bought or leased by country gentry who, at the beginning of the seventeenth century, had migrated to London in significant numbers. Many came for business or to educate their sons at schools such as St Paul's, Westminster, Charterhouse and at the other great centre of education, the Inns of Court. They also came to take advantage of favours meted out by the king and his courtiers, or simply to have a good time in the capital's theatres, cock pits, brothels and taverns.

So concerned was James I about the gentry neglecting their responsibilities on their country estates that at one stage he issued a proclamation ordering them home. He quipped, "Soon London will be all England." In 1632, under Charles I, some of these newcomers were even prosecuted in the Star Chamber for ignoring the order, but London continued to grow. While the West End attracted the gentry and self-made merchant princes, the suburbs to the north and east of the City were filling up even more rapidly. Immigrants from the country, sucked into the mushrooming urban conurbation, were joined by large numbers of people from the Continent fleeing religious persecution. By 1664 about 135,000 people lived in the eastern and western suburbs – more than in the City itself, which in 1695 recorded only 124,000 people. Locating seventeenth-century houses is difficult enough in the City and West End, but our know ledge of buildings of that period in the eastern suburbs is even more sketchy, as, in most cases, the archaeological evidence was carelessly scooped out of the ground during the digging of nineteenth-century basements.

One of the few examples of the scanty archaeological remains of seventeenth-century poor housing in the East End was preserved under railway sidings near Aldgate, which protected the remains for almost a century and a half until the area was sold for redevelopment. When the rails came up in 1974 a row of little houses with cesspits and a well was found. It was clear that these houses had been built over fields or gardens in the seventeenth century, and that associated workshops had made clay pipes in a kiln. Figurines were also manufactured from the pipe clay.

A late eighteenth-century warehouse complex built for the East India Company, between Aldgate and Bishopsgate outside the City wall, had also preserved remains of seventeenth-century houses and workshops beneath the warehouses. Now called Cutlers Gardens, the old East India buildings have been turned into offices. During the conversion archaeologists discovered the remains of houses, gardens and workshops; there were also cesspits made of brick or wood, and eight wells were found that had dried in the eighteenth century – perhaps because of a drop in the water table caused by the increased use of water in the new suburbs.

The area was alive with small industry in the seventeenth century: glassmaking; potteries, set up by Dutch immigrants, making tin-glazed "Delftware"; bell founding (there is still a bell foundry in Whitechapel Road using seventeenth- and eighteenth-century buildings); ivory turning; and clay-pipe production. But the most unusual find was of several hundred horn cores that had been used to line the sides of pits, with the tips of the horns all pointing out and arranged in lines. What process the pits were used for is not clear, but the horns themselves may provide researchers with useful information about the history of the early English breed of Longhorn cattle!

The find at Cutlers Gardens points up the need that London had for cattle as the population grew through the seventeenth century. In the areas around the city, farms were bought up by butchers and merchants, who took control of the whole food chain. Others loaned farmers money with which to increase their production, and the landscape itself was changed as market gardens were laid out in order to feed the capital.

Such was the demand for beef that animals were reared as far away as the North of England and Scotland for the London market. An analysis of bones found in pits at Smithfield confirms the existence of cattle from distant parts of the country; drovers brought them to farms in the shires near London where they were "finished" for the market and then driven to Smithfield.

Historians in recent years have also begun to build up a picture of seventeenth-century life in the suburbs. Michael Power's study of the surviving documents concerning the hamlet of Shadwell in the parish of Stepney has revealed much detail of the people and their properties. Less than 3 kilometres (2 miles) downstream from the City, Shadwell was just fields and ditches in 1600. But by 1650, according to a contemporary survey, 703 buildings had been laid out, like a small modern estate, by speculative builders. The biggest houses – just a few that had three storeys, a cellar and a garret – were built along the bank of the Thames, while the poorest inhabitants lived in sheds strung out along the road leading to the City. Most people seem to have had narrow (3.5-4.5 metres/12-15 feet) one- or two-storey timber-framed houses with a cellar or a garret. The average number of rooms was about four per house, though some had only two. Parish and tax records show that about three-quarters of the population were concerned in some way with the river and its shipping – rope makers, boat builders, lightermen, seafarers – and judging from the fact that only about 10 per cent were assessed for tax, most were poor compared with those living in the western suburbs. Most houses doubled as work places; shops were dotted about all over the suburb – Michael Power estimates that Shadwell residents had no more than 70 metres (75 yards) to walk to a shop – and although taverns were less common the ratio was one to every sixteen houses.

One of the major building projects in the growing London of the seventeenth century was the rebuilding of St Paul's Cathedral. Inigo Jones had worked on the restoration of the old building since 1620. Work stopped and started, depending on the availability of funds, but between 1628 and 1633 Jones and the Bishop of London, William Laud, raised the money, and the enthusiasm, to complete the first stage of the giant project. Houses that cluttered the edges of the building were demolished and shiploads of Portland stone were hauled up from the Thames to clad the old Romanesque and Gothic walls. The merchant Sir Paul Pindar contributed generously to the fund, and the king's promise of £500 a year for ten years gave Jones the opportunity to design a new west front. He built a long porch, inspired by a Roman temple, with ten huge Corinthian columns – a classical structure that could not be bettered in size anywhere in the Renaissance world north of the alps.

Soon after it was finished, in the 1640s, Civil War broke out. Londoners opted for Parliament and were therefore on the winning side when Cromwell executed Charles I and took control of the kingdom, but the cathedral, identified with popery by the Puritans, suffered badly. The portico was filled with shops; the nave was used as a stable for the cavalry; and part of the south transept collapsed from pillage and neglect.

All that remains of Old St Paul's: a few charred relics of the foundations of the chapter house and cloister area. They are preserved in a garden on the south side of the nave.

"Bring out your dead" was a cry that Londoners had heard on their streets many times since plague arrived in England in the fourteenth century. There had been several outbreaks since the beginning of the seventeenth century and thousands had died. But what came to be called the Great Plague was, for London, as lethal as the Black Death of the 1340s and '50s. Samuel Pepys first heard of the outbreak on 30 April 1665 and noted in his diary, "Great fear of the sickness here in the city, it being said that two or three houses are already shut up. God preserve us."

When someone died of the plague the authorities closed the house, marked the door with a red cross and posted a guard twenty-four hours a day; everyone remained inside until the patient recovered or died. Physicians, who knew nothing about the cause, could do little but apply poultices and lower the fever which accompanied the swellings around the groin and under the armpits. People became dizzy and delirious and, more often than not, died within a week. Pepys saw the epidemic spread as he went about London on Charles II's business: "Going in a Hackney Coach from Holborn, the coachman I found to drive very badly. At last he stopped, and came down hardly able to stand. He told me that he had been taken very ill and almost blind, and that he could not see. So I got down and went to another coach, with a sad heart for the poor man and fear for myself, in case he had been struck with the plague."

"Nurse keepers" had the job of caring for the sick and were themselves locked up for a month if any of their patients died. Other plague officials were the "searchers", who were paid a fee to examine bodies and confirm the cause of death, and "corpse bearers", whose carts rumbled back and forth to the burial grounds. Quacks did a roaring trade among an increasingly fearful population by selling bottles of "plague water" and potions made from ingredients that included pepper, frogs' legs, urine, herbs of various kinds and salt. The wearing of charms was another way to keep the plague away and attendance at church went up, as many people, believing that the disease was God's punishment for wrongdoing, sought divine forgiveness.

As the death toll increased in June 1665 the king moved out of London, leaving only a few members of the nobility, led by the Duke of Albermarle, to represent the court and the government. Large numbers of the gentry left as well. "I find all the town almost going out of town, the coaches and waggons being full of people going into the country," Pepys observed. But the country people shunned the Londoners who, in many cases, just drifted about from place to place, as the locals, fearful of infection, barred them from their towns and villages. Pepys sent his mother to the country in June and moved his wife to Woolwich soon after the king and his court had fled to Richmond, and later to Oxford, where Parliament had taken up temporary residence.

Fighting an enemy that was thought to have been in the air, Londoners were exhorted to keep the streets clean and smelling sweetly. Dogs and cats were rounded up and killed in case they spread the disease – about 40,000 dogs and 20,000 cats are thought to have perished at the hands of the specially recruited executioners. No one seems to have connected the disease with the rats which carried the infecting fleas!

By August Pepys reports that the streets of London were almost empty; the mayor had ordered a 9 p.m. curfew for able-bodied citizens so that "the sick may leave their domestic prison for air and exercise". But life in London, where grass had begun to grow in the streets, had virtually stopped. John Evelyn, another of the best known seventeenth-century diarists, wrote on 7 September: "Came home, there perishing now near 10,000 poor creatures weekly. I went all along the city and suburbs from Kent street to St James's, a dismal passage and dangerous, to see so many coffins exposed in the streets thin of people, the shops shut up and all mournful silence, as not knowing whose turn might be next."

The plague peaked at the beginning of November and only 152 people died during Christmas week. By 1 February the king thought it safe to return, and others who had sought a haven in the country, or on vessels moored out in the Thames, returned to add up the cost of human misery. Accurate figures are not available – at one stage too many were dying every day for records to be kept – but according to the official weekly "bills of mortality", 68,596 deaths had resulted from plague; the true figure is probably more like 100,000. Life in London had been snuffed out on a spectacular scale. But in less that a year those who had survived were to witness another catastrophe that spared the people but left them destitute and homeless.

Fire was a spectre that had been present in London since the Romans managed to burn down large sections of their city. In Norman London in the twelfth century William Fitz Stephen was forced to admit, "The only plagues of London are the immoderate drinking of fools and the frequency of fires", and in one of the worst fires four centuries later, in 1632, an area north of London Bridge, including a row of houses on the bridge itself, had been burnt down. John Evelyn graphically described London's shortcomings in an address to Parliament in 1661 when he complained of the amount of coal-fire smoke pollution in the air. He also thought it deplorable that "the buildings should be composed of such a congestion of misshapen and extravagant houses, that the streets should be so narrow

London burning: a contemporary illustration by a Dutch painter showing Londoners fleeing from the fire.

A back street scene of typical London houses from John T. Smith's Ancient Topography of London *(1815). Tinder dry after a hot summer, buildings like this would have burned like a bonfire.*

and incommodious in the very centre." But it is also true that London was a city of private splendour, with mansions built around quiet courtyards and, very often, a medieval hall as the centre of the seventeenth-century house.

"Some of our maids sitting up late last night to get things ready against our feast day today [2 September 1666], Jane called us up, about 3 in the morning, to tell us of a great fire they saw in the city. So I rose, and slipped on my nightgown and went to her window, and thought it to be on the back side of Mark Lane at the furtherst....I thought it far enough off, and so went back to bed."

Pepys could hardly have been blamed for thinking that it was a little local difficulty. Fires were common. Sir Thomas Bludworth, Lord Mayor, came to the same conclusion: he is supposed to have remarked, "Pish! A woman might piss it out!" and gone back to bed. When Pepys got up in the morning about 300 houses near the bridge had burned down and some on it were also alight. The Fishmongers' Hall was one of those that went up in flames, but not before the master and members of the company had thrown as many treasures as they could lay their hands on into the boats alongside the company's jetty. Pepys watched from a boat which he hired to take him through the bridge into what is now the Pool of London: "Poor people staying in their houses as long as till the very fire touched them, and then running into boats or clambering from one pair of stairs by the waterside to another." He watched pigeons, loth to leave their houses until their wings were burned by the fire, and then told the king that "unless his Majesty did command houses to be pulled down, nothing could stop the fire." The king agreed and sent Pepys off to find the hapless Lord Mayor, who "cried like a fainting woman" and said that people would not obey him.

The fire that had started in a baker's shop in Pudding Lane raged on towards the western end of the City, fanned by a strong east wind. The baker, Thomas Farynor, claimed that he had properly damped down his fires and had escaped with his wife and family over the roof tops when his house filled with smoke. One of his servants, however, failed to escape and was killed. The next day at four o'clock in the morning Pepys says that Farynor was given a cart and, clad in only his nightshirt, carried away his possessions to safety. As John Evelyn watched from the river-bank, others paid exorbitant prices for carts and boats: "Here we saw the Thames covered with goods floating, all barges and boats laden with what some had time and courage to save, as on another, the carts etc carrying out to the fields which for many miles were strewed with movables of all sorts, and tents erecting to shelter both people and what goods they could get away with."

On Monday 3 September the king took action; he set up fire posts manned by a hundred citizens and thirty soldiers, who were given the power to pull down houses and create fire breaks. The king's brother, James, Duke of York (the future James II), took overall control and, often with the help of Charles himself, fought the fire as it advanced westwards. Equipment was sparse: ladders, axes, buckets and fire engines consisting of a tank with a pump that directed a modest stream of water on to the fire. The most effective fire-fighting tools were ropes and hooks used to pull down timber-framed houses in the path of the blaze. But the fire raged on, through Cheapside, St Paul's and Fleet Street. Evelyn tried to follow its course: "I went on horseback and it was now gotten as far as Inner Temple; all Fleet Street, Old Bailey, Ludgate Hill, Warwick Lane, Newgate, Pauls Chain, Watling Street now flaming and most of it reduced to ashes, the stones of St Paul's flew like grenades, the lead melting down the streets in a stream and the very pavements of them glowing with fiery redness, so that as nor horse nor man was able to tread on them...." Meanwhile Pepys helped a friend to save some of his treasures: "Sir W. Batten, not knowing how to remove his wine, did dig a pit in the garden and laid it in there; and I took the opportunity of laying all the papers of my office that I could not other wise dispose of, and in the evening Sir William Penn [future

Facade of Sir Paul Pindar's house in Bishopsgate, dating from about 1600. Preserved now in the entrance hall of the Victoria and Albert Museum, the mansion had been turned into a pub by the time this picture was taken. It was demolished in 1890 to make way for the enlargement of Liverpool Street Station.

founder of Pennsylvania] and I did dig another, and my Parmesan cheese as well as my wine and some other things."

It was not until the third day that gunpowder was used to demolish houses when, with a high wind still fanning the flames, Whitehall itself was threatened. The fire had jumped the Fleet River and was burning along Fleet Street and through the Inns of Court. The Inner Temple lost its hall, but the Elizabethan hall of the Middle Temple was saved. The navy, who had been drafted in to blow up houses in the path of the fire, remarked to Evelyn that had they been brought in earlier much more of the City might have been saved. Tuesday night, eye-witnesses said, was even more dreadful, as the fire moved forward on all fronts, destroying as it went the great medieval Guildhall. Londoners, driven from house to house and street to street, were by now congregating with what possessions they had saved in the fields around the City.

Wednesday 5 September was the turning point. Fire fighters, led by the king and the Duke of York, seem to have used more gunpowder to create fire breaks. The wind also dropped for the first time. The fire stopped just before it could devour the medieval round church of the Templars; the suburb along the Strand was saved, and so was the northern part of the City, including the hospital of St Bartholomew. The thick stone walls of the Leadenhall stopped the fire in the east and, despite the continuing fierce burning of combustible goods stored in cellars, the worst was over.

Evelyn walked around the city on Friday, counting the cost, "clambering over mountains of yet smoking rubbish, and frequently mistaking where I was, the ground under my feet so hot, as made not only sweat, but even burnt the soles of my shoes." He lamented the loss of hundreds of thousands of books that had been stored in the crypt of St Paul's, the destruction of Inigo Jones's great portico, "the company halls, sumptuous building, arches, entries, all in dust". He described it as a dismal desert in which he found it difficult at times to get his bearings and to know where he was. About 13,200 houses were consumed, eighty-seven parish houses, forty-four company halls, the Royal Exchange, St Paul's and the Guildhall. Very few lives were lost, but, as Evelyn observed, the human misery was excruciating: "I then went towards Islington, and Highgate where one might have seen two hundred thousand people of all ranks and degrees, dispersed and laying along by their heaps of what they could save from the fire, deploring their loss and though ready to perish for hunger and destitution, yet not asking one penny for relief, which appeared a stranger sight than any I had yet beheld."

Chapter 7
Wren's London 1666-1723

THE GREAT FIRE OF LONDON had consumed 177 hectares (436 acres) of houses, churches and public buildings from the Tower to the Temple. Sifting through the wreckage, which had smouldered for days after the fire had been brought under control, Londoners, shocked by the devastation all around them, must have wondered if this once great city could ever be revived. Food was short and, to add to their miseries, winter was not far away.

Aware that civil unrest might follow, the king rode out among the refugees and tried to boost their morale by giving them tents, and allowing markets and temporary housing to be set up. One of the king's attendants, noted that Charles assured his destitute subjects that the fire was an act of God and not the result of some foreign plot to ruin the city; he had "found no reason to suspect anything of that nature; desired them to take no more alarms; he had strength enough to defend them from any enemy, and assured them he would, by the grace of God, live and die with them."

Such was the level of fear and xenophobia that when the committee of inquiry into the fire convened later in September, people came forward claiming that they had seen "foreigners" setting fire to houses. The war between England and Holland had recently flared up; English sailors had stormed ashore and put a Dutch town to the torch, as well as burning more than 150 Dutch vessels. The French were always treated with suspicion and when several French people in London were set upon, one man, a watchmaker from Rouen, confessed to starting the fire in the baker's shop. Although his confession was contradictory, confused and unbelievable, he was tried at the Old Bailey and hanged at Tyburn. The baker was one of those who gave evidence against him. After the trial and execution the master of the ship that had brought him to London testified that neither the ship nor the Frenchman had arrived until two days after the fire had started!

London reacted remarkably quickly in the aftermath of the fire. Within ten days several plans for rebuilding the City were submitted to the king, including one by John Evelyn and another by Christopher Wren, Savilian Professor of Astronomy at Oxford. Both suggested radical departures from the existing cramped medieval web of streets and, inspired by town planning in Paris and Rome, offered wide thoroughfares that started and ended in squares and circuses. A rigid grid of smaller interconnecting streets completed the scheme.

In the event neither plan was adopted for fear of the complications regarding ownership that would need to be unravelled and of the problem of agreeing compensation on such a large scale. But His Majesty's Commission, set up to rebuild the City, settled for a compromise that widened all the streets, created several new thoroughfares (including the present King and Queen Streets) and controlled the height of buildings. Smaller lanes were to be widened to over 4 metres (14 feet) and were to have two-storey buildings; bigger streets, or those overlooking the Thames, were allowed three storeys; on the main streets merchants' houses could be four storeys. The coal that London used was to pay for all this, through a tax levied on all imports into the capital.

The master plan having been approved by Parliament in February 1667, a Fire Court was set up to adjudicate over property disputes and, with the help of a huge influx of immigrant tradesmen and labourers, attracted by wages that could be 50 per cent higher than in other parts of the country, work went ahead. According to the inscription on the Monument to the Great Fire, the king set a time limit of seven years. Materials had to be brought to London from all over England; some bricks even came from Holland and wood for furniture and flooring was imported from Norway and Sweden.

Progress was slow at first. Each burnt-out property had to be cleared and pegged for the surveyors to inspect before rebuilding could begin. It took a year to build 150 houses. But every subsequent year saw thousands of buildings added to the stock of houses, churches and halls, and by 1676 a survey showed that most of the City had been restored, in a time scale not far from the target. The whole process, driven by a need to rehouse the population and the fear that London might lose its pre-eminent trading position, was a tribute to the remarkable organization and determination of City Fathers, royal officials and ordinary citizens alike.

By the time the rebuilding was completed, London's population, as well as its fabric, was significantly different. Many of the thousands of artisans, labourers and craftsmen from all over England and from across the Channel stayed on, while just as many thousands of Londoners who had been made homeless never returned.

Archaeologists have been able to dig right into the heart of the Great Fire. In parts of the City pockets of fire debris have been found undisturbed in seventeenth-century basements that were filled up with burnt rubbish and used after the fire as platforms for new buildings. During redevelopment in 1979–80 such a building was discovered in Pudding Lane, not far from where the fire started. Fire debris is not a novelty in London – as we saw in Chapter 1, the first great destruction, wrought by Queen Boudicca in AD 60, produced much of what we know about the earliest phase of Roman London; remains preserved in the debris of the Great Fire 1,600 years later have also been instructive.

I remember feeling very close to that catastrophe on the burnt brick floor of what had been a neighbouring basement of the king's baker of Pudding Lane when I visited that site in 1980. The archaeologists had removed an area of the thick layer of fire debris, among which were bricks, fragments of tiles, molten and twisted nails, floor tiles, clay pipes, parts of a hinge and a lock, earthenware storage jars and a worn Elizabethan sixpence.

Some substantial pieces of charred wood were also recovered. At the time we thought these might have been the remains of furniture, but after more of the scorched brick floor area had been dug out and the objects thoroughly cleaned and scientifically analysed, the charred wood turned out to be pieces of barrels. The staves and hoops of the barrels were covered with a substance that scientists concluded was "Stockholm Tar" – a refined resin from pine wood that was used as a waterproofing agent, perhaps for ships' hulls in the port not 100 metres (330 feet) from the cellar. Indeed, the cellar's contents may have played a crucial role during the first hours of the fire – once ignited, the barrels would have burnt long and hard, spreading the flames in all directions.

Eighty-seven of London's 109 churches were damaged or destroyed in the fire, but not all were rebuilt: it was decided that some parishes could be amalgamated. The job of reconstructing fifty-one churches fell to Christopher Wren, whose first building of any note, the Sheldonian Theatre in Oxford, was started only two years before the Great Fire. He had been consulted on the ruinous condition of old St Paul's in the early 1660s, but was better known as an astronomer and a founder member of the Royal Society – that enduring institution that led the advance of English science in the seventeenth century. By 1669, however, he was taken seriously enough as an architect to have been appointed chief architect to the Crown – Surveyor General – the position so ably held by Inigo Jones at the beginning of the seventeenth century.

Wren worked on an incredibly broad range of projects: plans for Winchester Palace that were never translated into bricks and mortar; several buildings within the precincts of the old Palace of Whitehall; the Monument to the Great Fire of London, built in 1671-7, whose inscription tells the story of the fire and of the plan to rebuild the City. If the 62 metre (202 foot) high column were laid on its side pointing down Pudding Lane to the east, it would reach the exact spot where the fire started on 2 September 1666. This was all in addition to the dozens of parish churches that were in the making, and his greatest building, St Paul's Cathedral.

He began work on the churches in 1670 with a small committee, including the architect and surveyor Edward Woodroffe and another distinguished scientist, Dr Robert Hooke. Wren, of course, could not have been responsible for every detail of every church, and although there are few documents to confirm it, he must have delegated much of the design and supervision, not just to his surveyors, but to an equally able team of masons.

The same must have been true of Grinling Gibbons, the Dutch-born craftsman whose outstanding carving earned him a post in the king's service as Master Sculptor and Carver in Wood.

Evelyn, who "discovered" Gibbons and introduced him to Wren, said of one typical Gibbons carving, "There being nothing even in nature so tender, and delicate as the flowers and festoons about it." But we must assume that many fine craftsmen, whose names have not been recorded against any specific pieces of work, were involved in the Gibbons "school".

The churches attributed to Wren are some of the most delightful aspects of modern London. You find them dotted about the City, often built at crazy angles, hidden away in courtyards and crouched defiantly beneath Victorian and modern office blocks. Each one is different; some simply followed the shape of what had been burned – oblong buildings with or without aisles, many with Wren's typical barrel-vaulted ceilings. Other sites, often misshapen corners of London, demanded more inventive solutions. In such cases Wren, with the architect's equivalent of a shoehorn, angled the buildings to fit the space.

Some of his interiors had galleries; one, St Clement Danes, had an apse; all had richly carved pulpits placed so the preacher could be seen by everyone and "the Word" clearly heard – a pre-requisite of the seventeenth-century English church. Wren's churches were also distinguished by the amount of light allowed in through their clear glass windows – a feature that Victorian restorers managed to undo with their predilection for stained glass, veiling the interiors in gloom and mystery.

Nineteenth-century restorers who tore down galleries, replaced box pews with benches and tiled the floors were, however, beneficent compared with Hitler's air raids. Most of Wren's fifty-one rebuilt churches were damaged. Some, like St Lawrence Jewry, St Clement Danes, St Bride's, St Giles Cripplegate, St Mary le Bow and St Andrew's Holborn, were completely gutted, leaving only the walls standing; others were left with only their tower and some ruined masonry, as in the case of Christ Church Newgate Street. When the churches were rebuilt after the war, subtle and sometimes not so subtle changes were inevitable. But how much poorer London would have been had the wartime damage not been repaired; in almost every case the architects and craftsmen of the 1950s and early '60s captured the spirit and the detail of Wren's London, and their work remains part of the architectural history of the City.

Wren made few attempts to replicate the churches burnt in the Great Fire – he simply started again. But in some cases he incorporated into his new design significant sections of the medieval ruin. When damage from a more recent fire was being repaired, St Mary-at-Hill was found not to have been completely destroyed during the Great Fire. Plaster rendering was taken off the exterior of the north wall, which was discovered to be medieval. Wren's circular window had been cut into the original pre-fire wall, which stands today to its full height.

His treatment of St Martin-within-Ludgate, a church that stood against the City's western wall from the twelfth century, was just as expeditious. He rebuilt it, after the fire had raced down

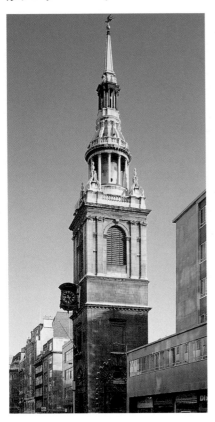

"The glory of the church is its steeple," wrote the architectural historian Nikolaus Pevsner of St Mary le Bow. Wren built the spire in 1678-80 and it remains his proudest work on any City church. It cost £7,388, compared with £8,033 for the rest of the church.

Ludgate Hill, using what has turned out to be a 17 metre (56 foot) high Roman and medieval stretch of the City wall for part of the church's west end.

St Vedast-alias-Foster, on the corner of Foster Lane and Cheapside, recently revealed another Wren secret when the exterior was cleaned after a long time. After the Great Fire, the church looked sound enough to be worth repairing and was one of the first City churches to be put back into service. In 1695, however, it was decided to rebuild it to a Wren design, and subsequent generations of architectural historians assumed that such a course would have meant the demolition of the patched up wobbly walls.

One of the loveliest of the City churches, St Mary-at-Hill has suffered a number of fires since Wren rebuilt it in the 1670s, but sensitive restoration over the centuries has preserved much of the style and atmosphere of the original.

The cleaning in 1992-3 revealed a different story. As the layers of grime came off a length of pre-fire wall standing to a height of 3 metres (10 feet), a blocked late medieval doorway was uncovered. Extraordinary that nobody had noticed it before! Moreover, it was found that the lower courses of the Wren tower were made of stone reused from the previous medieval church – perhaps an indication of the premium placed on stone during the post-fire rebuilding.

It has now emerged, after several other similar examples, that many Wren churches evolved in this way, using the shell of the previous buildings as the twentieth-century architects did with the same churches after the Second World War. Another aesthetic bonus at St Vedast is the colour you can now see in that cleaned stretch of the south wall. The rag-stone blocks carry a distinct tinge of orange which they acquired as the Great Fire swept along Cheapside more than three centuries ago.

One of the Wren churches least altered over the centuries is tucked away in a courtyard between King William and Cannon Streets. St Mary Abchurch (the meaning of its name has never been determined) is small, square and made of London brick with stone dressings. The plain building, with its tower and modest spire, hides one of London's most delightful surprises – a large dome 12 metres (40 feet) across, with allegorical scenes extravagantly painted in rich colours and supported by eight arches. The impression of great space created by this device is enhanced by the clear glass windows, white walls and the dark brown wood of the panelling, pulpit and pews contrasting with gilded details on the cornices above. The carved pews are original – a rare survival in London – and the reredos, the ornamental screen behind and above the altar, is the biggest in any Wren church; it is also one of the few authenticated works by Grinling Gibbons in a City church.

Wren's most spectacular parish church is alongside the Mansion House, in the heart of the City. St Stephen Walbrook (1672-9) appears to be just another grimy-looking London church with a door on to the street. But, having arrived at a lobby at the top of a flight of steps, the visitor is greeted by a breathtaking sight: a forest of Corinthian pillars in the centre of a church shaped like a Greek cross. The altar is straight ahead, while above, supported by a peristyle of columns, a great dome gives the church an impressive and spacious elegance. The ornately carved dark wooden pulpit is original, as are the altar rails, altar and font. An additional altar, in

St Mary Abchurch, Cannon Street. Built 1681-6, the square pale red brick church has a stone tower and lead spire, original carved furnishings by Grinling Gibbons and a painted dome by William Snow. The gallery, which was once used by boys of Merchant Taylor's School, has survived post-war restoration, as have the pews and the panelling.

the form of a large flat-topped sculpture by Henry Moore, directly under the dome, strikes an incongruous note for many admirers of the church. Weighing more than a ton, it was the gift of a twentieth-century millionaire property developer. Like many City churches without a significant congregation, St Stephen Walbrook sought an additional role for itself and the Samaritan organization was pioneered under its roof. St Stephen Walbrook represents Wren at his best among the parish churches. It is tempting to speculate that he took the opportunity of working for a comparatively wealthy parish to explore some of the engineering problems he would encounter when he embarked on the task of stretching a mighty dome over the crossing of St Paul's.

As Surveyor General Wren was also involved with the project to create new quays along the north bank of the Thames and on both banks of the Fleet. Under the master plan for London, the Fleet was to be canalized to a 12 metre (40 foot) width from the Thames to Holborn Bridge; a section of the City wall was to be demolished and both banks were to have 9 metre (30 foot) quays with warehouses, merchants' houses and high bridges that would allow for navigation. A cellar for one of the warehouses was found near Ludgate Hill and archaeologists digging 5 metres (16 feet) below the present ground level, at the corner of Seacoal Lane and Farringdon Street, came across the canal wall, built on a foundation of pine piles and oak planks. The wall itself was of chalk blocks faced with rag stone.

The work on the Fleet was completed in 1674, but the canal did not attract enough traffic. The section up stream of the Fleet Bridge was paved over in 1733 to accommodate a market and the rest of the canal met the same fate in the 1760s, when Blackfriars Bridge was built. One of London's "lost rivers" had become a drain under what are today Farringdon Road and New Bridge Street.

Remains of the burnt-out Fleet Prison were discovered during the same excavation. Its site, the island in the middle of the Fleet that the Normans had chosen six centuries earlier, survived only as a drain that encircled the prison and, for the first time, buildings abutted the prison walls. Since the Great Fire the prison had been destroyed and rebuilt twice; in 1846 it was finally demolished and its three million bricks offered for sale. That was the end of the curved perimeter walls, which had for so long marked the outline of the island in the Fleet that the Romans had first colonized.

One exciting find from the eighteenth-century prison was a pewter mug from the prison's privately run tap room. The owner, as well as dispensing beer, let the prisoners rooms at rates of four to eight shillings a week. The mug, which would have belonged to one such prisoner, was engraved with his name – John Hurst.

The Great Fire had claimed no fewer than forty-four out of the City's fifty-one company halls; most of them were rebuilt and most of the members of the companies, like the Fishmongers by London Bridge, had been able to rescue portable treasures from the path of the flames. Many items of that medieval and Tudor heritage survive today in alcoves and glass cases in the rebuilt company halls. The track record of survival for company buildings since then, however, makes gloomy reading. The Clothworkers, of which Samuel Pepys was master in 1677-8, date their first hall to about 1472; by 1633 they were on to their third, which burnt in the Great Fire. Rebuilt in 1668, it had become unsafe and was demolished in 1855. The fifth hall on the same site was opened in 1860 and destroyed by bombing in 1941. The present hall was finished in 1958.

Christopher Wren surrounded by evidence of his many talents. The Latin inscription tells us that the portrait was begun by Antonio Verrio and completed by Geoffrey Kneller and James Thornhill. It now hangs in the Sheldonian Theatre, Oxford, the first building of note that Wren designed.

Hanc Tabulam invenit & incepit Anton: Verrio. Perfecerunt Gothofredus Kneller & Joc: Thornhill Equites.

The Ironmongers' Hall was one of those not consumed by the Great Fire and when you see it today, among the stark concrete high-rise buildings of the Barbican, you could easily mistake it for one of those Tudor gems that everyone had forgotten to mention. It is in fact a modern building put on a new site after a First World War German raid destroyed the company's Georgian hall in Fenchurch Street. Relocated and rebuilt in 1925, it has a medieval-looking facade, finely crafted imitations of Tudor ceilings, richly carved panelling and a collection of treasures that came from the first hall. The banqueting hall has a minstrels' gallery, and the courtyard, with a fountain playing, has all the serenity of a medieval cloister. If only!

A surprising number of seventeenth-century halls were drastically altered, demolished or burnt down in the nineteenth century. The old facade of the Mercers' Company in Cheapside was dismantled in 1879 and incorporated into the Swanage Town Hall in Dorset four years later. It is still there, but the old Mercers' Hall has gone. It was another casualty of the Second World War; as we have seen, today's Mercers' Hall is part of a modern office block.

No City livery company has managed to keep a medieval hall nor has any post-fire hall of the seventeenth century survived intact. But many architectural fragments and even entire rooms, such as those in the Vintners' Hall, can lay just claim to being part of the London of Christopher Wren.

The "Tudor" gateway to the Ironmongers' Hall. Built in 1925, it is one of many features of bygone centuries that were skilfully reproduced on the hall's new site after the First World War.

One delightful example is the Tallow Chandlers' (candlemakers') Hall in Dowgate Hill. Rebuilt in 1672 and again after the Second World War, it has retained its pretty nineteenth-century Italianate courtyard and the original seventeenth-century panelling in both the parlour and the court room. Another hall in Dowgate, the Skinners' Hall, reached through an eighteenth-century ornamental gateway, is also arranged around a small courtyard. Brickwork of 1670 has survived on the front of the main building, and inside an original (post-fire) staircase takes you to the 1670 cedar-panelled court room. The Innholders' Hall and the Stationers' Hall also have substantial parts belonging to this period.

Of the thirty-six livery company halls standing in 1939 only the Apothecaries', in Blackfriars Lane, survived the Second World War without serious damage. A bomber scored a direct hit; the bomb went through the roof but failed to go off and the building was saved. Originally part of the Grocers' Company, the Apothecaries broke away and formed their own company in 1617, giving them the right, after 1630, to test all the medicines prepared and sold by apothecaries within an 11 kilometre (7 mile) radius of their hall. The Worshipful Society of Apothecaries also manufactured its own medicines, which, until the 1920s, were sold in the society's shop in the courtyard. They have kept, however, a vast collection of very valuable apothecary jars and unusual objects called "pill tiles" – large tiles on which medicinal mixtures were rolled out like fingers of pastry and cut into pills. The society once also had a lucrative monopoly to supply the Royal Navy, the East India Company, the army and the Crown Colonies, but today the members are all medical professionals working either in general medicine or in pharmaceuticals.

The building is special. It was part of the old Blackfriars Monastery guest house, which the Apothecaries acquired in 1632.

The site also included remnants of a "covered way" – the bridge over the Fleet to Bridewell Palace, built for the Holy Roman Emperor and his retinue when they visited Henry VIII in 1522. The society used these buildings in the mid sixteenth century to create their hall, court room and gallery, all of which were damaged in the Great Fire. But in the rebuilding the Apothecaries wanted to follow the layout of the original buildings and used whatever wall was still standing.

The reconstruction of 1671 remains largely intact, but with a late Georgian porticoed entrance from Blackfriars Lane that leads into an eighteenth-century courtyard. The grand staircase, built in 1671, leads to the court room and the parlour, which have their original seventeenth-century panelling and plaster. The walls, hung with oil paintings of famous masters and kings of England, reserve a special place for the apothecary to James I, Gideon de Laune, who it is said fathered thirty-seven children.

By the time the Apothecaries had repaired their hall in 1671 Wren was deeply involved in his greatest architectural project. His association with St Paul's had begun before the fire, in late 1663 or early '64, when it is believed that he was consulted by the Royal Commission set up to consider the deteriorating condition of the fabric of the cathedral. By May 1666, having spent the previous nine months studying buildings in Paris, he had written a report recommending that the inside of the nave should be refaced (Inigo Jones had reclad the exterior walls) and that saucer domes should replace the Gothic vaults of the roof. A tall dome, like a high tower, with a cupola was his suggestion for the crossing. According to Evelyn the scheme was adopted, but within days the Great Fire had rendered any plans useless.

When the wreckage was cleared away it was again possible to patch up the west end, where services were held while the royal court, the Church and the City Fathers grappled with the building's future in the context of a devastated city. The clergy and the king favoured the idea of using the nave of the old building as part of the rebuilding. Wren reluctantly went along with this and drew up plans, but in 1688 part of the nave collapsed and the decision to demolish and make a new start had to be taken.

Wren produced the first model for the new St Paul's in 1670. Although approved by the king, it failed to please the clergy and Wren was persuaded to think again. He came up with an imaginative design based on the shape of a Greek cross with a very short choir at the east end. The unusual form, with its large expanse of floor, was topped by a dome almost as broad as that of St Peter's in Rome. Both the first model and the wooden "Great Model" of 1673 are on display in the cathedral.

Again the clergy demurred. They wanted a conventional cross-shaped cathedral along medieval lines. Finally Wren gave them what they wanted – a design known as the Warrant Design (meaning that it was approved by royal warrant). His son Christopher explained in his book *Parentalia* that Wren had a get-out clause concerning

Detail like this foliage on the south transept of St Paul's was hardly visible until cleaning began in the 1960s. As centuries of soot were removed, a ball of cloth was found lodged among the carving. The cathedral architect at the time came to the conclusion that an eighteenth-century choirboy must have lost it during a game in the churchyard.

changes: "The king was pleased to allow him the liberty in the prosecution of his work, to make variations, rather ornamental than essential, as from time to time he should see proper." As a result, once building was underway, the tower and spire were replaced by a dome, the relative width of the nave and aisles reduced and an additional curtain wall designed for the exterior of the nave that would both help to support the new dome and screen the flying buttress.

The ruins of St Paul's after the fire, from a contemporary drawing.

At one stage Wren had to resort to gunpowder to loosen the medieval stone which was impregnated with molten lead from the roof, but most of the clearing of the site was done with pick axes and a battering ram manned by about thirty labourers. Wren noted that several Roman burials and potters' kilns were found and, contrary to the received wisdom of the time, he concluded that the Romans, and not some prehistoric super race, had founded the city. Much of the stone had to be brought by boat from the king's quarries in Portland, sailed around to London Bridge, transhipped into barges for the few last few hundred metres and then carted up the hill to the site. One ship full of stone became a prize of war, seized in the English Channel and taken to Calais where the stone was sold.

Work proceeded slowly as Wren decided to build the whole building gradually rather than complete the east end first in the conventional way. He was worried that a cathedral built in stages might fall victim to Treasury cuts and never be finished. In 1697 an exasperated Parliament suspended half his annual salary until such time as the job was finished, and in the same year the first Sunday services were held in the one part that was completed, the choir. The dome was in place by 1710 and Parliament declared the building finished in 1711, when Wren was seventy-nine.

The facade of Kensington Palace, designed by Christopher Wren and Nicholas Hawksmoor. Work started in 1689 when William and Mary acquired the house; the Wren/Hawksmoor additions culminated in the King's Gallery, begun in 1695.

While the restoring of the parish churches and the building of St Paul's were going on Wren started several new projects for the king, including the Royal Observatory at Greenwich and the hospital at Chelsea – the first of Wren's two monumental royal hospitals. Charles II is said to have been cajoled into providing for old soldiers by his vivacious mistress Nell Gwyn, but it is more likely that he was influenced by the example of the French king, Louis XIV, who had built a hospital for his army pensioners more than a decade before.

The Royal Hospital Chelsea was begun in 1682 to provide for about 500 old soldiers in a brick building about 3 kilometres (2 miles) up river from Westminster. Having had some practice on a few City churches such as St Mary Abchurch and St Benet, St Paul's Wharf, Wren now used brick on a large scale for the first time, in the construction of a huge three-sided court facing the Thames. The main north block, with its tall portico of giant Doric pillars and domed tower, contains the barrel-vaulted chapel on one side of a lofty octagonal vestibule, while the other side is balanced by the large panelled hall with a painting by Antonio Verrio of Charles II on horseback. The other two ranges are for the pensioners, who still use Wren's long colonnades and in their distinctive crimson jackets doze in the sun in the arcades thoughtfully aligned towards the south-west.

After the death of Charles II in 1685 his brother, James II, continued to fund the project, adding the outbuildings that now form such a harmonious whole. The main buildings, described by Evelyn as embodying monastic austerity, have hardly altered since Wren left them. Many of the interiors are also original and only the mullioned casement windows have been replaced with the present sash design. The best time to see the building is in May, when the Royal Horticultural Society holds the annual flower show that had its origins in the gardens of the Inner Temple.

Monarchs came and went regularly during Wren's reign as Surveyor General. James II, having set Wren to rebuild much of Whitehall Palace around Inigo Jones's Banqueting House, lasted only three years in the job. He fled from Westminster as the Glorious Revolution of 1688 overthrew his Catholic court, and Wren found himself with two new royal patrons, James's daughter Mary and her Protestant husband, William of Orange, who were invited by the anti-Catholic faction to rule jointly as William III and Mary II. William – the Dutch Bear, as Londoners called him – did not like

Whitehall Palace and chose to develop two other houses: a Jacobean mansion known as Nottingham House in Kensington and the old brick-built Tudor palace of Hampton Court, about 21 kilometres (13 miles) up river from Westminster.

Nicholas Hawksmoor also had a hand in the rebuilding of Kensington Palace. He arrived in Wren's office as his personal clerk in 1679 and ten years later was made Clerk of Works on the king's new house at Kensington, assuming a great deal of responsibility for both the design and the construction. The facade is much the same today as it would have been when Wren and Hawksmoor left it, but many additions and changes were made to the interior by successive monarchs – William III (1689-1702), Queen Anne (1702-14) and the first two Georges (1714-27 and 1727-60).

George III (1760-1820) preferred Buckingham House, as it then was, and although various minor royals continued to live in Kensington Palace, the state apartments there mouldered on into the nineteenth century, neglected and abandoned until they were refurbished and opened to the public in 1889, on the occasion of Queen Victoria's seventieth birthday. Victoria herself was born in the palace, and one of the most popular objects among the collection of uniforms, dresses, portraits and furniture – James II's bed is there – is the large dolls' house with all its original fittings that she played with as a child.

Fountain Court, one of Wren's seventeenth-century extensions to the Tudor palace of Hampton Court.

It was Mary, not William, who wanted money spent on Hampton Court, a great rambling Tudor palace with some superb buildings such as the hall and gatehouse. Wren's job was to enlarge it by adding four new buildings to each corner, and two new wings to be known as the King's and Queen's Galleries. Probably inspired by the

Louvre in Paris, Wren obliged Mary with a plan that swept away everything except the hall, which was to have become one of the focal points for the new complex.

Fortunately for us all there was a problem of money, so a modified scheme that left most of Henry VIII's palace intact was adopted and work was begun in 1689. By 1694, when the queen died of smallpox, the project was far from finished and, disheartened, William had the work stopped. Wren's additions might have remained unfinished had not all of Whitehall Palace, with the exception of Inigo Jones's Banqueting House, burnt to the ground in 1698. William's interest in Hampton Court was rekindled and the result is what we see today: the ranges along the south and east fronts and the restrained but pleasing arcades of Fountain Court.

The River Thames, London's great seventeenth-century highway was also the setting for Wren's finest royal palace. Greenwich Palace was an old site. Henry V's brother, Humphrey, Duke of Gloucester, had built "Bella Court" on the banks of the river in the early fifteenth century. Henry VI renamed it Placentia and several reigns later it became Henry VIII's favourite palace. Elizabeth I was born there and used it during the summer throughout her reign. But the Civil War finished it off. Cromwell, unable to sell it, stripped it of its treasures and left it derelict, so that on the Restoration of the Monarchy Charles II could only clear the site and start again. One fragment of the Tudor palace survived – an undercroft which is today under the Queen Anne Block of the Royal Naval Hospital.

Inigo Jones's pupil and later deputy, John Webb, produced a new design, which he started to build in 1664. It was to have been a palace around a three-sided courtyard facing the river, but only one wing, known as the King Charles block, was ever constructed. By the time it was finished Charles II was dead, his brother James had fled the country, and William and Mary had other ideas. They preferred, as we have seen, to live at Hampton Court and Kensington Palace, but for Greenwich the queen wanted a naval institution to mirror Charles II's Chelsea Hospital for old soldiers.

In 1694, therefore, Wren started on his last big secular project and, with the exception of St Paul's, his finest building in London. Inigo Jones's Queen's House, set back from the Thames in Greenwich Park, was in danger of being overwhelmed by the huge new complex of halls, wards and colonnades. Indeed Wren's first design would have made it completely invisible from the river. He was persuaded to come up with a second plan that included Webb's earlier range in a scheme of four huge buildings separated by a long "courtyard" open at both ends. His brilliant compromise was to allow a vista from the Thames through to the elegant Queen's House framed by the green swathe of the park. Wren had also designed the chapel and the Great Hall so that, from the river, their domes and a twin-columned colonnade acted as a frame for the little palace in the distance.

Work stopped and started as monarchs came and went. Over the years Wren's design was carried through with the help of some of England's finest architects, including Nicholas Hawksmoor, John Vanbrugh and Thomas Ripley, who completed that masterpiece of English architecture, the hospital's chapel. In 1704 the dome over the Great Hall was in place; the first pensioners arrived a year later.

But Wren did not live to see the completed baroque interior of what we know today as the Painted Hall. It took James Thornhill, Member of Parliament, Fellow of the Royal Society and father-in-law of William Hogarth, twenty years to perfect the oval ceiling's great expanse of flamboyant allegorical scenes celebrating the democratic benefits of the Glorious Revolution. Restorers managed to clean some fifteen coats of varnish from the ceiling in 1957-60, revealing in much greater clarity more than 200 figures swirling in colourful action around the stern-looking features of William and Mary at the centre of the tableau.

The Royal Naval Hospital took on its present role as a naval college in 1869, and the Queen's House is now part of the National Maritime Museum, which is also responsible for another Wren building, the Old Royal Observatory at the top of the hill in Greenwich Park. Wren's budget of £500 for the building had come from the sale of some spoiled naval gunpowder, but there was no question of new bricks. They were collected from a ruin at the old fort at Tilbury, while much of the stone was reused from a redundant gatehouse at the Tower of London.

Despite the royal penny-pinching, the observatory was completed in 1675 for the use of John Flamsteed, the first Astronomer Royal – though before he made any of his considerable contributions to scientific knowledge, he was obliged to go out and buy his own telescopes! The octagonal room, where Flamsteed made the first trustworthy catalogue of the position of the stars, has been carefully conserved by the National Maritime Museum to preserve its unique seventeenth-century character and today houses a collection of early telescopes.

As the burnt-out City of London was rebuilt, the suburbs began to expand as well. The squares of the West End which followed the examples of Inigo Jones's Covent Garden and Lincolns Inn Fields were being planned even before the fire: Evelyn noted in 1665 that the Earl of Southampton had started "a noble square or Piazza, a little towne" in what is now Bloomsbury Square. The earl had laid out building plots in a square around three sides of his mansion and let them at a peppercorn ground rent for people to build upon. The landowner retained the freehold and, when the leases fell in, the earl's successors owned everything. In the seventeenth century the square was on the list of sights to show foreign visitors but, although the north terrace dates from 1800, no original houses have survived.

The same pattern was followed by Henry Jermyn, Earl of St Albans, at St James's Square, off Piccadilly. After the Restoration he bought from the king some fields that were part of the St James's Palace estate, and, according to Pepys in 1663, "building in St James's by Lord St Albans is now about." The earl laid out the square with a view to capturing the quality end of the West End housing market, giving leases to his friends, and to speculative builders, to build large houses with gardens 60 metres (200 feet) long. Aristocrats fell over themselves to buy the houses and for more than half a century St James's Square was a *very* fashionable address. One of the gardens has survived, behind a house in the north-east corner, but the house was remodelled in the early eighteenth century. However, a surprising number of eighteenth-century houses, or their facades, still grace this aristocratic square and many others boast features designed by such architectural luminaries as Robert Adam.

That is also true of the streets running into and near the square – all part of the Earl of St Albans's development. Pall Mall, so called because of a French ball game similar to croquet called *palle-maille*, which used to be played nearby, is today a street full of monumental Victorian piles in which "gentlemen" relax in deep leather club chairs. One building, however, survives from the St Albans concept – Schomberg House, Pall Mall. Built for the Duke of Schomberg in 1698, it is one of only a few remaining seventeenth-century houses in London that is not part of a terrace. Made of brown and red bricks, its porch is decorated with slender caryatids, one of which is dated 1791. Haymarket is mainly nineteenth century except for one eighteenth-century shop front at the Piccadilly Circus end, and along Piccadilly itself nothing except St James's Church reflects anything of the bricks and mortar of the Earl of St Albans's time.

Canaletto's eighteenth-century view of Greenwich Naval College (Greenwich Hospital until 1869) from the River Thames. The Queen's House, designed by Inigo Jones, is visible between the domed towers of the central buildings. Artistic licence or faulty memory seems to have played a part in the painting: the Queen's House is not nearly as diminutive as Canaletto saw it.

The earl, a friend and patron of Christopher Wren, chose the architect to design a church for his "new suburb". The only one of Wren's churches to have been built on a virgin site, St James's foundation stone was laid in 1676. The church, which Wren himself thought was "beautiful and convenient", was completed in 1684, and largely paid for by the earl. Wren was particularly pleased with the number of people (about 2,000) he could pack in and the way that they could all hear and see the preacher.

Grinling Gibbons was given the job of carving the reredos and, unusually, he carved a font for the church in marble. The bowl, with reliefs showing Noah's Ark with the dove carrying an olive branch, is supported by a marble tree trunk – a representation of the Tree of Life – complete with Adam, Eve and serpent.

Miraculously, much of the woodwork did not burn when a bomb destroyed the roof in 1940. The gallery survived, as did the precious organ, an instrument ordered by James II for his palace at Whitehall and given to the church by Mary II in 1691. Pictures taken after the bomb fell show the church open to the sky, but at the west end the organ can be seen, with its delicate free-standing carved figures, also by Gibbons, in place on top of the pipes. The architectural historian John Summerson wryly commented, "The remarkably ugly spire which has disappeared from the tower was designed, not by Wren, but by a Mr Wilcox, a carpenter, who undercut Wren's estimate."

Throughout the latter part of the seventeenth century new London squares filled in the fields that once surrounded the city. Leicester Square, or Leicester Fields as it was first known, was developed by Robert Sidney, second Earl of Leicester, from about 1670. Nothing of the earl's original estate survives. Soho Square, or Kings Square as it was first called, followed in 1681, Hoxton Square in Shoreditch in 1683; and at Holborn Nicholas Barbon, one of London's first large-scale developers, built streets of houses against violent opposition from lawyers at nearby Gray's Inn. So incensed were they at the prospect of green fields disappearing under red brick that they fought a pitched battle with Barbon's workmen on the site. The lawyers lost, and Barbon's terraced houses, so admired today at Nos 36-43 Bedford Row, despoiled the lawyers' idyll.

The same speculator also developed a large area of what was once the garden of the Duke of Buckingham's York House to the south of the Strand: George Street, Villiers Street, Duke Street and Buckingham Street. More than a dozen seventeenth-century houses can still be seen, including No. 12, the house in which Pepys lived from 1679 to 1688, but all that remains of the duke's mansion is the York Watergate (1626) which is now stranded high and dry in the Embankment Gardens.

Barbon also built Essex Street on the site of Essex House, between the Strand and the Embankment, and some of those red-brick houses – Nos 11, 14, 19 and 34 – built in 1675 have survived, many of them with original interior fittings such as staircases. In the same area, Gough Square on the northern side of Fleet Street has one house left from the post-fire rebuilding. Its famous eighteenth-

Queen Anne's Gate, developed in 1704, has several houses that are original. Built of brown brick with red brick window dressings, some of the houses retain their elaborately carved canopies over the front door. The exterior of No. 17 is the most original in the square, thanks to the fact that its early eighteenth-century gabled dormer windows at the attic level have survived.

century tenant, Dr Samuel Johnson (who coined the maxim "When a man is tired of London he is tired of life"), has ensured the survival of the house. He lived there from 1748 to 1759, and today the building is maintained as a small museum house displaying Johnsonian memorabilia and the garret room where his great dictionary was compiled. Nearby Racquet Court has a row of houses which also dates from the 1680s.

A statue of Queen Anne completes the symmetry of one of the most attractive squares in London – Queen Anne's Gate, on the Westminster side of St James's Park. Started in 1704 with a row of twenty-four houses, it still boasts several of the originals with their elaborate door canopies and carved door frames. Such carvings were banned by the 1707 Building Act as a measure against the continuing risk of fire, making the survival of these exterior features even more remarkable.

Wren designed the dome of St Paul's, over 30 metres (100 feet) wide at its base, in two parts: an outer skin topped by a ball and cross 110 metres (365 feet) above the pavement, and a lower inner dome on which Sir James Thornhill painted his tableau of the life of St Paul. Even when he was in his eighties, Wren inspected the building once a week, being hoisted up to the dome in a basket; but he left the final inspection to his son as the last stone was laid in 1710. By this time the City skyline was sprinkled with Wren spires and dominated, as it would be for 250 years, by the dome of St Paul's.

In the City itself Wren's rebuilt London survives in corners that are best explored on foot. Laurence Pountney Hill, which runs between Cannon Street and Upper Thames Street, has two buildings from the period. Said by architectural historians to be two of the best surviving examples of the post-fire rebuilding, Nos 1 and 2 have richly carved hoods over the doors, while the door frames are decorated with friezes of carved foliage. A small raised churchyard opposite is all that is left of the church of St Laurence Pountney after it was burnt in the Great Fire and not rebuilt. The adjacent "Rectory House" in Laurence Pountney Lane is another seventeenth-century building but eighteenth- and nineteenth-century alterations have made it less authentic.

As one might expect, the area around St Paul's Cathedral is rich in seventeenth-century buildings. Wren's tall brick chapter house in the churchyard was restored to its present condition having been burned out during the Second World War; the Deanery in Dean's Court dates from 1670; and, almost hidden from view in a lane called Amen Court, off Warwick Lane, is a row of houses that Wren built for the clergy of St Paul's.

During his years in office, which started under Charles II and ended under George I, Wren designed some of the kingdom's most elegant, innovative and enduring buildings. Perhaps his only mistake was to stay too long as an arbiter of taste and style. Some critics wanted him out; the Earl of Shaftesbury wrote in 1712, "Thro' several reigns we have patiently seen the noblest publick buildings perish, if I may say so, under the hand of one single Court-Architect; who if he had been able to profit by experience, would long since at our expense, have proved the greatest Master in the world. But I question whether our patience is like to hold much longer." Other forces were also working against Wren. Even when he was putting the finishing touches to St Paul's he was thwarted over his plan to surround the cathedral with a wrought-iron fence. Cast iron was imposed on him and when he protested about the addition of a balustrade to his cathedral's walls he was ignored – what he described as "an edging" went ahead.

The office he had inherited fifty years before was bound to change. Queen Anne had begun the process and a change of government after her death in 1714 hastened reform. A Board of Commissioners was appointed to run the Office of Works. In recognition of Wren's long service and eminence he was permitted to retain his title, but only a fraction of the power he had once had. His ability as an administrator came under attack and the axe finally fell in 1718, when he was dismissed from office.

He made a dignified defence of his position, pointing out that as titular head of the commission he had no real power and "as I am dismissed, having worn out (by God's mercy) a long life in the royal service, and having made some Figure in the World, I hope it will be allow'd me to Die in Peace." He retired to a house on the Thames at Hampton Court, granted to him some years earlier by Queen Anne, and divided his time between that and another house he had in St James's Street, where he died in 1723, aged ninety-one.

He was buried in the crypt of St Paul's under a plain black slab with an inscription that simply says, "Reader, if you seek a monument, look around you."

*The Palm Room at Spencer House.
Perhaps the most exotic room in the
house, it was used as a typing pool
during the 1950s. The gilt chairs are
copies of originals made for the room.*

Chapter 8
A Georgian Postscript 1714-1830

WREN LIVED JUST LONG ENOUGH to see the arrival of Georgian London. Its focus came from the young Earl of Burlington who, before he was twenty-one, made a Grand Tour of Italy that filled his mind with images of classical architecture. He returned to London in 1715, a year after the accession of George I, and remodelled Burlington House in Piccadilly along the lines of an Italian palace that had impressed him on a visit to Vicenza. The pitched roof with dormer windows was replaced by a flat roof hidden by a balustrade, and the facade was dramatically changed to include Ionic columns and pedimented windows.

For Londoners this transformation must have had a familiar look – it was reminiscent of the classical style that Inigo Jones had introduced after his time in Italy a century earlier. But where Jones had had only limited success in popularizing these ideas, the Burlington Palladians established an architectural style that was to be unassailable in London and throughout England for a century and more.

Although Burlington House was altered again in the nineteenth century, the youthful third earl's ideas can still be seen in much of the exterior fabric of the main house. Many of his interiors, which now provide a background to Royal Academy exhibitions, survive to be admired.

In 1717 Lord Burlington, with the help of William Kent, Colen Campbell and Giacomo Leoni, a Venetian whom his lordship had befriended on tour, set about developing the estate around Burlington House. Streets laid out under their influence include Burlington Gardens, Savile Row, Old Burlington Street and Clifford Street. The Palladians, following the strictures of their sixteenth-century master, designed their houses with the first floor – the *piano nobile* – as the principal one, with the highest ceilings and therefore the tallest windows; each successive floor had smaller windows until, in the purest Georgian form, those of the top floor were shrunk to a perfect square.

Some of the original houses on the Burlington Estate survive with few alterations – Nos 4-9, 16, 17 and 18 Clifford Street are examples worth examining. Another important pair, Nos 31 and 32 Old Burlington Street, are relics of the first uniform London terrace of the Palladian revival, designed by Campbell and built in 1718-23. In Savile Row Nos 3, 11-14, 16 and 17 survive from another early eighteenth-century terrace, and on the corner of Savile Row and Burlington Gardens, Leoni designed Queensberry House. Although altered in 1785 and 1855, it still conveys a clear impression of the Palladian revival spearheaded by Burlington and his friends, and is considered by some experts to be the first example of the ubiquitous Palladian London town house.

Other architects, including Wren's protégé Nicholas Hawksmoor, carried on apparently unimpressed by the Burlington clique and, empowered by Queen Anne's Act of Parliament for the building of fifty new churches (1711), made such baroque contributions as the City church of St Mary Woolnoth (1716), St George's Bloomsbury (1721) and Christ Church Spitalfields (1714-29). James Gibbs's St Mary-le-Strand (on an island in the Strand outside the BBC's Bush House) was started in 1714; and his impressively pedimented St Martin-in-the-Fields followed in 1722-6. Thomas Archer built the ill-fated St John's Smith Square (1713-28); it was gutted during the Second World War and is now used as a concert hall and restaurant.

As the bricks and mortar of Georgian London began to smother tracts of land that had lately been pasture, the main beneficiaries were the great landowning families fortunate enough to have had estates on the edge of London. The fashion for West End houses, started by the Earl of St Albans after the Great Fire, lost none of its appeal during the eighteenth century and, as the medieval city's population declined, Londoners with money and social pretensions moved west. By 1759 there were houses all along Piccadilly and Mayfair's remaining pastures had been replaced by fashionable pavements, squares and streets of Georgian houses conforming to a strict planning grid.

The Grosvenor Estate was – and is – the largest of these properties. It was put together in 1677 when Sir Thomas Grosvenor, a landowner from Cheshire, married a twelve-year-old heiress whose dowry happened to include 40 hectares (100 acres) of fields in Mayfair. She also brought to the marriage more than 130 hectares (half a square mile) of property between Hyde Park and the river. The next generation of Grosvenors began to exploit their potential riches by laying out Grosvenor Square and a surrounding grid of expensive streets in 1737.

The smaller Berkeley Estate, including Berkeley Square, was carved out of the Grosvenor holdings as the result of a settlement over a marriage between two minors that did not take place. Several eighteenth-century houses survive on the west side of Berkeley Square, of which No. 44, designed by William Kent, is a perfect illustration of the lavish interiors that lay behind an often austere facade. While the gentry and merchant princes commissioned architects to design lavish and flamboyant colonnaded mansions on their rural estates, they seemed content with, even proud of, the restrained dignity and uniformity of the London Georgian town house. But the insides of these houses often had another message – one of innovative design and pride in sumptuous decoration.

Kent, perhaps Burlington's closest ally in the promulgation of the Palladian style, was also responsible for a mansion which has recently been restored by the Eagle Star Insurance Company at 22 Arlington Street, behind the Ritz Hotel on Piccadilly. Its exterior and the approach from the street have been changed, but many of Kent's rooms, now restored by the company for their own entertaining and for hire, are another worthy tribute. His best surviving public buildings are in Whitehall – the old Treasury building and the spectacular Horse Guards.

The second Earl of Oxford was responsible for Portland Place, Cavendish Square and the grid that includes Harley and Wimpole Streets (both family names), between Oxford Street and Marylebone Road. He had planned a grand scheme for Cavendish Square, but the recession of 1731 knocked him off balance and meant that the centrepiece of his plan, a palatial town house, had to be abandoned. Fortunately, two fine buildings that were erected, with their stone porticos and Corinthian columns, still stand on the northern side of the square.

In the 1760s Henry William Portman made Portman Square the starting point for a vast tract of London, reaching from north of Oxford Street to the edge of Regents Park, that still contains any number of Georgian terraced houses. By this time, the second wave of Palladians was being challenged by a new group of architects who wanted change. Robert Adam, a talented and energetic Scot whose architectural features such as fireplaces fetch astronomical prices today, was the best known member of the group that came to be known as the Neo-Classicists. Adam's style retained most of the perceived Palladian virtues but drew its inspiration from archaeological sites he had visited during almost a decade of travelling throughout the ancient Mediterranean world.

The Neo-Classicists sometimes used more decoration on their facades than the Palladians, but their interiors, with their imaginative use of space and decor inspired by archaeological themes, were different enough to surprise and delight fashionable London. One of Adam's buildings for the Portman Estate was Home House at 20 Portman Square. The modest moulded exterior decoration of panels of draped foliage on a blue background gives little warning of his revolutionary approach to the interior. Apparently his series of grand reception rooms and a monumental staircase for the septuagenarian Countess of Home, all squeezed into a London terrace, were made possible by the fact that the countess required only one bedroom, which Adam decorated in the Etruscan style.

Robert Adam's brother James worked with him on many projects. Of these, Chandos House in nearby Chandos Street still stands, although it has become somewhat neglected looking in recent years. One wing of Lansdowne House in Berkeley Square remains (another was lopped off to widen a road into the square and was subsequently shipped to the Metropolitan Museum in New York). No. 20 St James's Square, Apsley House at Hyde Park Corner, and the south and east sides of Fitzroy Square (for the third Duke of Grafton) all survive as monuments to the Adams' genius. The exterior of Apsley House was remodelled by James Wyatt in 1828, but retains some Adam interiors.

William Kent's interior of 44 Berkeley Square. Built in 1742-4, it has the finest staircase and drawing room of any eighteenth-century Georgian terraced house.

But of their greatest contribution to London's townscape, the Adelphi on the Strand, only a few fragments survive. The brothers acquired a ninety-nine-year lease on the site of Durham House, one of the old Thamesside mansions, and began a speculative building project in 1772. The imposing range of eleven high-class houses stood on a wide terrace that had to be built above the river-bank and supported by a series of wide arches and vaults. The concept was inspired by a visit that Robert had made to the Dalmatian coast, where he saw the remains of the Roman Emperor Diocletian's palace overlooking the Adriatic; a large number of Scots, encouraged by regular playing of the bagpipes, laboured on the site, while the interiors were painted by some of the best artists of the day; marble fireplaces designed by Robert Adam decorated the rooms and everything was of the highest quality.

The whole scheme should have been a runaway success, but part of the financial package behind it was the anticipated income from letting the extensive vaults below; when these proved to be undesirable due to occasional flooding, the financial consequences were disastrous. The brothers ran out of funds just before the houses were finished, and to remain solvent they hit upon the idea of running a private lottery to dispose of everything. They escaped bankruptcy and the houses were finished and occupied.

The sumptuous music room designed by Robert Adam at 20 Portman Square.

Today, blocks of offices line the Strand where the Adelphi once stood. In the words of Nikolaus Pevsner, "The greed of Londoners destroyed nearly its whole front in 1936. Let what stands in its stead speak for itself." Would Paris have demolished Gabriel's buildings fronting the Place de la Concorde, Pevsner mused in his survey of *The Buildings of England*? The Adelphi, he maintains, was in the same league.

For those who would like to search out what might have been, there are fragments in the streets behind the the Strand, near Charing Cross. Some of the substructure for the vaults is visible in Lower Robert Street off York Buildings and there are houses standing in Adam Street – Nos 8, 9, 10 and 18. No. 7 Adam Street has giant pilasters, topped by a pediment, that carry the original decorative scheme of honeysuckle in high relief. John Adam Street still has Nos 4 and 6, and No. 8 is the Royal Society of Arts, built in 1772-4. In addition to its neo-classical facade, the building retains many Adam features inside.

The Cadogan Estate, which still owns great swathes of Chelsea, owes its origins to Sir Hans Sloane, a distinguished scientist and physician, who made a fortune during his lifetime and acquired vast stretches of land along the river in Chelsea, much of which was

The Adam brothers' greatest achievement, the Adelphi, shortly after its completion in 1772.

given to the Earl of Cadogan when he married Sloane's daughter in 1771. Sir Hans's name lives on in the streets of Knightsbridge and Chelsea and is even more revered in Bloomsbury, where his vast "cabinet of curiosities" plus 50,000 books and 3,500 manuscripts ended up as the core of the British Museum collection, established by Act of Parliament in 1753 and housed today in early nineteenth-century grandeur.

As we have seen, the Bedford family were in at the start of London's rush to develop the western suburbs. The first earl, John Russell, with the help of Inigo Jones, created Covent Garden and set a trend of regulated suburban leasehold development that was followed by landowners and developers for the next two and a half centuries. The Earl of Southampton's urban estate in Bloomsbury was another seventeenth-century success, and the two estates were joined through marriage in 1669 to create the wealthy and powerful Bedford Estate, which in 1775 began work on Bedford Square.

Built at a time when the conscience of eighteenth-century Londoners had been prodded into providing new hospitals, better policing and better drained streets, Bedford Square reflected some of London's new-found civic pride. It was the finest example of Georgian town planning and the first square to have been designed and built all of a piece. One feature is the way the doorways are highlighted by "coade stone", a paste named after a Mrs Coade of Lambeth whose factory made it from china clay mixed with flint, sand and glass – a durable concoction that could be turned into moulded blocks or lofty pilasters.

In 1775 a country house in the west of London became a royal palace. Built by the Duke of Buckingham in 1703, it overlooked St James's Park and so irritated Queen Anne that she forbade the duke to use the royal park as access to the front entrance of his house. George II tried to buy it in 1723 but could not agree a price; it was left to George III to tidy up the edge of the park by buying the house for £28,000 in 1762 and moving in thirteen years later. Buckingham House was never palatial and when George IV became king in 1820 he set about the additions that led to the monumental building that is such a potent symbol of London today. The works were the cause of many rows between the king and his government, who had sanctioned £250,000 for repairs and improvements. George IV, typically, took no notice of the budget and gave John Nash, London's great Regency architect, his head. Nash was sacked in 1830, Edward Blore finished the building and the bill soared towards £700,000. Further additions by other nineteenth-century architects brought the total number of rooms to about 600 and in 1912-13 Sir Aston Webb replaced the east front with Portland stone.

The present Royal Family occupies only a small number of rooms in the north wing of what we now know as Buckingham Palace, overlooking Green Park; to the great disappointment of the many thousands of tourists who since 1993 have been admitted to the state apartments during the summer months, the Queen's bedroom is out of bounds.

During the latter part of the eighteenth century the Adam brothers shared the architectural limelight with another Scottish architect, Sir William Chambers. Born in Sweden, Chambers drew his inspiration from visits to the Far East and many years studying in France and Italy. Like all successful eighteenth-century architects he accepted commissions from landowners for a variety of buildings that ranged from town houses and great country houses to follies and monumental gateways throughout the British Isles.

Unlike Adam, Chambers was later drawn into designing for the state and succeeded to Wren's old job of Surveyor General. His greatest achievement came towards the end of his career when George III's government decided to build an enormous office block to accommodate their main departments. The site of the old royal palace of Somerset House on the Strand was chosen and the first stone laid in 1776 for a building that would rival the adjacent Adelphi, begun only eight years before.

Somerset House was conceived on a grand scale, even by today's standards. The buildings are arranged around a huge quadrangle measuring 76 by 92 metres (250 by 301 feet), with a terrace and riverside range almost 250 metres (800 feet) long that sits on top of a series of monumental arches, the biggest of which once served as the watergate. A colonnaded triple gateway set into the Strand wing leads into a wide stone courtyard where, in some wings, government offices continue to function. In 1990, however, a move was made to open up some of this fine building to cultural organizations: the Courtauld Institute now uses the splendid and elegant range of rooms facing the Strand to house its famous art collection.

Architects like Chambers and Adam had little to do with the other half of their divided city. While those with money were enjoying the new, cleaner and quieter suburbs in the west, waves of immigrants from other parts of the British Isles and the Continent washed up on the Thames shore and settled into the sprawling shanty town of the East End. By the time of the first census in 1801 London's population was just under one million and, according to one stipendiary magistrate at the time, one in eight of them was a vagrant or beggar.

The chapel of the former Ironmongers' Almshouses, now part of the Geffrye Museum in Shoreditch, with the monument to their benefactor, Sir Robert Geffrye, described as "Knight, Alderman and Ironmonger", above the entrance.

Johann William von Archenholtz, a German visitor to London in 1794, remarked on the east-west divide: "The East End, especially along the shores of the Thames, consists of old houses, the streets there are narrow, dark and ill paved; inhabited by sailors and other workmen who are employed in the construction of ships and by a great part of the Jews. The contrast between this and the West End is astonishing; the houses here are mostly new and elegant; the squares are superb, the streets are straight and open.... If all London were as well built there would be nothing in the world to compare with it."

While the elegant residences of the West End have survived in large numbers, the rooming houses of the East End, where one room per family was not uncommon among the Irish immigrant community, were either pulled down or fell over. The sheds and lean-tos of Shoreditch and Shadwell may only have lasted a generation and the small shops and factories where the workforce sweated towards an early grave survive only as archaeological sites which the experts rarely have an opportunity to explore.

Huguenot weavers' houses still stand in Spitalfields, a corner of relative prosperity in the eighteenth century, and can be seen in Fournier Street. No. 4, built in 1726, is a fine example of a silk weaver's house and some smaller houses in Hambury Street retain the garrets where the weavers worked their twelve-hour day. The 1743 Huguenot church in Brick Lane survives as a mosque for the area's latest immigrant community – Muslims from the Indian sub-continent – and Hawksmoor's eighteenth-century church at Spitalfields is another heritage landmark.

Shoreditch, another early East End parish, has not fared as well. St Leonard's Church (1736-40), the work of George Dance the Elder, is one of only two important Georgian buildings left. The other, the Geffrye Almshouses built in 1715, when Shoreditch still had fields and farms in the parish, was a bequest in the will of Sir Robert Geffrye, a former Lord Mayor and master of the Ironmongers' Company. Set in extensive gardens, they are typical almshouses of the time, with a central block and two wings forming three sides of a triangle. The chapel, attendance at which was obligatory for Geffrye's pensioners, is the focal point of the red brick building.

This rare example of East End almshouses was almost lost at the turn of the twentieth century when the Ironmongers' Company, recognizing that Shoreditch had deteriorated into something close to a slum, decided to sell the site and move the pensioners to a more leafy location in Kent. Most of the other City company almshouses had already taken that course. The Geffrye buildings would have been demolished and high-density housing built on the site had not the newly formed National Trust and the Society for the Protection of Ancient Buildings taken up the cause. Many local councillors also recognized the value of the buildings to Shoreditch and enough noise was raised to persuade the London County Council to intervene with a substantial contribution to the cost of buying out the Ironmongers. The LCC bought the old buildings in 1911 and soon afterwards opened them as a local museum.

The almshouses themselves are a more than worthy artifact, but in the course of the last eighty years the museum has also built up a fine collection of furniture, paintings and objects associated with London's history. Its most valuable contribution is the way it now exhibits rooms from London houses – some of them original interiors rescued from demolition sites – ranging from the seventeenth through to the mid twentieth century.

Another important and little-known building is the East End's oldest surviving domestic house, which dates from the time when Hackney was a village in a countryside dotted with "country" houses for Tudor merchants and courtiers. Built in 1535 and called Sutton House after the seventeenth-century merchant and philanthropist who founded the Sutton Hospital and Charterhouse School on the site of the old Carthusian monastery, the building has suffered many alterations over the centuries. Since the late 1600s it has been used as a school, a church institute for working men, a trades' union office, a social services office and finally a squat.

The National Trust acquired it in 1938 in an attempt to save it from demolition, but allowed it to run down in the hands of various tenants. In the mid 1980s squatters moved in and many of the fittings were looted; the place was subsequently boarded up. The Trust admits that in desperation they planned to let a developer convert parts of the old mansion into flats; local people objected and a pressure group, the Sutton House Trust, was formed. It persuaded the National Trust to reverse its earlier decision and restore the house as a whole.

When conservation began in 1990 all sorts of original features, such as Tudor fireplaces and panelling, were found behind later additions; seventeenth-century decoration emerged from beneath coats of whitewash and the panelling and many fittings sold by the squatters were returned by the dealer concerned. The house, fully opened in 1994, is not only an authentic frame in which to display part of London's history but a delightful setting for the regular recitals of chamber music and other events that have brought the house to life again.

One curious outcome of recent years of study of the building and its records is the inconvenient fact that Thomas Sutton did not live there after all. It is now clear that another prominent Tudor family had the house and that Sutton's establishment, long since demolished, was next door!

Sutton House, Hackney: built in 1535, it is the oldest surviving domestic house in the East End and is now the property of the National Trust.

Much of London's architectural history has been highlighted by needless demolition and neglect of the built heritage, and nowhere has that been more apparent than in the case of London's private palaces. The royal palaces have been inviolate, but until the first quarter of the twentieth century the West End was dotted with many more great houses that generations of gentry and aristocratic families had maintained as their London base. The economic depression of the 1920s and '30s, and the Second World War took a great toll on such palaces: Devonshire House, Grosvenor House, Dorchester House, Chesterfield House, Aldford House and Norfolk House all succumbed to commercial and other pressures, though part of the music room of Norfolk House survives in the Victoria and Albert Museum.

Spencer House, a great Palladian palace of the mid eighteenth century, is one of the few to escape destruction or redevelopment. Credit for its survival must be given to the tenacity of the seventh Earl Spencer (1892-1975), grandfather of the Princess of Wales, who, although forced to live elsewhere, hung on to the house when his peers sought other solutions to rising costs.

The house, designed by John Vardy and built between 1756 and 1766, overlooks Green Park. The enormous wealth of the first earl ensured that the best craftsmen, painters and designers of the day had a hand in its construction and decor: Robert Adam, James Stuart and, later in the eighteenth century, Sir Robert Taylor and Henry Holland worked on it. For almost two centuries, Spencer House was one of London's great centres of political and social influence.

Soon after the outbreak of the Second World War Lord Spencer packed up the furniture and any fittings he could prise from the walls, and transported them in a convoy of vans to the family seat of Althorp, near Northampton. Although bombs fell on all sides of Spencer House, no direct hit was suffered, but many

A detail of the Jacobean wall painting on the West Staircase of Sutton House

rooms were badly shaken and the plasterwork dislodged in places. The eighteenth-century gates were removed by government order – as was so much of London's wonderful wrought and cast iron work, most of which was found to be unsuitable for munitions and had to be dumped – and the house was requisitioned as the HQ of the war effort's Nursing Corps.

Cleaned up after the war, it was partitioned and let to various tenants, until in 1985 the Rothschild group of companies acquired the lease and obtained the agreement of English Heritage to use the servants' quarters and private rooms for offices. In return they would restore the state rooms and open them to the public, for a fee, for the first time in the history of the building.

The deal was done. The great plaster ceilings have been restored, missing architectural features meticulously copied, original furniture tracked down and acquired – a unique set of sofas and chairs made for Spencer House which had been on display at Kenwood House in Hampstead is now back in its original home – and the state rooms are as they would have been when the house was in its heyday.

The facade of Spencer House in St James's, a rare survival of the great town houses of the eighteenth century.

In a rare reversal of a consistent trend towards attrition, Spencer House has been added to London's stock of Georgian buildings. It has to be said, of course, that despite the ravages of the second half of the twentieth century London retains an extraordinary number of fine eighteenth century buildings and that those who predicted something approaching the total destruction of Georgian London have fortunately been proved wrong.

The balance between the commercial needs of a modern city and the protection that should be afforded to the past is a delicate one; the heritage of the Victorian developments that followed the Georgians into the nineteenth century has yet to be fully appreciated for its Gothic innovation and the ebullient expression of a city at the peak of imperial expansion. The search for fragments of the past described in the early chapters of this book underlines the fragility of the physical signs of our cultural heritage and the speed with which familiar old buildings and ancient archaeological sites can disappear in a city of constant change.

Select Chronology

The following is a selective list of major events in London and elsewhere in Britain during the period covered by this book. Events of national importance such as the deaths of monarchs are listed as "elsewhere" although many of them occurred in London.

London	AD	National Events
	43	Romans invade Britain
Foundation of Roman Londinium	c.50	
Londinium sacked by Boudicca	60	Revolt of Boudicca
Londinium rebuilt	61	
	70–84	Roman conquest of Wales and Scotland
Basilica and forum built	70–125	
Londinium destroyed by fire	c.120	
New waterfront built		
	122	Emperor Hadrian visits Britain; Hadrian's Wall begun
Building of city wall begun	c.190	
Temple of Mithras built	240	
	270s	Renewed economic growth in Britain
London mint established	c.290	
	c.296	Britain becomes a civil diocese in four provinces
	306	Constantine the Great proclaimed emperor at York
	340–69	Severe disorder; harassment by barbarians
	398–400	British victories over Picts, Scots and Saxons
	410	Fall of Rome; end of Roman rule in Britain
	c.450	Hengist and Horsa settle in Kent
Britons defeated by invading Anglo–Saxons; Londinium disappears from historical record	457	
	c.477	Saxon settlement of Sussex
	c.495	Saxon settlement of Wessex
	597	St Augustine's mission arrives in Kent
Saxon London built along the Strand	c.600	
Building of St Paul's Cathedral begun	604	
Mellitus appointed Bishop of London		
St Mary Overie nunnery established	606	
on present site of Southwark Cathedral		
	624	Redwald of East Anglia dies and is buried at Sutton Hoo
	731	Bede completes his *Ecclesiastical History*
	757	Offa becomes King of Mercia
	793	Danish raids on Lindisfarne
	796	Death of Offa
Viking attack on London	842	
	865	Landing of Danish "Great Army"
	870	East Anglia falls to Danes
Danes occupy London	871	Danes attack Wessex; Alfred becomes king

London recaptured by Alfred the Great	874	Mercia falls to Danes
	878	Alfred defeats Danes at Edington
	899	Death of Alfred;
		Edward the Elder becomes King of Wessex
	919	Norse kingdom of York founded by Regnald
	924	Death of Edward the Elder; Athelstan becomes king
	940	Death of Athelstan; Edmund becomes king
	946	Death of Edmund
	959	Edgar becomes king
	975	Death of Edgar;
		Edward "the Martyr" becomes king
	979	Murder of Edward;
		Ethelred "the Unready" becomes king
	1002	Ethelred orders massacre of all Danes in England
	1003	Danish invasion led by King Swein
	1013	Danelaw accepts Swein as king
	1014	Death of Swein; Canute elected king by Danish army
Canute captures London	1016	Death of Ethelred; Edmund Ironside and Canute proclaimed king in different parts of England
		Death of Edmund;
		Canute becomes king of all England
	1035	Death of Canute
	1037	Harold Hardrada becomes king
	1040	Death of Harold; Hardecanute becomes king
	1042	Death of Hardecanute;
		Edward the Confessor becomes king
William the Conqueror grants London its charter	1066	Death of Edward; Harold of Wessex becomes king
		Harold defeats and kills King Harold of Norway at the Battle of Stamford Bridge
		Duke William of Normandy defeats and kills Harold at the Battle of Hastings
		William "The Conqueror" crowned king at Westminster Abbey
Tower of London built	c.1067	
	1086	Domesday Survey
	1087	Death of William I; accession of William II ("Rufus")
Bermondsey Abbey founded	1089	
	1100	Death of William II; accession of Henry I
	1106	Henry captures Normandy
Building of St Bartholomew's Priory and Hospital	1123	
	1135	Death of Henry I; accession of Stephen
	1139–53	Civil War in England between Stephen and his cousin,Empress Matilda (Maud)
Priory of St John of Jerusalem established at Clerkenwell	1140	
	1141–5	Geoffrey of Anjou, husband of Matilda, conquers Normandy
	1152	Henry of Anjou (later Henry II) marries Eleanor of Aquitaine
	1154	Death of Stephen; accession of Henry II, son of Geoffrey and Matilda, first Plantagenet king
Vinter's Company granted charter	1155	
	1162	Thomas Becket appointed Archbishop of Canterbury
	1170	Becket murdered in Canterbury Cathedral
Building of London Bridge	1176	
Fitz Stephen, London historian, gives first description of the medieval city	1180	
First mention of Goldsmiths' Company		

Temple Church consecrated	**1185**	
	1189	Death of Henry II; accession of Richard I ("the Lionheart")
	1190	Richard leaves on Crusade
Mayor and aldermen establish own court	**1192**	
	1199	Death of Richard I; accession of John
First building regulations introduced	**c.1199**	
Southwark Cathedral founded	**1212**	
St Thomas's Hospital established at Southwark	**1213**	
	1215	John forced to sign Magna Carta; civil war in England
	1216	Death of John; accession of the infant Henry III
	1221–4	Arrival of Dominicans and Franciscans (Blackfriars and Greyfriars) in England
St Paul's Cathedral extended in Gothic style	**1256**	
	1272	Death of Henry III; accession of Edward I
First mention of "Flete Strete"	**1274**	
	1282–3	Edward's conquest of Wales
Expulsion of Jews from London ghetto in Old Jewry	**1290**	
Wall extended from Ludgate to Fleet River	**1294**	War with France
	1307	Death of Edward I; accession of Edward II
First meeting of the Common Council of the City of London	**1327**	Deposition and death of Edward II; accession of Edward III
	1337–1453	Hundred Years' War with France
	1346	English victory at Crécy
	1347	English capture Calais
The Black Death – 10,000 people buried at West Smithfield	**1348**	Plague (the "Black Death") arrives in England
138 shops built on London Bridge First Goldsmiths' Hall built	**1358**	
Charterhouse monastery founded	**1371**	
Effigy of Edward III placed in Westminster Abbey	**1377**	Death of Edward III; accession of Richard II
	1381	Peasants' Revolt provoked by heavy taxes being levied to finance war with France
First Custom House founded	**1382**	
First of Richard Whittington's four terms as Lord Mayor	**1397**	
	1399	Deposition of Richard II; accession of Henry IV, first king of the House of Lancaster
First Guildhall built	**1411**	
	1413	Death of Henry IV; accession of Henry V
Sheen Palace built by Henry V	**1414**	
	1415	English conquest of Normandy; victory at Agincourt
	1422	Death of Henry V; accession of the infant Henry VI
First reference to the Honourable Society of the Inner Temple	**1440**	
	1455	Wars of the Roses break out between Houses of York and Lancaster
	1461	Deposition of Henry VI; accession of Edward IV, first king of the House of York
	1470	Deposition of Edward IV; restoration of Henry VI
	1471	Restoration of Edward IV; death of Henry VI
	1477	William Caxton produces first book to be printed in England
	1483	Death of Edward IV; accession, deposition and presumed murder of Edward V (with his brother Richard, Duke of York, "the Princes in the Tower"); accession of Richard III

London		World/National events
	1485	Death of Richard III at Battle of Bosworth Field; accession of Henry VII, first of the Tudor monarchs, marks end of Wars of the Roses
Lambeth Palace gatehouse built	**1490**	
First printing press set up in Fleet Street	**1501**	
	1502	Death of Arthur of Brittany, Henry VII's eldest son
St Paul's School founded	**1509**	Death of Henry VII; accession of Henry VIII, followed by his marriage to his brother's widow, Catherine of Aragon
	1515	Thomas Wolsey appointed Lord Chancellor
Henry VII chapel at Westminster Abbey completed	**1519**	
Bridewell Palace built	**1522**	
	1527	Henry VIII's divorce crisis begins
	1529	Fall of Wolsey; Sir Thomas More appointed Lord Chancellor
	1533	Henry VIII divorces Catherine and marries Anne Boleyn
	1534	Act of Supremacy: Henry VIII becomes head of the Church of England.
	1536	Dissolution of the Monasteries Union of England and Wales
	1543	War with France
	1547	Death of Henry VIII; accession of nine-year-old Edward VI; Earl of Somerset becomes Lord Protector
	1553	Death of Edward VI; accession of Mary I
First mention of the George Inn, Southwark	**1554**	
	1555	Persecution of Protestants begins
	1558	Death of Mary I; accession of Elizabeth I
	1570	Papal Bull excommunicates Elizabeth
Middle Temple Hall built	**1571**	
Birth of Inigo Jones	**1573**	
Gresham College founded	**1579**	
	1580	Francis Drake circumnavigates the globe
	1585	War with Spain
Rose Theatre built in Southwark	**1587**	
	1588	Defeat of Spanish Armada
John Stow's *Survey of London* published	**1598**	
Globe Theatre built in Southwark	**1599**	
Plague causes c.25,000 deaths	**1603**	Death of Elizabeth; accession of James I, first of the Stuart monarchs
	1605	Gunpowder Plot, a Catholic conspiracy against the Protestant king, led by Guy Fawkes
Charterhouse School founded by Thomas Sutton	**1611**	Publication of Authorized Version of the Bible, also known as the King James Bible
Queen's House built at Greenwich	**1616–35**	
Banqueting House built in Whitehall	**1619–25**	
	1620	Pilgrim Fathers sail for America
	1624–30	War with Spain
	1625	Death of James I; accession of Charles I
	1629	Charles I dissolves Parliament and begins eleven years of personal rule
Birth of Christopher Wren	**1632**	
Birth of Samuel Pepys	**1633**	
Covent Garden piazza built	**1635**	
Hyde Park opened for public use	**1637**	
London sides with Parliament in Civil War; Royalist army defeated at Turnham Green	**1642**	Charles attempts to arrest five Members of Parliament; Civil War breaks out between Parliament and Royalists

	1644	Parliamentary ("Roundhead") armies win vital battle at Marston Moor
	1646	Charles I surrenders
	1649	Charles I executed in Whitehall; Royalists proclaim his son King Charles II
	1651	Charles II defeated by Cromwell and forced into exile
Death of Inigo Jones	1652	
	1652–4	First Dutch War
	1653	Oliver Cromwell becomes Lord Protector
	1655–60	War with Spain
	1658	Death of Cromwell; succeeded by his son Richard
	1659	Richard Cromwell overthrown
	1660	Restoration of the Monarchy; Charles II returns to England
	1662	Royal Society receives its charter
The Great Plague causes c.100,000 deaths	1665	
	1665–7	Second Dutch War
The Great Fire	1666	
Rebuilding of City churches by Christopher Wren and Nicholas Hawksmoor	1670–1700	
Monument to Great Fire	1671–7	Third Dutch War
	1672–4	
Foundation of Royal Observatory, Greenwich	1675–6	
St Paul's Cathedral rebuilt	1675–1711	
Royal Hospital Chelsea founded	1682	Death of Charles II; accession of James II
	1685	
	1688	The "Glorious Revolution": deposition and exile of James II; accession of William (III) and Mary (II)
	1690	Battle of the Boyne: William defeats Irish and French armies
	1694	Death of Mary II Bank of England founded
Berkeley Square begun	1698	
Bedford Row begun	1700	
	1702	Death of William III; accession of Anne
Buckingham House (later Palace) built	1702–5	
Death of Pepys	1703	
	1707	Union of England and Scotland
	1714	Death of Anne; accession of George I, first monarch of the House of Hanover
	1715	Jacobite rebellion led by James II's son, James Stuart, the "Old Pretender", fails
Cavendish Square begun	1717	
Death of Wren	1723	
	1727	Death of George I; accession of George II
	1728	Birth of Robert Adam
	1739	Anglo-Spanish Naval War
Mansion House built	1739–53	
	1745	Jacobite rebellion led by Bonnie Prince Charlie, the "Young Pretender"
	1746	Jacobites defeated at Battle of Culloden
Dr Johnson's *Dictionary* published	1755	
	1756–63	Seven Years' War against France, Austria, Russia and Spain
	1760	Death of George II; accession of George III
City wall demolished and removal of gates begun	1766	
Adelphi begun	1772	
Somerset House	1776	Declaration of American Independence
	1793	War with France

	1801	First census of population
	1805	Battle of Trafalgar
	1815	Battle of Waterloo; defeat of Napoleon brings peace to Europe
George IV begins additions to Buckingham House that will make it a suitable royal residence	1820	Death of George III; accession of George IV
	1830	Death of George IV; accession of William IV

A Brief Guide to City Churches

All Hallows by the Tower
Byward Street, EC3

Founded in 675, the later medieval church survived the Great Fire but was largely destroyed during the Second World War. The seventeenth–century brick tower survived, and the bombing brought to light a Saxon arch and Roman bricks. The church was restored by 1957.

Features include a museum which houses part of a Roman pavement, a centre for brass rubbing and a good bookshop.

All Hallows London Wall
London Wall, EC2

The first church on this site was built between 1100 and 1135. The second, dating from the thirteenth century, survived the Great Fire but by the eighteenth century had fallen into decay. A new church was built between 1765 and 1767. Badly damaged during the Second World War, it was reconsecrated in 1962.

A victim of recent terrorist bombings, this church will be closed until further notice.

The Dutch Church of Austin Friars
Austin Friars, EC2

The original church on this site dated from 1253. The Protestant Edward VI provided a place of worship for the Dutch community in 1550. The church survived the Great Fire but was completely destroyed in 1940, rebuilt and reopened in 1954.

Features include the altar stone from the original thirteenth-century church, and a kaleidoscope of stained glass.

Church of the Holy Sepulchre without Newgate
Holborn Viaduct, EC1

First mentioned in 1137, this church was rebuilt in the fifteenth century, destroyed by the Great Fire, rebuilt and substantially altered in the nineteenth century; it survived the Second World War. This is the largest parish church in the City, measuring 46 by 49 metres (150 by 162 feet).

Features include a Renatus Harris organ from 1677 and a hand bell (now housed in a glass case) that was in nearby Newgate Prison rung outside the cell of a prisoner about to executed.

St Andrew by the Wardrobe with St Ann's Blackfriars
Queen Victoria Street, EC4

A manuscript in St Paul's Cathedral dates the founding of this church back to 1244. It was destroyed by the Great Fire, rebuilt by Wren (1685-95), gutted by fire bombs in December 1940 and restored in 1961.

Features include two seventeenth-century sanctuary chairs, a figure of St Andrew dated to about 1600 and two eighteenth-century chandeliers.

St Andrew's Holborn
Holborn Circus, EC1

A charter in Westminster Abbey mentions a Saxon church on this site as early as 951, but only the medieval tower (1446) exists today. The remainder of the church survived the Great Fire only to fall into decay and be rebuilt by Wren (1687). Gutted by the Second World War, it was restored in 1961.

Features include a sunken churchyard whose seats provide a haven from the roar of nearby traffic; a gold-encrusted organ once played by Handel; and a superb lectern of wrought iron.

St Andrew Undershaft
Leadenhall Street, EC3

First mentioned in the twelfth century, rebuilt in the fourteenth and sixteenth and restored in 1634, the church survived both the Great Fire and the Second World War – one of only four City churches to do so – yet tragically has fallen victim to recent troubles. Two terrorist bombs, in 1992 and 1993, damaged parts of the building.

Features include the fifteenth-century door complete with sanctuary knocker; communion rails that are a fine example of seventeenth-century ironwork; and a monument to London's first historian, John Stow, whose parish church this was.

St Anne's and St Agnes'
Gresham Street, EC2

First mentioned in the thirteenth century, the church was damaged by fire in 1548 and destroyed by the Great Fire. Rebuilt by Wren(1676-87), it was gutted again during the Second World War and restored by 1968.

Features include a superb example of Charles II's royal coat of arms, a beautiful dome supported on four Corinthian columns and a bust believed to be of Wren.

St Bartholomew the Great
West Smithfield, EC1

The most likely date of foundation is 1123. Extended in the thirteenth and sixteenth centuries, the church survived the Great Fire only to fall into decay. No serious attempt at restoration was undertaken until 1897.

Features include the oldest "ring" in London – five medieval bells that are still rung for Sunday services; a Norman choir; and a Lady Chapel dating from 1370 with vaulted crypt below. St Bart's also houses the tomb of its founder, Rahere, constructed about 1405.

St Bartholomew the Less
Cloth Fair, EC1

1184 is the earliest date for a church on this site. It survived the Great Fire and the fifteenth-century tower was incorporated into the restoration, which took place between 1760 and 1820. Damaged during the Second World War, the church was reopened in 1951.

Features include stained glass depicting St Bartholomew and the founder of the hospital, Rahere; two brasses in the vestry dating from the fifteenth century; and particularly attractive brasswork.

St Benet Paul's Wharf
Queen Victoria Street, EC4

Founded in 1111, consumed by the Great Fire, rebuilt by Wren (1677-85) and repaired in 1836, the church escaped the ravages of the Second World War but was badly damaged by fire in 1971.

Features include the pulpit – although it is modern, the date 1685 can just be made out on one of the panels; a seventeenth-century altar table with its inlaid top supported by angels; and two sanctuary chairs, again seventeenth century.

St Botolph's Aldersgate
Little Britain, EC1

1050-1350 are the dates for the first church on this site. The second church survived until the middle of the eighteenth century, having escaped the Great Fire. Completely rebuilt between 1789 and 1791, it remained intact throughout the Second World War.

Features include the Wedgwood blue ceiling beneath which are marble pillars; and the only eighteenth-century transparency in the City.

St Botolph's Aldgate
Aldgate, EC3

There is reference to a church on this site in 1125. It escaped the Great Fire but fell into decay and had to be rebuilt in 1744; surviving the Second World War, it was damaged by fire in 1966. The church now does valuable work with London's homeless, 250 of whom rely on its charity and support.

Features include a wooden carving of King David surrounded by musical instruments and a Renatus Harris organ dating from 1676.

St Botolph's without Bishopsgate
Bishopsgate, EC2

The earliest mention of a church on this site is 1212. It survived the Great Fire but was demolished in 1742. Rebuilt by James Gold in 1748, it survived the Second World War but fell victim to damage from a terrorist bomb in 1993.

Features include a large, well-kept churchyard and a beautifully carved ceiling in white and gold, supported on tall Corinthian columns with oak bases.

St Bride's Fleet Street
Bride Lane, EC4

This claims to be the first church in London where Christianity was practised – it is possible that there has been a church on this site since the sixth century. Church number four was built by the fifteenth century; it was destroyed by the Great Fire, rebuilt by Wren (1670-5), badly damaged during the Second World War and restored by 1957.

Features include the famous "wedding cake" spire, a wonderful painting of the crucifixion and an eye-catching black and white marble floor.

St Clement's Eastcheap
King William Street, EC4

A charter of 1067 mentions St Clement's, which Stow accurately describes as "a very small church". Destroyed by the Great Fire, it was rebuilt by Wren (1683-7) and much altered by the Victorians. Undamaged by the Second World War, it was further altered in 1949.

Features include a seventeenth-century pulpit of Norwegian oak, a wonderful gilded sword rest and a dole cupboard, also seventeenth century. This was used to store bread that was "doled out" to the poor of the parish.

St Dunstan in the West
Fleet St, EC4

It is possible that a Saxon church existed on this site, but the first mention of the medieval church comes in the 1180s. It survived the Great Fire but was completely rebuilt between 1829 and 1833, badly damaged during the Second World War and reopened in 1950.

Features include a stone statue of Elizabeth I dating from about 1586, a superb clock complete with temple above and a beautifully painted screen, a gift from the Romanian Church.

St Edmund the King
Lombard Street, EC3

Little is known of the early history of this church, though 1150 is a possible date for its foundation. Destroyed by the Great Fire and rebuilt by Wren (1670-9) with the help of his surveyor Robert Hooke, this church suffered damaged during both world wars and was rebuilt in 1957.

Features include some fine seventeenth-century woodwork, including the communion table; a rather strange semicircular ceiling above the altar that looks incomplete; and a handsome black and gold clock.

St Ethelburga the Virgin within Bishopsgate
Bishopsgate, EC2

Founded in 1250 and rebuilt in 1390, this church survived the Great Fire and two world wars, only to be partly demolished by a huge terrorist bomb in April 1993. As yet no decision has been taken on the future of what was the City's smallest and finest medieval church.

St Giles without Cripplegate
Fore Street, EC2

1090 is the first date for a church on this site and three more had been built by 1550. Surviving the Great Fire, St Giles was restored in the eighteenth and again in the nineteenth century; destroyed during the Second World War and reopened in 1960.

The parish of St Giles suffered terribly in the Great Plague of 1665–8,000 people died and on just one day, 18 August, there were 151 funerals.

Features include a sword rest that bears the arms of the last four Aldermen of Cripplegate to serve as Lord Mayor and a particularly fine wood-panelled ceiling.

St Helen's Bishopsgate with St Martin Outwich
Bishopsgate, EC2

Founded in 1161, this church, like St Ethelburga, survived the Great Fire and two world wars, but fell victim to terrorist bombs in 1992 and 1993. One of the City's most important churches, it is often described as the Westminster Abbey of the City because of its medieval monuments. The earliest date for its reopening is 1995.

St James's Garlickhythe
Upper Thames Street, EC4

1170 is the earliest recorded date for this church. It was rebuilt in 1320 and again in the first half of the seventeenth century, only to fall victim to the Great Fire. Rebuilt by Wren (1676-82), it was damaged in the Second World War, restored by 1963 and damaged again in September 1991 when part of a crane fell through the roof. An exhibition of photographs in the church tells the story.

Features include the tallest interior of any City church; a wig stand on the pulpit; and large and unusual carvings of a unicorn and lion on the front of the pews.

St Katharine Cree
Leadenhall Street, EC3

A church called St Katharine de Christ Church at Aldgate is recorded from 1280. The third church on the site was built between1628 and 1630 and survived both the Great Fire and the Second World War.

Features include an enchanting churchyard complete with fountain, a ceiling with coloured bosses representing seventeen of the City livery companies, and a door case of 1693 through which the garden can be reached.

St Lawrence Jewry
Guildhall, EC2

First mentioned in 1136, the church was destroyed by the Great Fire, rebuilt by Wren and consecrated in 1677. Gutted during an air raid in 1940 (the walls survived), it was restored by 1957.

Features include the font, which dates from 1620, eight ornamental brass chandeliers and a superbly carved altar piece.

St Magnus the Martyr
Lower Thames Street, EC3

A stone church on the site is mentioned in 1067. It was rebuilt by Wren (1671-87). Fire and the widening of London Bridge brought changes in the eighteenth century and a major refurbishment was carried out in the 1920s. St Magnus suffered minor damage during the Second World War and was restored by 1951.

Features include the 56 metre (185 foot) steeple of Portland stone, together with its impressive clock; an altar piece as ornate as any in the City; and seventeenth-century wrought iron communion rails.

St Margaret's Lothbury
Lothbury, EC2

First mentioned in 1181, St Margaret's was rebuilt in the fifteenth century, destroyed by the Great Fire, rebuilt by Wren (1687-1700) and escaped damage during the Second World War.

Features include the fine white stone tower with its lead steeple; a wonderfully carved wooden screen in four parts which stretches right across the interior; and lunchtime concerts which are very popular with City workers.

St Margaret Pattens
Eastcheap, EC3

"St Margaret de Patins" is first mentioned in 1275. A second church, completed in 1538, was destroyed by the Great Fire and rebuilt by Wren (1684). Badly damaged during the Second World War, it was restored by 1956.

Features include the needle-like spire; canopied pews with the initials "CW", possibly standing for Christopher Wren; and the little Lady Chapel complete with wig pegs, formerly used by parishioners in hot weather.

St Martin within Ludgate
Ludgate Hill, EC4

There may have been a church on this site as early as 600, but the earliest confirmed date is 1174. Rebuilt in 1437, the church was destroyed by the Great Fire, rebuilt by Wren (1677-87) and undamaged by the Second World War.

Features include the churchwarden's "double" chair with "1690" carved on the top; the marble font (1673) with the words "Wash my sin not my face only"; and a superb brass candelabrum which originated in the West Indies!

St Mary Abchurch
Abchurch Lane, EC4

First mentioned towards the end of the twelfth century, this church was destroyed by the Great Fire, rebuilt by Wren (1681-7) and damaged during the Second World War, although the bombing led to the discovery of a fourteenth-century crypt.

Features include a painted domed ceiling, unique in a Wren City church; a Grinling Gibbons altar screen; and panelled box pews that include a kennel for dogs.

St Mary Aldermary
Watling Street, EC4

1080 is the earliest mention of a church on this now very busy site. All except the tower of the sixteenth-century church was destroyed by the Great Fire and the church was rebuilt by Wren (1682, tower 1701). 1876 saw a dramatic Victorian restoration. All but the stained glass survived the Second World War undamaged.

Features include the intricate ceiling with rosettes; a seventeenth-century pulpit and font; and an intricately carved sword rest dating from 1682.

St Mary-at-Hill
Eastcheap, EC3

The Norman church dating from 1177 was damaged but not destroyed by the Great Fire. Wren incorporated the surviving tower and walls into his rebuilding (1670-6). The church survived the Second World War and repairs were undertaken in the 1960s.

Features include the most attractive churchyard in the City; a collection of six sword rests; and the only complete set of box pews in a City church.

St Mary le Bow
Cheapside, EC3

Founded in 1090, the Norman crypt still remains (and houses a lunchtime restaurant aptly named The Place Below). Destroyed by the Great Fire, rebuilt by Wren (1670-83), destroyed again during the Second World War, the church was not rebuilt until 1964.

Features include the famous "Bow Bells", within the sound of which true Cockneys are born; a glorious steeple topped by a weather vane representing a 3 metre (9 foot) long golden dragon; and a pale blue and green ceiling giving the church a sense of calm and tranquillity.

St Mary Woolnoth with
St Mary Woolchurch Haw
Lombard Street, EC3

A Saxon church may have existed on this site, but 1198 is the earliest definite date. Two more churches were built in the fifteenth century, the latter damaged by the Great Fire and restored by Wren. The building became unsafe and was replaced by a new church designed by Nicholas Hawksmoor (1716-27) – his only City church. It then survived numerous attempts by the Railway Board to acquire the site for an underground station, and the Second World War.

Features include four great circular headed windows which allow the blue and gilt ceiling to "light up", and a forest of impressive Corinthian columns, twelve in all.

St Michael's Cornhill
Cornhill, EC3

A Saxon foundation, this church was restored and a new tower built in the fifteenth century. Damaged by the Great Fire and rebuilt by Wren, it became unsafe in 1715 and repairs were finally completed in 1722. The tower (1818-24) is by Hawksmoor. Heavily "Victorianized" in the mid nineteenth century, the church came through the Second World War intact.

Features include a spectacular carving of a pelican feeding its young (1775); an intricate poor box supported by two dolphins; and an organ originally by Renatus Harris but altered several times, which Purcell may have played.

St Michael Paternoster Royal
College Street, EC4

First mentioned in 1219, St Michael's was rebuilt in the fifteenth century, destroyed by the Great Fire, rebuilt by Wren (1686-94),destroyed again in 1944 and restored by 1968. This was Dick Whittington's parish church – he lived next door and supplied the money for it to be rebuilt in the fifteenth century.

Features include an outstanding candelabrum stamped 1644 and post-Second World War stained glass depicting the young Dick Whittington with his cat.

St Nicholas Cole Abbey
Queen Victoria Street, EC4

Founded in 1144, the church was destroyed by the Great Fire, rebuilt by Wren (1671-81), destroyed during the Second World War and restored by 1962.

Features include an unusual, trumpet-shaped lead spire, abstract stained glass and an excellent collection of photographs depicting the bombed-out church and its subsequent rebuilding.

St Olave's Hart Street and
All Hallows Staining with St Katherine Coleman
Fenchurch Street, EC3

It is possible that a place of worship existed here in Saxon times, but 1222 is the earliest date that can safely be used. Rebuilt in the fifteenth century, the church escaped the Great Fire but was badly damaged during the Second World War and reopened in 1954.

Features include the macabre touch of a skull and crossbones above the gateway; a seventeenth-century carved pulpit; and a monument to Samuel Pepys, who referred to St Olave's as "our own church".

St Paul's Cathedral
St Paul's Churchyard, EC4

King Ethelbert founded a church dedicated to St Paul in 604; it is possible but not proven that it was on the site of the present cathedral. Wren's masterpiece, completed in 1711, is at least the fifth church to occupy the site.

Features include the Whispering Gallery high up inside the dome; exterior carving by Grinling Gibbons; and Wren's monument in the crypt.

St Peter upon Cornhill
Cornhill, EC3

St Peter's claims a foundation date of 179, which would make it the oldest place of worship in the City. 1040 is a safer date. Destroyed (apart from part of the tower) by the Great Fire, the church was rebuilt by Wren in the 1680s and survived the Second World War.

Features include the 43 metre (140 foot) high tower with its pre-fire base; a seventeenth-century long wooden table; and a marble font dating from 1681.

St Stephen's Walbrook
Walbrook, EC4

Founded in 1096, the church was rebuilt in the fifteenth century and destroyed by the Great Fire. Rebuilt by Wren (1672-7), it was badly damaged during the Second World War and restored by 1954. This church is often cited as Wren's masterpiece among the parish churches and a prototype for the dome of St Paul's Cathedral.

Features include the dome, which weighs 50 tons and is supported on eight arches; the jet black pulpit with its large canopy; and an altar by Henry Moore.

St Vedast-alias-Foster
Cheapside, EC3

There has been a church on this site since the twelfth century. Damaged but not destroyed by the Great Fire, it was rebuilt by Wren, who incorporated the remains into his reconstruction (1695-1700). Only the tower and spire survived the Second World War, but the church was restored by 1962.

Features include the remains of the medieval walls on to which Wren built, their stone coloured orange by the flames of the Great Fire; a carved organ case from the seventeenth century; and a wonderfully ornate ceiling painted with silver and gilt.

Temple Church
Inner Temple, King's Bench Walk, EC4

A church was consecrated on this site in 1185. It escaped the Great Fire, was refurnished by Wren in 1682, badly damaged in 1941 and restored by 1954.

Features include the "round" which, at 800 years old, is the earliest part of the church; the thirteenth-century effigies of knights lying on the floor; and the use of blue and grey Purbeck marble.

Other London Churches Mentioned in the Book

Christ Church Spitalfields
Commercial Street, E1

Built between 1714 and 1729 by Nicholas Hawksmoor, at a cost of £40,000. Struck by lightning in 1841 and subsequently repaired, the church fell into decay as the parish became short of funds; it was closed in 1958. A recent surge of interest culminated in the formation of the Friends of Christ Church Spitalfields, which has in turn led to concerts and religious services being held in the church once more.

The Queen's Chapel of the Savoy
Savoy Place, WC2

A chapel existed on this site in the fourteenth century but was not consecrated until 1515, when it became a hospital chapel. A new church built in 1723 was taken over by the Duchy of Lancaster in 1772; they have since been responsible for appointing the chaplain. Badly damaged by fire in the mid nineteenth century, the chapel came through the Second World War relatively unscathed.

St Clement Danes
Strand, WC2

Alfred the Great permitted the Danes to settle this area in 886. The first church was built in 1022 and remains of it are incorporated in the base of the existing tower. St Clement Danes survived the Great Fire but was rebuilt by Wren; it was then badly damaged during the Second World War. Rebuilt by 1955, it is now the church of the Royal Air Force.

St Etheldreda's
Ely Place, EC1

This chapel is all that remains of the former London palace of the Bishops of Ely, built in the late thirteenth century. The roof and the stained glass suffered in the Second World War, but one interior wall and the timber floor are medieval.

Forced to convert to Protestantism after the Reformation, St Etheldreda's reverted to Catholicism in the nineteenth century.

St George's Bloomsbury
Bloomsbury Way, WC1

This grand church with its portico of six huge Corinthian columns and colourful interior was designed by Nicholas Hawksmoor in 1730. Apart from internal refurbishment in 1781, the church has remained true to Hawksmoor's design.

St Giles in the Fields
St Giles High Street, WC2

Founded in 1101 as a chapel to a leper hospital, the church was rebuilt in the 1620s and again in 1734 at a cost of £8,000. "Modernized" in the late nineteenth century, it survived the Second World War. It has a superb steeple that even the nearby Centre Point cannot spoil. The churchyard is a public garden.

St James's Piccadilly
W1

The church was designed to hold 2,000 people, the maximum number Wren thought practicable for a religious service. He completed work on it in 1684 and a spire was added in 1699. Badly damaged in the Second World War, it was restored by 1954. The Grinling Gibbons font depicting Adam and Eve in the Garden of Eden is exquisite.

St John's Smith Square
SW1

Built by Thomas Archer between 1713 and 1728; gutted during the Second World War and now used as a concert hall and restaurant.

St Martin-in-the-Fields
St Martins Place, WC2

The first mention of a church on this site comes in 1222; it was rebuilt by Henry VIII in 1544 and again in 1721, when the Tudor church was considered too small for a parish of 40,000 people. The architect was James Gibbs. The famous steeple with its unusual concave spire was completed in 1842.

The church is best known for its concerts and for its work with the homeless, which has rightly earned it the title "the parish church of London".

St Mary le Strand
Strand, WC2

1147 saw the foundation of this church, where Thomas Becket was rector. It was demolished in 1549 by the Duke of Somerset to enable him to complete his new mansion, Somerset House. A new church of Portland stone was consecrated in 1723, the architect being James Gibbs.

St Paul's Covent Garden
Bedford Street, WC2

Built between 1631 and 1633 by Inigo Jones for the Earl of Bedford, it was destroyed by fire in 1795 and rebuilt in 1798. The church has long been associated with the world of entertainment – as early as 1662 Samuel Pepys watched a Punch and Judy show there.

Grinling Gibbons is buried here, and plaques on the walls commemorate many famous actors.

Southwark Cathedral
Montague Close, SE1

The Priory of St Mary Overie was established on this site in 1106. After some rebuilding, the church survived the Reformation and the medieval tower and transepts remain. The nave was rebuilt in the nineteenth century.

Features include the monuments to several great poets and dramatists, notably John Gower, John Fletcher and Philip Massinger. Shakespeare's brother Edmund is also buried here.

Access to Sites Mentioned in this Book

The livery companies are not generally open to the public, but visits can be arranged through the City of London Information Centre, telephone 071-332 1456.
Ring in February or March for visits in July or August.
Much of the architectural beauty of the Inns of Court can be appreciated from the outside, but there is strictly speaking no right of access to the interiors. However, members of the public can telephone and make individual arrangements at the Inns' discretion.

Chapter 1

Museum of London
150 London Wall, EC2
071-600 3699
Access: 10.00-6.00 Tues-Sat, 12.00-600 Sun
Cost: £3; free after 4.30

The "Stone of London"
Oversea Chinese Banking Corporation
111 Cannon Street, EC4
Access: The "stone" can be seen through a glass inlay in the wall
Cost: Free

Guildhall
Guildhall Yard, EC2
071-606 3030
Access: 10.00-5.00 Mon-Sat, and Sundays from 1 May to 30 September
Cost: Free
The excavation of the Roman amphitheatre under the Guildhall should be open to the public by mid 1995

Temple of Mithras
Temple Court
11 Queen Victoria Street, EC4
Access: Visible from the street

British Museum
Great Russell Street, WC1
071-636 1555
Access: 10.00-5.00 Mon-Sat, 2.30-6.00 Sun
Cost: Free

Remains of the Roman Wall can be seen at: Tower Hill, EC3, in the garden to the east of the north entrance of Tower Hill underpass; Coopers Row, EC3, in a courtyard by the bank; Emperor House, Vine Street, EC3, outside the entrance and at the rear of the building; Dukes Place EC3 – wall and bastion; in the gardens of St Alphege, London Wall, EC2; Bastion House, London Wall, EC2 (restricted access – ask permission at Bastion House); Noble Street, EC2, at both the north and the south end; south of St Giles Cripplegate, EC2; and at 1 America Square, EC3, where a 30 metre (100 foot) stretch of wall may be seen by appointment only.

Chapter 2

Westminster Abbey, SW1
071-222 5152
Royal Chapels
Access: 9.00-4.45 Mon-Fri, 9.00-2.45 Sat
Cost: £4; concessions available
Chapter House and **Pyx Museum**
Access: 9.30-6.00 16 March-15 October, 9.30-4.00 16 October-15 March
Open seven days a week
Cost: £2.10; concessions available
Access to the nave and cloisters is free.

The ruins of the bath house of the Billingsgate villa are not open to the public.

Chapter 3

Tower of London
Tower Hill, EC3
071-709 0765
Access: 9.00-6.00 Mon-Sat, 10.00-6.00 Sun (Closes 5.00 Nov to Feb)
Cost: £7.95; concessions available

Public Record Office
Chancery Lane, WC2
081-876 3444
Access: 9.30-5.00 Mon-Fri
Cost: Free

"Clerkenwell"
14-16 Farringdon Lane, EC1
Access: Individual arrangements can be made through Finsbury Library on 071-278 7343
Cost: Free

Order of St John
St John's Gate, EC1
071-253 6644
Access: 10.00-5.00 Mon-Fri, 10.00-4.00 Sat
Guided tours Tues, Fri, Sat at 2.30 are the only way to gain admittance to the crypt.
Cost: Free

Bakers' Company
The Hall, Harp Lane
Lower Thames Street, EC3
Access: See preamble

Dyers Company
The Hall
10 Dowgate Hill, EC4
Access: See preamble

All Hallows Staining
Mark Lane, EC3
Property of the Clothworkers' Company, Dunster Court,
Mincing Lane, EC3, telephone 071-623 7041

The thirteenth-century arch from Holy Trinity Priory
is visible at Swiss Re House, Leadenhall Street, EC3.

Chapter 4

Crosby Hall
Cheyne Walk, SW3
Now a private house

Palace of Westminster
Parliament Square, SW1
071-219 4272
Access: Queue for admission when Parliament is in
session. Otherwise contact your MP or phone for an
individual booking.
Cost: Free

Vintners' Company
The Hall
Upper Thames Street, EC4
Access: See preamble

Mercers' Company
The Hall
Ironmonger Lane, EC2
Access: See preamble

Barnards Inn (Gresham College)
Holborn, EC1
071-831 0575
Access: See preamble

Staple Inn
High Holborn, WC1
071-242 5240
Access: See preamble

Grays Inn
8 South Square, WC1
071-405 8164
Access: See preamble

Lincolns Inn
Lincolns Inn Fields, WC2
071-405 1393
Access: See preamble

Inner Temple
EC4
071-353-2553
Access: See preamble

Middle Temple
Temple Lane, EC4
071-353 4355
Access: See preamble

Clink Exhibitions
1 Clink Street, SE1
071-403 6515
Access: 10.00-6.00 seven days a week
Cost: £2; concessions available

The Rose Window of the Bishop of Winchester's Palace
is visible in Clink Street, SE1.

Chapter 5

Lambeth Palace
Lambeth Palace Road, SE1
071-928 8282
Access: By appointment only.
Organized tours Wed and Thurs.
Cost: Free

St Mary at Lambeth
Museum of Garden History
Lambeth Palace Road, SE1
071-261 1891
Access: 11.00-3.00 Mon-Fri, 10.30-5.00 Sun
Closed Sat and 12 Dec-4 March
Cost: Free

Charterhouse
Charterhouse Square, EC1
071-253 9503
Access: Chapel 9.45 Sun, guided tour Wed 2.15 April-July
Cost: Free

George Inn
77 Borough High Street, SE1
071-407 2056
Open: 11.00-11.00 Mon-Sat, 12.00-3.00 Sun
Still a functioning pub

Canonbury Tower
Canonbury Place, N1
071-22 5111
Access: By appointment only
Cost: Free

The Rose Theatre Trust
P.O. Box 1587, SE15,
071-732 4067
Will have a small exhibition open to the public from 1995.

Henry VIII's wine cellar, Great Close tennis court and Small Close tennis court are neither open to the public nor visible from the street.

Prince Henry's Room
17 Fleet Street, EC4
071-936 2501
Access: 11.00-2.00 Mon to Sat except Bank Holidays
Cost: Free

Chapter 6

Queen's House
Greenwich, SE10
081-858 4422
Access: 10.00-5.55 Mon-Sat, 12.00-5.55 Sun
Cost: £4.95; concessions available. The ticket includes admission to the National Maritime Museum and the Royal Observatory

Banqueting House
Banqueting Hall
Whitehall, SW1
071-839 3787
Access: 10.00-5.00 Mon-Sat
Cost: £2.90; concessions available

Sir John Soane's Museum
13 Lincolns Inn Fields, WC2
071-430 0175
Access: Tues-Sat 10.00-5.00, guided tour 2.00
Closed Bank Holidays
Cost: Free

Fishmongers' Company
The Hall
London Bridge, EC4
Access: See preamble

Cutlers' Warehouses, Cutler Street, E1 are visible from the street.

Chapter 7

Clothworkers' Company
The Hall, Dunster Court
Mincing Lane, EC3
Access: See preamble

Ironmongers' Company
Ironmongers' Hall
Barbican, EC2
Access: See preamble

Tallow Chandlers' Company
The Hall
4 Dowgate Hill, EC4
Access: See preamble

Apothecaries' Company
The Hall
Blackfriars Lane, EC4
Access: See preamble

Skinners' Company
The Hall
8 Dowgate Hill, EC4
Access: See preamble

Royal Hospital Chelsea
Royal Hospital Road, SW3
071-730 0161
Access: 10.00-12.00 & 2.00-4.00 Mon-Sat, 2.00-4.00 Sun
Cost: Free

Hampton Court Palace
East Molesey
Surrey
081-781 9500
Access: 10.15-6.00 Mon, 9.30-6.00 Tues-Sun
Cost: £7; concessions available

Buckingham Palace
Buckingham Gate, SW1
071-493 3175
Access: 9.30-5.30 7 Aug-2 Oct seven days a week
Cost: £8; concessions £5.50

Dr Johnson's House
11 Gough Square, EC4
071-353 3745
Access: 11.00-5.30 Mon-Sat, closed Bank Holidays
Cost: £3; concessions available

The remains of Christ Church, Newgate Street, EC1 and the **York Water Gate,** Water Gate Walk, WC2 are visible from the street.

Chapter 8

Royal Academy of Arts
Burlington House
Piccadilly, W1
071-439 7438
Access: 10-00-6.00 seven days a week
Cost: £4.50; concessions available. Other prices apply for special exhibitions

22 Arlington St
22 Arlington St, SW1
Owned by Eagle Star Insurance Company; not open to the public.

Courtauld Institute of Art
Somerset House
Strand, WC2
071-873 2777
Access: 10.00-6.00 Mon-Sat, 2.00-6.00 Sun
Cost: £3; concessions £1.50

The Geffrye Museum
Kingsland Road, E2
071-739 9893
Access: 10.00-5.00 Tues-Sat, 2.00-5.00 Sun
Closed Mon except Bank Holidays (2.00-5.00)
Cost: Free

Sutton House
2 Homerton High Street, E9
081-986 2264
Access: 11.30-5.00 Wed & Sun
Cost: £1.50; children 50p

Victoria & Albert Museum
Cromwell Road, SW7
071-938 8441
Access: 12.00-5.50 Mon, 10.00-5.50 Tues-Sun
Cost: Free, but a donation is requested

Spencer House
27 St James's Place, SW1
071-409 0526
Access: 10.45-4.45 Sun, closed August & January
Cost: £6; concessions £5

Bibliography

Chapter 1

Barker, F. & Jackson, P. *London: 2,000 Years of a City and its People* Papermac, 1983

McCann, W. (ed.) *Fleet Valley Project Interim Report* Museum of London Archaeology Service, 1993

Campbell, J. *The Anglo-Saxons* Phaidon, 1982

Chapman, H. *Discoveries* Museum of London, 1986

Dillon, J., Jackson, S., Jones, H. "Excavations at the Courage Brewery and Park Street 1984-90" *London Archaeologist Vol. 6 no. 10* Museum of London Offprint 21

Geoffrey of Monmouth, Thorpe, L. (trans.) *The History of the Kings of Britain* Penguin, 1966

Hobley, B. *Roman and Saxon London a Reappraisal* Museum of London, 1985

Hume, I. N., "Into the Jaws of Death Walked One" *Collectanea Londiniensia* LMAS Special Paper no 2, 1978

Hunting, P. *Ludgate Broadgate Properties*, 1993

Ireland, S. *Roman Britain* Croom Helm, 1986

MacKenna, S.A., & Ling, R. "Wall Paintings from the Winchester Palace Site" *Southwark Britannia XX11*, 1991, Museum of London Offprint 24

Marsden P. *The Roman Forum Site in London* HMSO Books, 1987

Marsden, P. *Roman London* Thames & Hudson, 1980

Merrifield, R. *The Roman City of London* Benn, 1965

Milne, G. (ed.) *From Roman Basilica to Medieval Market* HMSO Books, 1992

Milne, G. *The Port of London* Batsford, 1985

Perring, D. *Roman London* Seaby, 1991

Schofield, J. & Dyson, T. *Archaeology of the City of London* City of London Archaeological Trust, 1980

Stenton, F.M. *Anglo-Saxon England* Oxford University Press, 1971, pbk 1989

Salway, P. *The Oxford Illustrated History of Roman Britain* Oxford University Press, 1993

Thomas, C. *Celtic Britain* Thames & Hudson, 1986

Chapter 2

Brooke, C. *The Saxon and Norman Kings* Batsford, 1963, Collins Fontana, 1986

Campbell, J. *op. cit.*

Garmonsway, G.N. (ed.) *The Anglo-Saxon Chronicle* Everyman, 1972

Grimes, W.F. *The Excavation of Roman and Medieval London* Routledge, 1968

Hodges, R. *The Anglo-Saxon Achievement* Duckworth, 1989

Kennedy, C.W., *Beowulf* Oxford University Press, 1978

Keynes, S. & Lapidge, M. (eds.) *Alfred the Great: Asser's Life of King Alfred and Other Comtemporary Sources* Penguin, 1983

Loyn, H.R. *The Vikings in Britain* Batsford, 1977

Loyn, H.R. *The Governance of Anglo-Saxon England* Edward Arnold, 1984

Myres, J.N.L. *The English Settlements* Oxford University Press, 1989

Stenton, F. *op. cit.*

Taylor, H.M., & Taylor, Joan *Anglo-Saxon Architecture* Cambridge University Press, 1980

Vince, A. *Saxon London* Seaby, 1990

Webb, J.F. & Farmer, D.H. (trans.) *The Age of Bede* Penguin, 1983

Whitelock, D. *The Beginnings of English Society* Penguin, 1987

Chapter 3

Barlow, F. *Thomas Becket* Weidenfeld & Nicholson, 1986

Barlow, F. *Edward The Confessor* Eyre Methuen, 1979

Billings, M.J. *The Cross and the Crescent* BBC Books, 1987

Brooke C.N.L., & Keir, G. *London 800-1216: The Shaping of a City* Secker, 1975

Chibnall, M. *Anglo-Norman England 1066-1166* Blackwell, 1987

Colvin, H.M., & Taylor, A.J. *The History of the King's Works* Vol. 1, HMSO, 1963

Dyson, T. *The Medieval London Waterfront* Museum of London, 1987

Fitz Stephen, William *Description of the Most Noble City of London*, English translation in Stow's *Survey*, Wheatley, H.B. (ed.), Everyman, 1956

Gillingham, J. *The Angevin Empire* Edward Arnold, 1984

Hibbert, C. *The English – A Social History 1066-1945* Grafton, 1987, pbk 1988

Parnell, G. *The Tower of London* Batsford, 1993

Poole A.L. "From Domesday Book to Magna Carta, 1087-1216" *Oxford History of England Vol. 3* Oxford University Press, 1955

Rowley,T. *The Norman Heritage 1066-1200* Routledge, 1983

Schofield, J. *The Building of London* Colonnade, 1984

Wilson, D.M. *The Bayeux Tapestry* Thames & Hudson, 1985

Chapter 4

Bolton, J.L. *The Medieval English Economy 1150-1500* Dent, 1985

Butt, R. *A History of Parliament – the Middle Ages* Constable, 1980

Colvin, H.M. & Taylor, A.J. *op. cit.*

Grainger, I., Hawkins D., Falcini, P. & Mills, P. "Excavations at the Royal Mint Site 1986-1988" *London Archaeologist Vol. 5 No 16* 1988, Museum of London Offprint 3

Milne, G. (ed.) *op. cit.*

Paris, Mathew *Historia Anglorum* (English history, from the year 1235-1273), 3 vols (Bohms Antiquarian Library) G. Bell, 1852. o.p., AMS Press, New York, reprinted 1852 edition

Prestwich, M. *Edward I* Methuen, 1990

Preswich M. *The Three Edwards: War and State in England, 1272-1377* Methuen, 1981

Rowley, T. *The High Middle Ages – 1200-1500* Routledge, 1986

Schofield, J. *op. cit.*

Schofield, J., Allen, P. & Taylor, C. "Medieval Buildings and Property Development in the Area of Cheapside" *London and Middlesex Archaeological Society Vol. 41*, 1990

Ross, C. *The Wars of the Roses* Thames & Hudson, 1976, pbk 1986

Southern, R.W. *The Making of the Middle Ages* Pimlico, 1993

Stow, John *The Survey of London* Everyman, 1956, reprinted 1987

Chapter 5

Barratt, M., & Thomas, C. "The London Charterhouse" *The London Archaeologist, Vol. 6, no. 11*, 1991, Museum of London Offprint 22

Beir, A.L., & Finlay R. *London 1500-1700* Longman, 1986

Burford, E.J. *The Bishop's Brothels* Robert Hale, 1993

Colvin, H.M., & Taylor, A.J. (eds) *op. cit.* Vol. III

Guy, J. Tudor *England Oxford University Press*, 1988, pbk 1990

Stow, John *op. cit.*

Palliser D.M. *The Age of Elizabeth* Longman, 1983

Reese, M.M. *Shakespeare: His World and His Work*

Simon, J. *Education and Society in Tudor England* Cambridge University Press, 1979

Schofield, J. *op. cit.*

Chapter 6

Clay, C.G.A . *Economic Expansion and Social Change – England 1500-1700* 2 vols, Cambridge University Press, 1984

Colvin, H.M., & Taylor, A.J. (eds.) *op. cit.*

Coward, B. *The Stuart Age* Longman, 1980

Defoe, D. *A Journal of the Plague Year* Penguin, 1986

Eccles, C. *The Rose Theatre* Nick Hern Books, 1990

Evelyn, J. *The Diary of John Evelyn* ed. E.S. de Beer, Oxford University Press, 1959

Hill, C. *God's Englishman – Oliver Cromwell and the English Revolution* Penguin, 1990

Milne, G. *The Great Fire of London* Historical Publications, 1986

Sharpe, J.A. *Early Modern England* Arnold, 1988

Stone, L. *The Causes of the English Revolution, 1529-1642* Ark Publications, 1986

Summerson, J. *Inigo Jones* Pelican, 1966

Wedgewood, C.V. *The Trial of Charles I* Penguin, 1984

Chapter 7

Colvin, H.M., & Taylor, A.J. (ed) *op. cit.* Vol. V

Wren, Christopher *Life and Works of Sir Christopher Wren from the Parentalia or Memoirs by his son Christopher*, ed. E.J. Enthoven, 1903; Royal Institute of British Architects facsimile edition 1965

Pepys, S. *The Diary of Samuel Pepys*, ed. R. Latham & W. Mathews, 11 vols, Bell, 1971

Summerson, J. *Architecture in Britain 1530-1830* Yale University Press, 1993

Whinney, M. *Wren* Thames & Hudson, 1971

Worden, B. (ed.) *Stuart England* Phaidon, 1986.

Chapter 8

Burton, N. *The Geffrye Almshouses* Geffrye Museum, 1979

Byrne A. *London's Georgian Houses* Georgian Press, 1986

Colvin, H.M., & Taylor, A.J. (eds.) *op. cit.*

Friedman, J. *Spencer House* Zwemmer, 1993

George, M. *London Life in the Eighteenth Century* Penguin, 1992

Jenner, M. *London Heritage* Michael Joseph, 1988

Summerson J. *op. cit.*

Weinreb, M., *London Architecture* Phaidon, 1993

NB. All chapters have also benefited from the two inestimable reference works on London buildings and places:

Pevsner, N. & Cherry, B. *The Buildings of England* Penguin, Vol. I 1957, Vol. II 1983

Weinreb, B. & Hibbert, C. *The London Encyclopedia* Papermac, 1983

Index

Page numbers in *italic* refer to the illustrations and captions

Picture Acknowledgements

The author and publishers would like to thank the following for
their assistance in providing pictures for this book and for permission
to reproduce copyright material

National Maritime Museum London: frontispiece and
pages 135, 166

Museum of London: pages 7, 10, 18, 22, 26, 27, 37,
43, 48, 126, 147

A.F. Kersting: pages 8, 60, 112, 114, 115, 125

Museum of London Archaeology Service: pages 14,
15, 20, 28, 30, 86, 95, 98

Michael Holford: pages 39, 51, 58, 59 (general view of
the Tower), 154

British Library: page 38 (Cotton MS Tiberius C II f5
verso)

Bodleian Library, University of Oxford: page 45
(MS Hatten 20 fol 1R)

Ashmolean Museum, Oxford: page 46

Peter Jackson Collection: pages 49, 56, 73, 116, 117,
118, 137, 140, 145, 148, 161, 168, 176

Corporation of London Records Office: page 55 (AF
628)

Crown Copyright (the Tower of London): page 59
(photo of the Crown Jewels by Tim Graham)

Public Record Office: page 62

Guildhall Library, Corporation of London: pages 65,
67, 69, 88, 101

**Royal Commission on the Historical Monuments of
England © RCHME Crown Copyright**: pages 68, 71,
89, 102, 109, 133, 136, 141

Order of St John: pages 74, 75

Dean and Chapter of Westminster: pages 78, 79, 106

English Heritage: pages 82, 83

Vintners' Company: page 90

Mercers' Company: page 94

Arcaid: pages 107 (photograph by Steve Lyman), 142
(photograph by Richard Bryant)

**His Grace the Archbishop of Canterbury & the
Trustees of Lambeth Palace Library**: page 110 (MS 3
f. 6)

Michael Jenner: pages 122, 138, 139, 155, 163, 167,
174, 175, 178, 182

Press Association: page 127

National Trust Photographic Library: © pages 131
(photograph by Michael Caldwell), 181 (photograph by
John Bethell)

Trustees of the Victoria & Albert Museum: page 149

Pitkin Pictorials Ltd: page 156

Thomas Photos Oxford: page 158

Ironmongers' Company: page 159

Dean and Chapter of St Paul's Cathedral: page 160

Barnabys Picture Library: page 162

Mark Fiennes: page 170

James Morris: page 180

The diagrams and maps on pages 11, 24, 44, 53 and 61
are by Tamasin Cole. Pages 24 and 61 are based on
information in the Museum of London's Fleet Valley
Interim Report.